Western
Trips & Trails

Western Trips & Trails

HIKES, DRIVES AND CAMPS
in 50 prime areas

Written and Photographed by
E. M. Sterling

With Maps by Helen Sherman

Stackpole Books

WESTERN TRIPS AND TRAILS

Copyright ©1974 by
E. M. Sterling

Published by
STACKPOLE BOOKS
Cameron and Kelker Streets
Harrisburg, Pa. 17105

Printed in the U.S.A.

Library of Congress Cataloging in Publication Data

Sterling, E   M
    Western trips and trails (hikes, drives, and camps
in 50 prime areas).

    1. The West--Description and travel--1951-
--Guide-books. I. Title.
F595.2.S73   917.8'04'3   74-649
ISBN 0-8117-2035-7

To
My Wife
with appreciation and affection

Contents

    (Note: The general location of the various parks, monuments, wilderness areas, etc. may be seen by matching the topical numbers shown below with circled numbers on the Master Map.)

COLORADO

IDAHO

UTAH

ARIZONA

WASHINGTON

OREGON

CALIFORNIA

acknowledgments

IT WOULD BE impossible here to recognize in detail the tremendous debt owed others in the preparation of this book. To start with, there is the unassessable debt owed all those of the past who had a hand, large or small, in preserving the features we cover here. And there is the similar debt owed all those living who still carry on the fight to protect and preserve these wonders.

But, still, there are particular debts for specific help which cannot be ignored. Debts owed, for instance, to district rangers and staff members of the U.S. Forest Service, superintendents and staff members of the National Park Service, and the many individuals and officials of state parks particularly in Washington, Oregon and California all of whom suggested material for this book and then reviewed it all before publication. Credit for accuracy belongs to them. I accept full responsibility for all errors.

Thanks too must go to Cal Fanders, who produced and processed all of the pictures, for his helpful advice and counsel, to Joyce Woody for her careful and thoughtful work in typing the final manuscript, and to the many friends in Seattle for their constant encouragement and help.

The greatest thanks, however, must go to my wife without whose patience, encouragement and tremendous help the book could not have been written at all.

E. M. Sterling.

introduction

IF THIS BOOK has any one premise it's that the best things in the West are reserved for those willing to hike. And if it has any one purpose, it's to identify those places for anyone planning a trip or vacation there.

Listed here, certainly, are places that can be reached by automobile. Each section contains a review of the best scenic drives in every area. Most of the identified roads are paved. A few are graded gravel and some are even rough, narrow and twisting logging or mining roads that lead to remote areas which can be reached no other way. But all can be driven in a standard passenger car with ease if approached with caution and care.

Public campgrounds are also covered here with information in each section about the facilities, locations and suggestions on how to avoid heavy-use periods and crowds.

But the major emphasis is on walks and hikes to the greatest spectacles of the West—the waterfalls, ice caves, glaciers, flower meadows, ocean beaches, gorges, moraines, alpine lakes and even groves of trees and cactus plants that make it famous.

Mileages for the hikes here are listed in terms of distance, one-way. And no effort is made to estimate the time it will take to make each trip. And the reason is simple. Few walkers will cover the same ground in the same period of time.

Generally, however, a hiker can expect to hike between one and two miles an hour, seldom less and seldom more. Few mountain trails are level. Most of them when they're not climbing steeply are dropping as sharply, making walking always a slow process even for a seasoned hiker. Novices and family groups should probably allow an hour for every mile to start with, limiting beginning hikes to half-day trips until they have hardened their muscles and acclimated themselves to mountain elevations.

One word, too, about pace. If you find yourself having to stop and rest every few minutes, you're walking too fast. Drop to a lower gear. You'll get there just as fast. And remember, a four-mile destination is at least two hours away. So pace yourself, even at the start, to take that long.

And if children are hiking with you, an even slower pace should be considered. Hikes here are supposed to be enjoyed, not suffered through. Dawdling is to be encouraged, not condemned. And all children should be allowed time to kick pine cones, whistle at marmots, play in streams, feed chipmunks and pick up toads while wives and mothers admire flowers, pause at vistas, enjoy waterfalls and cool off in the shade of every tree.

Little special equipment is required to hike any of these mountain, desert or seashore trails. Good hiking shoes may be the most essential item. Tennis shoes will do in a clinch. But regular city shoes won't do at all on trails that are sometimes muddy, often rocky and occasionally even covered with snow.

Sturdy ankle-high mountain shoes with rubber-lugged soles, available at outdoor mountaineering equipment stores, are preferred. And make certain they are well broken in. Wear them around the house for a week or two, at least, before starting down any trails. Don't buy them the day you leave town.

Hikers are also advised to carry a light rucksack full of emergency equipment including a warm sweater and light rain gear. Mountain weather can change almost instantly from warm to freezing, or from dry to drenching. Extra clothing is mandatory. And in addition, take along sunglasses, bug and suntan lotion, a knife, emergency matches, fire starter, first aid kit, flashlight, compass and a map.

But probably more important than what you carry *in* on the trails covered here is what you carry *out*. Lettering is strictly *verboten*. For if everyone who hiked today left a beer can at the end of a trail there would soon be no beauty left. So carry out all trash. Stuff nothing under trees. Throw nothing into creeks. Leave nothing behind except the scenery.

And stay on all trails. Only the inexperienced hiker shortcuts established trails. First, shortcutting sets up erosion paths that can quickly destroy a trail system and, second, it creates a danger of rocks falling on hikers below.

Backpacking is not discussed in detail here. But hikers who plan backpack trips should buy a small mountain stove. Even in forest settings today, wood is becoming scarce. So don't chop down trees—anywhere. Cook on a stove.

And one closing note: Trails and particularly trailheads change from year to year due to the activities of both men and nature. If you discover some change or inaccuracy in the book and would like to help us keep the directions here accurate and current, drop a note to the author in care of Stackpole Books, Cameron and Kelker Streets, Harrisburg, Pa. 17105.

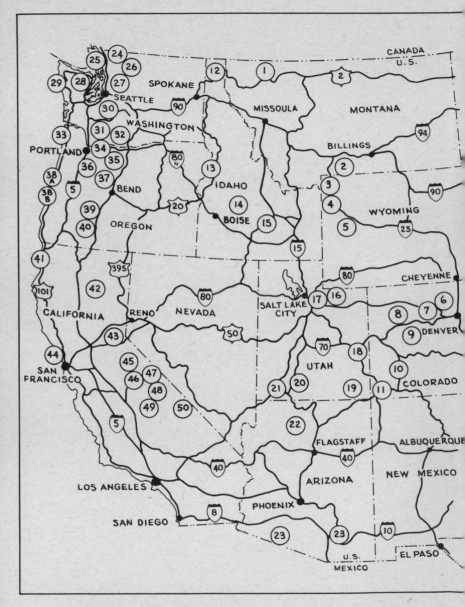

Master Map. (Circled numbers show locations of the various areas as identified and numbered in Table of Contents.)

MONTANA

glacier national park

MORE THAN JUST a sample here of all the glories of the mountain West.

From trails and even roadways—towering mountains, misty waterfalls, green lakes, flower meadows, glaciers and even white goats grazing on cliffs. And a great place to learn your mountain skills.

The park embraces more than 1600 square miles of mountain scenery offering hikers more than 700 miles of trail. Reviewed here, however, is just one small section—the Many Glacier area on the east side of the park.

To reach the area: From the east, drive west on U.S. highways 89 or 2, turning north toward St. Mary. From St. Mary continue north about 9 miles to Babb, turning left there on the Many Glacier road. Many Glacier in 12.8 more miles.

To reach Many Glacier from the west, drive east on U.S. 2 to the park's West Glacier entrance. Cross the park on the spectacular Going-to-the-Sun road, turning north again at St. Mary to the Babb and Many Glacier road.

The park receives its heaviest use during the school vacation periods, starting to peak early in July and tapering off in the last week of August. Use is heavy all week long during the summer season with slightly higher pressures on weekends.

September to many, however, offers the park's "best" camping and hiking. Although many of the campgrounds are closed after Labor Day, some are kept open and there's always space available. Backcountry trails are likewise without crowds.

Supplies may become a problem. Many of the concessionaires in and near the park close down as the season ends. But some facilities are always available.

During the summer season, the Park Service offers a variety of naturalist programs, including a series of guided "Eco-Treks" into the backcountry. These three-day backpacking trips are designed to develop an understanding of man's impact on his environment.

Slide programs are presented at campfire programs in the major campgrounds every night. Guided day hikes are also offered in each major area on a daily basis. Information on the programs can be obtained at visitor centers and entrance stations.

Visitors should come prepared for almost every kind of weather in the park. Days can be warm. Nights are always chilly. And rain is not uncommon, although the park enjoys its best and driest weather during July and August.

Temperatures in July and August range in the low 60s with highs in the upper 80s and lows in the mid 40s with occasional drops to freezing at higher elevations.

Glacier is also bear country. Grizzlies live here. And visitors are warned to keep food locked in their cars and to be alert for animals when hiking.

WHERE TO DRIVE

The highway spectacles here are unequaled anywhere. Sweeping vistas at every turn. Weeping walls, lily meadows, waterfalls, lakes, gorges, creeks and peaks—in an ever changing parade.

Going-to-the-Sun road—a 50 mile drive—is an absolute must no matter which section of the park you visit.

Start either at West Glacier or St. Mary and follow the constantly winding paved two-lane road over the top of Logan Pass

(6664 feet) and then back down again. And give yourself lots of time. A motorist guide will help you enjoy your trip.

Automobile and trailer combinations over 30 feet long and more than 8 feet wide are barred from the twisty road between Avalanche Campground on the west side of the pass and the Rising Sun Campground on the east during July and August. The limitation is extended to 35 feet at other times.

Waterton Lakes—Follow the Chief Mountain Road from Glacier into the Waterton Lakes National Park of Canada just across the border.

Drive 4 miles north from the Many Glacier junction with U.S. 89 at Babb, turning left at a well marked junction. Cross the border in 15 miles, reaching the Waterton lakes area in another 13 miles. Long mountain vistas down the lake. Views as you travel too of Chief, Sentinel and Sofa peaks along the Rocky ridge.

WHERE TO HIKE

Trails here for every level of skill and to every type of scenery. Trails past waterfalls, to glaciers, lakes and vista points. Trails where hikers look up and others where hikers look down, where a hiker must work or where a walker may stroll.

It's a great place to develop a mountain "sense"—to get used to the deceptions of distance and size that every mountain newcomer must learn to understand.

Opportunities here also to start your learning process with experts. Park rangers conduct daily hikes into many of these areas with visitor groups.

Bullhead and Redrock Lakes—An easy 3-mile stroll from the Many Glacier campground to two lakes tucked in a valley below towering Grinnell (to the southwest) and Wilbur mountains (to the north).

Find the trailhead off the end of the campground road just beyond the store. From a junction with the Iceberg Lake trail in a few hundred yards, the trail crosses a bridge and then climbs slightly through timber to views through trees down on Fishercap Lake in less than a half mile.

The path, almost level from now on, reaches Redrock Lake in 1.5 miles and then climbs slightly past the modest but noisy

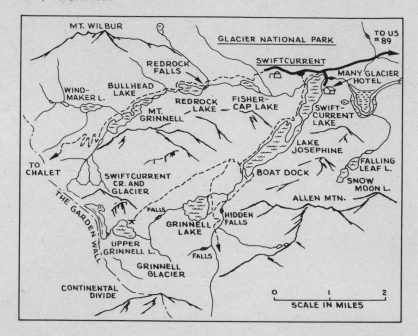

Redrock Falls to a brushy flat and the long Bullhead Lake. Walk through the brush here for reflected views of the mountains on the lake.

End your walk either at the lake or continue on about a half-mile up switchbacks (more strenuous now) to views from the trail down on the lakes and out the valley. The trail continues up the mountain to the Granite Park Chalet. From the lake, another 4.5-mile trek, one way.

Watch for goats. An easy afternoon or morning walk.

Grinnell Lake—Hike 3 miles to a pretty gray-green lake tucked in a steep mountain cirque below Grinnell glacier.

Find the trailhead off a picnic area about .3 miles west of the campground on the south side of the Many Glacier road.

The trail crosses to Swiftcurrent Lake, skirts the lake and then climbs a slight ridge to Lake Josephine. At the upper end of Lake Josephine watch for a junction leading to the left downhill to the head of the lake and boat dock. Turn right (west) at the next junction and follow the well-worn path to Grinnell Lake, another .8 miles.

Camping by permit at the outlet end of Grinnell. But picnic as you will. Pictures here of the lake, the east side of the Garden Wall and Grinnell Falls as it tumbles off the glacier shelf.

Grinnell Glacier—A standard hike, of sorts. Park naturalists take groups there almost every day. But it's still one of the most exciting hikes in the Many Glacier area—with a naturalist or without. 5.5 miles.

The glacier is normally the "goal" of this trip. But the mountain cliffs dotted with goats, the view down and back on the valley lakes and the end-of-the-trail vista clear back to the plains outside the park are the real reasons for taking this day-long trek.

Here again, the trail starts from the picnic area on the south side of the road just east of the campground. After passing Swiftcurrent and Josephine lakes (see Grinnell Lake hike) the glacier trail cuts sharply uphill in a series of short switchbacks and then continues to climb (gradually but seldom steeply) until it nears the top of the rock cirque above Grinnell Lake.

From here on the trail climbs a little and drops a little as it makes its way ledge-by-ledge to a picnic area just below the barren glacial slopes. The trail here gives the hiker a good idea of how mountains are formed as the trail drops down the inclined slope of one upthrust plane of rock and then climbs over the exposed end of another upthrust layer.

Trail to Grinnell Glacier

From the picnic area, trails climb uphill to views toward the plains, Upper Glacier Lake and the ice field itself. *Don't* hike out on the glacier unless you've been trained or are with a ranger group. Glaciers *are*, not can be, dangerous.

To shorten your trip—if you must—take a cruise boat up Swift-current and Josephine lakes from the Many Glacier Hotel, hiking to the trail from the head of Josephine Lake. Save about 2.5 miles each way.

Highline Trail—Although not in the Many Glacier area, a hike here of whatever length leads to some of the most spectacular vistas in the park. Views (constantly), flowers (every month) and spectacle (beyond belief).

The trail starts from the Going-to-the-Sun road at Logan Pass and climbs gradually to Granite Park Chalet in 7.6 miles. Find the trailhead across the highway from the visitor center parking lot. The trail drops down slightly immediately, cuts around the face of a rock bluff and then wends gently up and down toward the chalet through a seemingly endless series of flowered slopes.

Although the trail travels just above the highway, the road's presence soon is forgotten. As the road drops, the trail climbs, leaving the hiker alone with the mountains.

You can either hike to the Chalet and return, or drop over Swift-current Pass east of the Chalet ending your hike at Many Glacier (a 15 mile trip) or simply walk out the trail a few miles, eat lunch by a stream and walk back.

BACKPACKING OPPORTUNITIES

Backpacking opportunities in Glacier seem almost unlimited. But heavy use of the backcountry has brought controls.

Backpackers must now obtain permits for any overnight trip and are required to camp only at established campsites.

The park also limits the number of campers permitted in each site and length of stay and assigns backpackers to specific areas on a first-come-first-served basis. No mail permits are issued. If an area is "full", park officials will suggest alternatives sites.

Backpackers should also bring cooking stoves. In some areas open fires are prohibited. Hikers are urged to write the park for backcountry information before planning any trip. Occasionally an area may be closed to camping because of use or bear problems.

Permits can be obtained, in person, at ranger stations or visitor centers.

WHERE TO CAMP

There are over 1000 auto campsites available in Glacier offering campers a wide variety of camping experiences. The larger campgrounds, as you'd expect, are also the most crowded. Campers willing to brave narrow dirt roads, however, can usually find privacy at remote camps in such places as Kintla and Bowman lakes.

Most campgrounds fill each night during the peak season with the most popular camps filling by noon. Information on the campground situation can be obtained at entrance stations.

Commercial campgrounds are available outside the park near all of the major entrance stations.

Persons visiting Many Glacier can camp at the campgrounds listed below. Other camps are available on the west side of the park.

Many Glacier—117 sites on well designed loops at the end of the Many Glacier road. Generally fills during the rush season by mid-morning. Flush toilets. Piped water. Open from early June through September.

St. Mary Lake—156 sites off the Going-to-the-Sun road about a half mile west of the St. Mary entrance station. Generally fills late in the day. A lower elevation camp. Flush toilets. Piped water. Open late May through September.

Rising Sun—82 sites on pleasant spruce forested loop on a bench above—but well away—from St. Mary Lake. 5.6 miles from St. Mary entrance. Generally fills by mid-morning. Flush toilets. Piped water. Open early in June through mid-September.

Where to Get Information

For details on the park write:

> Superintendent
> Glacier National Park
> West Glacier, Mont. 59936

beartooth country

CAMP AND HIKE here to glimpse the wild beauties of the Beartooth backcountry, just outside Yellowstone National Park.

From campgrounds near Cooke City, Mont., only 3.5 miles from Yellowstone's Northeast entrance, trails lead into the wild lakes and barren plateaus of the Beartooth primitive area. More than 400 lakes here, many of them at over 9000 feet, in a 230,000-acre tract.

To reach the area: Drive east from the Yellowstone Northeast entrance on the Beartooth highway (U.S. 212) or drive west from Red Lodge, Mont., on the same highway. 65 miles. The highway between Cooke City and Red Lodge is closed in the winter.

Campgrounds and lowland trails, mostly to lakes, open generally in mid-June and remain open through mid-September, depending on the weather. Higher country trails open later as the snows melt.

The area gets its heaviest hiking and camping use during the vacation season from July 4 to mid August, tapering off quickly as schools open. Fall camping and hiking are attracting increasing numbers in late August and early September despite occasional storms and even snow. Cool days, crisp nights, an absence of crowds—and bugs—makes the area particularly attractive then.

Temperatures here remain in the cool range day and night all summer. Daily maximums range in the 70s and minimums stay near freezing. Snow can be expected any month at higher elevations. Warm clothing is a must for low country or high country campers or backpackers.

Afternoon thundershowers are common, lasting an hour or two—or sometimes only a matter of minutes—and then passing on. Bugs can be a problem for both campers and hikers until mid-July.

The Forest Service generally presents campfire slide programs several nights each week in the Cooke City amphitheater during the summer rush period. Schedules are posted in Cooke City and in campgrounds.

Find tourist facilities in Cooke City, a small and old gold mining and trapping center which has been active (but never very) since 1869.

WHERE TO DRIVE

Clay Butte Lookout—The 65-mile Beartooth highway is worth a drive all by itself. New vistas from every curve. But for a short spectacular sample of the grandeur here visit the Forest Service lookout atop Clay Butte.

To reach the lookout, drive east from Cooke City on the Beartooth highway for 22 miles turning north on a well-maintained gravel spur road. The lookout at the end of a 3-mile climb.

Perched atop a high meadow knob, the lookout affords 360-degree views of the Beartooth mountains to the north, the North Absaroka Wilderness to the south and the Cooke City landmarks—Pilot and Index peaks—to the west.

Blankets of mountain flowers too. Hawks, eagles and occasionally a band of sheep.

The Forest Service has provided a special viewing room for visitors in the bottom of the tower where a visitor can identify nearby peaks, valleys and landmarks. If you have time, climb up and talk with the person manning the lookout too.

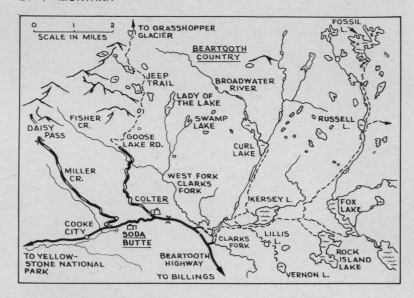

Daisy Pass road—Drive 4 miles up a rough mining road to vistas down two river drainages, a lake and an old abandoned mining operation.

Drive east from Cooke City, turning north onto the Daisy Pass road in about 1.5 miles. The seldom-maintained road switchbacks up a ridge and then climbs steadily toward the pass, first through timber and finally over open meadows.

Note the evidence of prospecting above and below the road as you cross the open meadows below the pass and see the results of an actual mining operation at the top. Green rolling mountains on one side of the crest. Brown and barren tailing piles on the other.

Probably not to be driven in any low-slung passenger car. But other vehicles will make it with ease—if driven with care. Be particularly careful in crossing the erosion ditches dug across the road.

Grasshopper Glacier—A popular local tourist trip. Local packers offer vehicle and horse trips into this ice field which contains the frozen remains of thousands of grasshoppers trapped and embedded in the glacial ice some 2000 years ago.

The trip should not be attempted by passenger car and hiking is over a steep four-wheeled vehicle trail (never pleasant). An 11-mile trip, one way.

WHERE TO HIKE

Day hikes here will get you to the edge of the wilderness country and that's about it. But a glimpse of the spectacles hidden here is better than no view at all.

Broadwater Lake—Hike 3 miles past a broad river (truly) to two mountain lakes tucked in granite mountain clefts.

Find the trailhead for all of these Beartooth trails at the end of a short spur road a mile east of the Colter campground on the north side of the road. It's generally marked as a foot trail starting point.

Take the trail north out of the parking area, dropping over a bridge and then climbing over a slight ridge to a junction with the main Beartooth horse trail in about a quarter mile.

Take the main trail to the right. It's a mire of mud here all season. Four-wheeled vehicles are not barred in this section.

Watch for a junction in another quarter mile. The Broadwater trail branches off to the left, crosses a stream and then climbs uphill rather steadily along an old road. As the road turns downhill keep a sharp lookout for a spur trail, again to the left, in about a quarter mile. (The road continues on to the upper end of Kersey Lake.)

From that junction, the trail passes a soggy meadow and then starts climbing again, sometimes rather sharply, over a series of benches, first to a narrow section of the Broadwater River and then to a very broad section of the stream. (Is this where it got its name?) From the broad section, the trail climbs inland again over a granite ridge and rock bluffs before dropping down above Curl Lake. Keep alert for blazes here. It's easy to miss the trail if you don't pay attention.

At Curl Lake (2.5 miles) the trail passes a collapsing old prospector's cabin before dropping down to the water. From here the trail becomes more primitive, following the lake shore to the Broadwater outlet in a long half-mile.

As you hike this trail, note the tin cans nailed to trees, particularly along the broad stretch of the Broadwater. These cans served as marten traps for local trappers. A trap was placed inside each can along with bait. A stick was propped to the can from the ground so the marten could reach the bait. Little trapping is done in this area today.

Russell Lake in Beartooths

Russell Lake—Hike 6 miles through pleasant forest and up an exciting boulder-plugged gorge to a high granite-girded mountain lake. A full introduction here to the greater beauties offered by the rest of the Beartooth backcountry. An all-day trip.

The trail starts from the hiker trailhead (see above) dropping over a bridge and climbing a ridge before joining the muddy horse and vehicle trail to the right. After about a half-mile the mud and vehicles cease and the trail starts up a rocky slope to the outlet of forested Kersey Lake. Take the trail along the south side of the lake, over the shoulder of a bluff above the lake and then down past a meadow.

At 2 miles, the trail passes a junction with the Rock Island lake trail and continues uphill slightly to wind through level open and pleasant stand of pine.

At about 4 miles the trail starts climbing again, first over a ridge to Russell creek and then into the canyon just below Russell Lake.

For the last 1.5 miles the trail climbs first along the sides of the rock canyon and then through a section where massive boulders have buried the stream, finally switchbacking up the side of the waterfall outlet of the lake. Look back here at the Index and Pilot peak landmarks south of Cooke City.

Russell Lake, tucked below granite mountains and surrounded by rock, offers limited camping at the upper end. The Forest Service has closed some sites to camping in an effort to protect the fragile lake shore from further human destruction. So give the area tender care and obey the signs. Picnic but don't camp. Enjoy but don't destroy.

Rock Island Lake—An easy hike to a pretty wooded lake guarded by barren bluffs and dotted with islands of rock. About 3 miles.

Find the trailhead off the hiker's parking lot, again, following signs toward Kersey and Russell lakes. After passing Kersey Lake and climbing over the ridge at the end of the lake, the trail crosses a meadow and then starts uphill gradually to a junction in 2 miles with the Rock Island Lake trail.

Take the trail to the right past two swampy meadows to the lake in three-fourths mile. Camping and picnic spots near the lake. An easy half-day walk.

BACKPACKING OPPORTUNITIES

Backpackers here should check with forest officials before starting any overnight trips into the Beartooth backcountry.

Permits may be required and hikers may be asked to limit camping to specific areas as the Forest Service attempts to protect some of the more fragile areas from overuse.

Backpackers can either follow established trails or find their own way, particularly in the barren high plateaus of the primitive area.

A popular trail is one that leads first to Russell Lake (see above) then easterly past Mariane, Picket and Jordan lakes to a junction with the trail that loops back past Widewater and Fox lakes to the Russell Lake trail again. A three-day trip. But again, check with forest officials before planning any trek here. Inquire in Cooke City for the location of the local ranger.

WHERE TO CAMP

Campgrounds near Cooke City fill every day during the summer rush although many may have sites open as late as 7 p.m. The campgrounds are opened and closed on an as-needed basis early in the year and after Labor Day.

Soda Butte Campground—A half-mile east of Cooke City on the south side of the highway. 21 units. Vault toilets. Piped water. Well-spaced sites in open forest along a single spur road.

Colter Campground—2 miles east of Cooke City on the north side of the road. Pleasant sites on forest loops. Lots of privacy. Pit toilets. Piped water. 23 sites.

Where to Get Information

For information write:

District Ranger
Gardiner Ranger District
Gallatin National Forest
Gardiner, Mont. 59030

WYOMING

yellowstone national park

THE GRANDFATHER OF all parks, this. The first national park in the world. But still one that lends itself to exploration. In fact, the 1,000 miles of maintained backcountry trails in this great park have, in the past at least, been seldom used at all.

Covered here is only a sampling of park trails in one part of the park—the steaming thermal country around Old Faithful in the southwest section.

Not covered are the many heavily used footpaths that lead from busy roads to nearby mudpots, geysers and hot springs. Information on these crowded trails can be obtained at park visitor centers.

Drives are suggested, however, into other areas of the park so that no visitor misses the vast variety of wonders to be seen here.

To reach the park: To reach the park from the east, drive northwest from Rawlins, Wyo., on U.S. 287; west from Cody on U.S. 16, or southwest from Billings on U.S. 212. Several roads lead north to the park from U.S. I-80. From the west, take U.S. 191

from Idaho Falls, Idaho, and Bozeman, Mont. From the north, take U.S. 89 from Livingston, Mont.

Tourist travel in Yellowstone is heaviest in July and August with the numbers reaching almost crowd proportions at times around some of the more popular park features such as Old Faithful Geyser.

The people impact is generally week-around during the rush season with the heaviest crowds reported mid-week rather on weekends.

The park season opens in May and generally closes at the end of October—as always, depending on the weather. September is thought by some to be the "best" month in which to visit the area. Camping sites then are usually available. Crowds have disappeared—along with the bugs. Some naturalist programs are still being offered. But commercial services are being reduced to a minimum as the month progresses.

June is the rainiest month in the park, on the average, with July, August and September having only occasional showers.

Daytime temperatures range in the mid 70s in July and August with evening temperatures averaging in the high 30s. Snow is possible at any time. In September, nighttime temperatures drop to the near-freezing range. Warm clothing here is essential all summer long.

In addition to evening campfire programs at all the major campgrounds, the Park Service schedules daily walks and hikes from centers throughout the park. Get information at visitor centers. Formal self-conducting nature trails, including one for the blind, are also found. The Park Service has established a series of radio transmitting stations near major features. Tune to 1606 on your car radio.

Thermal areas pose particular hazards to the unwary and careless. Water roiling from many of the geysers, springs, pools and paint pots is often at scalding temperatures. And the ground surface in many thermal areas consists of little more than a thin crust over still more boiling pools.

Because of the number and variety of animals in this park, visitors are particularly warned to give them all wide berth. None should be approached. All are wild. And any met on a trail should be passed with caution. Grizzlies should be avoided at all cost.

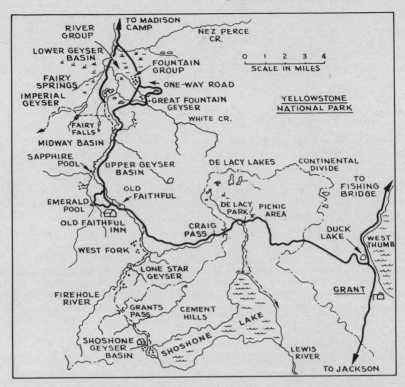

WHERE TO DRIVE

If Yellowstone is nothing else, it's a park designed for the automobile. In fact, almost every important feature can be visited by road and a short walk—not hike—from the curbline. But the off-the-beaten-track drives remain interesting.

Listed here is a slim cross-section of the drives offered in the park. Study park maps to identify other trips of your own.

Firehole Lake Drive—A 3.5 mile one-way loop road off the Madison-Old Faithful road about 9 miles south of the Madison (7 miles north of Old Faithful) junction leads past Great Fountain Geyser, White Dome Geyser and steaming Firehole Lake with its nearby Three-senses Nature Trail designed for both the sighted and the blind. Directions and interpretation are in braille as well as print.

A witch's cauldron here of spouting water, bubbling ponds and hissing steam.

Hayden Valley—A late evening or early morning drive on the 16-mile stretch of road through this valley, between Lake junction and Canyon, is almost guaranteed to bring views of wildlife— moose, buffalo, deer, elk and bear—as they leave the forest to graze on river flats and hillside. Park on turnouts along the road.

But don't disturb the animals, both for your own safety and theirs.

Moose here feed belly-deep in the river. Buffalo amble over flats and bear—sometimes even grizzlies—feed discreetly on far hill-sides. Waterbirds too—by the dozens—in valley ponds and streams.

Bring binoculars and wait.

Grand Canyon of the Yellowstone—Drive—almost—to views down on the Upper and Lower falls on the Yellowstone River near Canyon junction. The colors of the wind-eroded cliffs in the canyon are almost as spectacular as the falls themselves.

Drive south on the Hayden Valley road about 2 miles from Canyon junction, turning east across Chittenden bridge to the South Rim Drive.

For views down on the Upper Falls, stop at the Uncle Tom's parking area walking (not hiking) about 100 yards to the west and a formal viewpoint. To see the Lower Falls drive to the end of the road at Artist Point, walking maybe 200 yards this time to long views back at that falls. Other vistas from the North Rim drive. Information at the Canyon visitor center.

Firehole Canyon Drive—A one-way 2-mile drive off the Madison-Old Faithful road through a pretty river canyon with a waterfall and cascades. Don't hurry here.

Turn west off the main road about a half-mile south of the Madison junction returning to the road just beyond a cascades along the Firehole River.

WHERE TO HIKE

Not every geyser, mudpot or lake here is overwhelmed by crowds. Some can still be viewed in relative privacy. If you're willing to hike a ways.

Imperial Geyser and Fairy Falls—Hike 3 miles on an almost level trail to your own private waterfall and geyser.

Find the trail at the end of a short trailhead spur road to the west of the Madison-Old Faithful road about 1.3 miles south of the Midway Geyser basin parking area.

The trail starts out as an abandoned road, crossing the Firehole river and then following the southern boundary of Midway geyser basin. Watch for a trail to the left in about a mile. It's signed.

The new branch starts out on an old two-track road finally becoming a legitimate one-track trail in about a half mile, reaching the base of Fairy Falls in nearly another mile. A wispy stream here plumes 200 feet into a greenery-set pool. No formal vistas. Find your own.

To reach the geyser, hike another .7 mile beyond the falls. The trail, less used now, crosses a soggy meadow (there's a signed junction here, turn left) then wends through forest to the geyser in an open area at the base of a mountain.

Allow plenty of time to ponder the wonders here. The geyser boils almost constantly in its own clear lake, spouting jets occasionally as high as 60 feet. And examine, too, the sputtering mud pot and bubbling pools nearby. Note also the heavy signs of moose and elk in the clearing area.

Lone Star Geyser—Walk about 2.4 miles to another private view of one of the showiest geysers in the park. But with warnings, this time.

You may be totally disappointed unless you find out when the geyser is expected to erupt *before* you start. The geyser here only spouts once every three hours and unless you know about what time it's due you may have a long time to wait! So check with returning hikers or bicyclists—and hope.

Find the path (unfortunately you must walk the whole way on an old paved road) just off the Old Faithful-West Thumb road about 2.7 miles east of the Old Faithful underpass. A spur leads to a parking area south of the road. Find the geyser at the end of the trail road.

The geyser, with one of the largest cones in the park, spouts water 30 to 40 feet in a slanting jet during its eruption periods. It does little more than grumble and steam during its three-hour dormant time.

If you have to wait for the display watch the nearby meadows for elk.

De Lacy Creek trail to Shoshone Lake—A 3-mile stroll through green meadows and along a meandering stream to a wilderness lake.

Find the trail here about .2 miles west of the De Lacy picnic area on the Old Faithful-West Thumb road, 9 miles east of the Old Faithful junction. The trail starts on the south side of the road. Parking on the north side. So be careful when crossing the highway.

The path climbs first over the highway bank and then drops for about 50 yards down to the level of the creek, ambling sometimes up and sometimes down all the way to the lake.

The trail starts in timber but soon moves into open meadows near the creek ending up in timber again as it nears the lake. Watch the meadows for moose and elk and occasionally a pair of big sandhill cranes. You may also meet some on the trail. Your

Imperial Geyser reached only by trail

primal residual sense of danger will probably alert you at such times.

When the path reaches the lake—no powerboats here at all— turn right (the main trail continues on the left side of the lake) following the sandy shore to a formal camping site in a half-mile more. Picnic where you wish. Camping, however, only by permit.

BACKPACKING OPPORTUNITIES

Permits are required for all backcountry overnight hiking in Yellowstone. Campsites are assigned before you begin your trip.

Obtain permits at the ranger station in the district in which you plan your hike. All are issued "in person" at the time of use. None can be obtained by mail.

Suggested here is a hike into the Shoshone Geyser Basin on Shoshone Lake via the Lone Star Geyser trail (see above.) This 7-mile trail wends through forest to camping areas near the west end of the lake. Thermal areas lie alongside the trail. Several active geysers here and many bubbling pools. *But* use care. These are fragile features for which *you* are wholly responsible. So approach them gently so that they may continue to function for others to see.

A two-day trip, at least. Stay longer if you can.

WHERE TO CAMP

Four campgrounds serve the Old Faithful area.

Norris—116 sites 1 mile north of the Norris junction. Open through August. Piped water. Flush toilets.

Madison—292 sites on forest loops a quarter-mile west of the Madison junction. Open through September. Piped water. Flush toilets. Sewage dump.

Grant Village—433 sites near, but not on, the West Thumb of Yellowstone Lake. 2 miles south of West Thumb junction. Open into early September. Flush toilets. Piped water. Sewage dump.

Lewis Lake—100 sites on pleasant forest loops near Lewis Lake. Open through October. Piped water. Pit toilets. Fills later than some other camps.

If park campgrounds fill, visitors can find commercial facilities outside the park at the West Entrance.

Sites can also be reserved through the nationwide American Express-Park Service reservation system by contacting local American Express travel offices, Ramada Inns or Hertz offices.

Where to Get Information

To get information on the park write:

        Superintendent
        Yellowstone National Park, Wyo. 82190

grand teton national park

NO WAITING FOR mountains here. Peaks leap to more than 13,000 feet from an almost level plain.

Spectacle comes easy from the highway. But the true splendors of this park will be enjoyed most by the camper willing to walk or hike into the towering mountain wildness.

Short hikes provide samples of the grandeur. But longer trails that climb to vistas and subalpine lakes will give fuller meaning to what these mountains mean.

To reach the area: From the west and south, take U.S. 89 north from Jackson. From the east, take U.S. 26 and U.S. 287 from Casper and Rawlins. From the north drive U.S. 89 from Yellowstone.

The park season here generally begins in mid-June. But trails at higher elevations often don't open for another month with snow remaining on some high passes until August 1.

Opening and closing of trails here is almost a direct function of altitude and weather with lower trails open the longest and upper trails the shortest period of time. Low trails may stay open until late September. But higher trails generally are closed by snow shortly after Labor Day.

Temperatures in the Tetons range from cool to cooler. In the summer, day maximums range through the upper 70s and low 80s with nighttime minimums dropping into the upper 30s. Freezing temperatures, however, are possible in every month.

Rains are usually heaviest in June, dropping off dramatically in July, August and September. Afternoon thundershowers are common in July and August. But despite their bluster and threat, they seldom last long.

Use in the park, as one would expect, is heaviest during the school vacation periods through Labor Day with steady use the week-around. June and post-Labor Day visitation, however, has been increasing. Camping space is no problem then. There are no crowds. Visitor services within the park, however, may be limited.

Visitors, not familiar with mountains, should approach these peaks and rivers with care. All of the trails are safe although some can be deceivingly steep. The rivers, however, are all deceptively swift, racing at 5 to 8 miles an hour even in quiet stretches.

The mountains which rise so suddenly from the plain look easy to climb. But no one should attempt such a feat without proper conditioning and training. Climbing instruction is available in the park.

Park naturalists offer a variety of afternoon and morning walks throughout the park as well as special hikes for children. Some day-long hikes are also scheduled. Get information at visitor centers and entrance stations.

WHERE TO DRIVE

No matter where you enter the park, be sure to drive the main north-south Teton Park road from the South Entrance at least to Colter Bay.

Vistas here change constantly as the mountains are put in new perspectives by distance, angle and light. The Teton peaks look entirely different from Jenny Lake than from Signal Mountain. And different again from Colter Bay.

Lots of turnouts and formal vista points. And remember to take the one-way loop road past Jenny Lake.

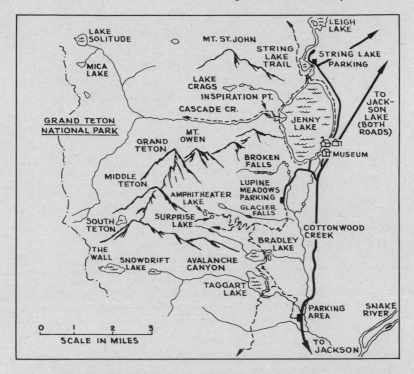

Signal Mountain—Drive a 5-mile paved road—no trailers here—to a series of vista points on the 7731-foot Signal mountain.

Turn east off the Teton Park road about 1 mile south of the Signal Mountain campground.

In 2 miles stop at the Jackson Lake overlook. In another 2.5 pause at the Jackson Point overlook for even broader views. Drive a half-mile more for a still different view, this one down on Emma Matilda Lake and the Snake River.

But the best view is the last, at the end of the road. A 360-degree vista here of the whole shebang.

WHERE TO HIKE

Hike a long way to long views and a short distance to shorter ones. But gain a sense of mountains on all of them. For once on the trail, the range becomes a physical reality rather than just a post-card view.

Surprise and Amphitheater lakes—Two high and pretty mountain lakes are the goal here but the vistas enroute alone make the trip very worthwhile.

A 4.8-mile all-day trek. Carry water.

The trail starts from the end of the Lupine Meadow parking area. Turn west off the Jenny Lake-Headquarters road about three-fourth mile from the Jenny Lake junction. Trailhead in 1.5 miles.

The trail starts out fairly level for the first half-mile but then starts climbing up a ridge and never stops. At 1.7 miles leave the Valley trail and continue on uphill.

From the junction, the trail climbs eight long switchbacks (rest at a vista point with views to the north over Jenny Lake at the end of the series) and then continues up 10 more shorter ones before reaching the first lake, Surprise.

It would be unfair to say that the trail is steep. But it would be a downright lie to infer that it is anywhere near level. It climbs without respite. If you've never hiked in mountains before this is certainly no place to start. In fact, even if you're an experienced hiker you'll wonder more than once enroute why you started at all.

But, actually, the effort is all worthwhile, even if you don't go all the way. In the first mile, views out over Bradley Lake, Taggart Lake and the valley. And the further you climb the bigger the vista.

Surprise Lake—the first goal—lies tucked in a rocky basin surrounded by trees. You'll rest here for sure. Amphitheater lake lies .2 miles beyond at the base of a rock wall in a truly alpine setting. Another resting spot.

This is a popular trail, heavily used by young backpackers. And a good example of what a stiff mountain trail can be.

Taggart and Bradley lakes—A 5-mile loop trail leads through forest and meadows to two pleasant wooded mountain lakes.

Find the trail westerly from the Taggart Lake trail parking lot off the Jenny Lake road about 3¾ miles south of the Jenny Lake junction. 1.6 miles to Taggart lake. Another 1 miles to Bradley and 2 miles from Bradley back to the trailhead.

The trail here starts out across a barren plain but soon plunges into pleasant forest. Turn right at the first junction in a quarter mile. In a mile, turn left following the trail to still a third junction, this with the Valley trail at Taggart Lake.

From Taggart Lake follow the Valley trail to the right (north)

Surprise Lake

first along the lake and then over a ridge to Bradley lake. From Bradley lake, take the cutoff trail back to the parking lot. (Watch for the trail, to the right, as you near the lake.) But don't turn back as soon as you reach the junction. Dawdle awhile by walking up Bradley Lake on the Valley trail to the bridge across the outlet channel. Views all along the lake of the surrounding peaks.

The trail from Bradley Lake climbs over two slight ridges and then through a series of grassy meadows (views here down on Taggart lake) before joining the Taggart Lake trail again a mile from the parking area.

Jenny Lake-Hidden Falls-Inspiration Point—An easy hike here to a pretty waterfall and vista point. And all around a pleasant lake.

There must be a half-dozen ways to visit the falls, the vista point and tour Jenny Lake by boat, trail or both.

Suggested here is an easy hike from String Lake, just north of

Jenny, to the falls and vista point with a trip back across Jenny Lake by boat, returning to String Lake by trail again. About 5.5 miles by trail.

Find the String Lake trailhead parking area just off the Jenny Lake loop road about 3.5 miles from the north Jenny Lake junction. Trail drops to the String Lake outlet. Cross the bridge, turning downstream (left) to reach the head of Jenny Lake in about a quarter mile.

The trail then climbs above the west shore of Jenny Lake reaching a junction with the boat-dock trail at 2 miles. Stay on the main tread here (don't cross the creek) following a foot trail uphill to Hidden Falls in a few hundred yards.

To reach Inspiration Point and its view back over Jenny Lake, continue a half mile past the falls and on up the Cascade Canyon trail as it switchbacks steadily up the face of a cliff. Watch for practicing mountain climbers here. Park climbing schools conduct classes on this cliff. The vista point is marked.

To return to String Lake, take the boat (there's a nominal charge) back to Jenny Lake Campground. Then hike north along the west side of Jenny Lake.

Find the trail here across from the store just west of the road, away from the lake. The trail remains on the east side of a slight ridge for about a quarter mile before dropping down to the lake.

Reach the parking area again in about 3 miles.

BACKPACKING OPPORTUNITIES

The Grand Tetons abound with backcountry backpacking opportunities. But the Park Service, in an effort to protect the fragile backcountry, limits the number of backpackers, bans open fires and requires all backpackers to obtain a no-charge permit.

Hikers must camp in designated places, assigned at the time of departure.

Overnight hikers—no permit is required for day hiking—can obtain permits either by mail or at the park for specific dates and areas.

Hikers unfamiliar with the park should use care, however, in planning trips in advance and seeking permits from afar. Effective hiking distances here often have little to do with distances on a map.

WHERE TO CAMP

Campgrounds are almost always filled to capacity in July and August with the more popular camps filling by mid-morning. Entrance stations have late information on possible camping opportunities.

Sites can also be reserved through the nationwide American Express-Park Service reservation system by contacting local American Express travel offices, Ramada Inns or Hertz offices.

Overflow camping is available in nearby Forest Service campgrounds and in commercial campgrounds south of the park.

Larger campgrounds include:

Jenny Lake—85 sites on forest loops near—but not on— Jenny Lake. A popular area restricted to tents and small camping vehicles. Trailers, walk-in campers, motor homes and buses are excluded. Flush toilets. Piped water.

Signal Mountain—86 sites on loops of lodgepole pine near Jackson Lake. Most sites have small views of the lake through trees. Flush toilets. Piped water.

Colter Bay—525 campsites near Colter Bay Village on loops near Jackson Lake. Flush toilets. Piped water.

Gros Ventre—408 sites on a series of loops above the Gros Ventre river. About 4 miles east of U.S. 26 at Gros Ventre junction. Often has vacancies in the late afternoon.

Where to Get Information

For information on the park write:

Superintendent
Grand Teton National Park
Moose, Wyo. 83021

bridger wilderness

STRICTLY HIKING COUNTRY, this. And already very heavily used.

Vistas from valley roads only hint at the virgin beauties to be found in the mountains of this vast area.

But from the trails! No signs of roads. No clearcut slopes. No distant views of smoggy towns. Just mountains and valleys as they were meant to be.

The Bridger Wilderness stretches 90 miles, covering over 383,300 acres and embracing more than 1,300 lakes. Only a small corner is covered here, however—the Green River Lakes entrance to the very north.

To reach the area: From Pinedale, Wyo., 100 miles north of Rock Springs, drive west from town about 5 miles, turning north (right) onto the Green River road. The Green River Lakes campground and the end of the road in another 45 miles.

The river road starts out paved but soon changes to gravel getting narrower and rougher the closer it gets to the end. Drive at usual cruising speed at the start. Speed, at only 20, near the end.

The Bridger gets its heaviest backcountry use during July and August when campgrounds, particularly in the Green River Lakes area are almost always full.

Most campgrounds open by mid-June. But backcountry trails generally don't open until mid-July.

The camping and hiking season often continues through September with pleasant periods of Indian summer after the equinox. Snows, however, can close trails then at any time.

Summer thundershowers are common in the afternoon, rolling through with almost the regularity of a clock, streaming hail, rain and wind. And the sound of the storms here can be awe-inspiring as thunder echoes and re-echoes through the mountains. Beautiful!

Altitude and bugs (particularly in early summer) may pose the greatest problems to campers and hikers. Trails here all range from 8,000 to 10,000 feet in elevation which means lowland hikers may find themselves short of breath until they've acclimated themselves. Bug levels usually drop off late in August. But hikers may still want to carry repellant.

The Forest Service here offers no formal campground programs. Information about the area, however, can be obtained weekdays and weekends at the ranger station in Pinedale, a block south of the main street in the middle of town.

And just one other important note: Give this area your finest care! The beauties here depend on man. Your trash, your waste, your fire can destroy in an instant all that time has built. So be kind. Be thoughtful. So others in the future can also enjoy what you come here to see.

WHERE TO DRIVE

View drive opportunities are rare in this part of the Bridger area. Roads in the valleys afford distant views of the Wind River peaks. But the number of forest roads that climb to close views is limited.

Skyline Drive—Drive 15 miles from Pinedale above Fremont Lake to look into the wilderness area and out over the many foothill lakes.

Find the road at the end of the Pinedale main street at the east end of town. Signs indicate Elkhart Park and Fremont Lake. Turn

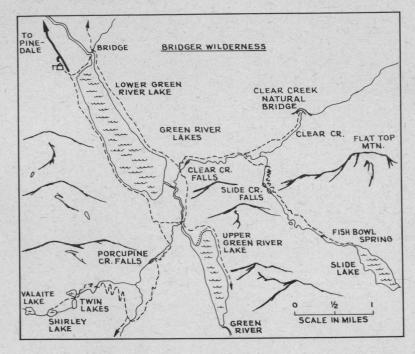

toward Elkhart (right) at a junction in about 3 miles.

From viewpoints along the road look down on Halfmoon Lake (to the south) and over Fremont Lake (to the north). Elkhart campground and trailheads at the end of the road.

Green River Lakes drive—No tall mountains here. But in late evenings watch for moose and antelope on a valley floor.

Drive north from the Green River Lakes Campground on the entrance road. No fixed distance. Keep a sharp eye for aminals as they move out to graze near the river.

Lots of water birds and eagles too, including if you're lucky, glimpses of trumpeter swans.

WHERE TO HIKE

The day hikes listed here offer only a tiny cross-section of the great spectacles hidden in these wilderness valleys. Longer, several-day hikes seem here to be the rule. Trails stream with backpackers either going into the wilderness or coming out.

But shorter one-day hikes can be rewarding too. Splendors at trip-ends found nowhere else.

Upper Green River Lake loop—Hike less than 4 miles to a classic view of Bridger's Square Top Mountain towering over Upper Green River Lake.

All the reason one needs to call the Bridger spectacular. If you take no other hike, take this.

Find the head of the trail which leads around the west side of Lower Green River Lake at the far end of the Green River Lake campground, about 50 yards to the west of the boat-launch road. It starts behind a campsite at a stile over the campground fence.

The trail at first climbs away from the lake into timber for about a half-mile then out to views over the lower lake and at surrounding mountains. After dropping down to the lakeshore, the path then climbs into timber again as it nears the head of the lake, looping to the left and a stream crossing. Watch for a spur trail here to the sandy beaches which stretch clear across the head of the lake. Explore if you have the time.

The main trail now goes eastward past a junction with the Porcupine Trail, across a meadow and a bridge to a junction with the lake's east-side Highline Trail. Turn right (south) here, reaching the upper lake in another half-mile. Watch for moose. But if you meet one treat it with great respect.

At the upper lake—once you've absorbed the initial glories of the vista—follow fisherman trails (noting where you left the main trail) to the right along the lakeshore to a camping site on the outlet cove.

To return to the campground via the trail along the east side of the lower lake, follow the main trail back to the lower lake junction, continuing on the Highline trail along the *east side* of the Green River outlet, across Mill creek to a path in sagebrush on the east side of the lower lake. Constant views now back at the mountains and down the lake.

At the outlet on the lower lake, cross the bridge bearing to the left along the lakeshore to find paths back to the campground.

Clear Creek Natural Bridge—Certainly nothing here to compare to the spectacular rock bridges of the southwest. This is a juvenile bridge in the early stages of formation. But add Clear Creek, its meadows and a glimpse of two waterfalls and it's a hiking package worth the time.

A 5 mile hike to the bridge.

Take the Highline trail along the east side of Lower Green River lake watching for a trail uphill (to the left) just north of the Clear Creek, in about 2 miles.

Take any one of several sharply climbing paths for about a quarter mile to the top of a bluff and an overlook for Clear Creek Falls. To see the falls at the bottom of a gorge walk about 25 yards to the right of the trail.

From the falls overlook, continue up the valley (the trail is almost level now) along the edge of the grassy Clear Creek past the Slide Lake junction watching the far ridges for glimpses now of the snow-white face of Slide Creek Falls.

The trail reaches the end of the meadow about 2 miles from the lake, then winds into open timber along the creek, reaching the natural bridge in still another mile.

Square Top over Upper Green River Lake

From the downstream side, the bridge looks more like a giant spring with water gushing from a gash in the rock. But from the upstream side (take a trail uphill over the ridge to the left) one can see a large full-size bridge in the process of being formed.

Twin Lakes—Hike 7 miles and climb nearly 3,000 feet to a pretty brace of lakes nesting high in Bridger mountain peaks. An all-day trip.

Take the trail from the campground along the west side of the lower lake. Find the trailhead near a stile about 50 yards west of the boat-launch road at the end of the campground.

The trail travels about 3 miles along the lake, turning eastward to meadows and a junction with the Porcupine Trail at 3.5 miles. Turn right (south) here following the Porcupine trail first through level meadows to a crossing of Porcupine Creek and then up a series of stiff switchbacks for 2 miles. Watch for a viewpoint here of Porcupine Creek falls.

At the top of a ridge, the trail flattens out (thankfully) for about a half-mile to another creek crossing and a junction with the Twin Lakes trail at the edge of a meadow just across the creek.

Bear to the right here on the Twin Lakes trail as it crosses a meadow and then climbs again through increasingly thinning timber to the lake outlet stream, switchbacking then to a clearing with spectacular views out at Square Top mountain and the snow-capped peaks beyond. The first lake in another half-mile.

The two lakes set side-by-side in a mountain cirque. Places to camp on the far side of the larger lake.

And take time here to examine the sandy bottom of the shallow far shore of the larger lake. Lots of caddis larvae here, dressed in cases of sticks and sand. Watch closely and you can see them move. These larvae later will change into delicate flies providing, of course, some hungry trout doesn't eat them first—cases and all.

A fainter trail continues past Twin Lake up over a ridge to Shirley Lake in another half-mile and Valaite Lake in a mile.

BACKPACKING OPPORTUNITIES

Identification of all of the loop and long one-way backpack trips in this wilderness would require an entire book.

A few hikers start at one end of the wilderness and hike toward the other. Some start in the middle and hike one way or the other. And still others work out loop trips from any of the several entrance roads.

From Green River Lakes, hikers can take a number of loop trips up the Green River and back down the Porcupine Trail. Some hike as far as Trapper Lake (16 miles). Others pick shorter routes.

For an easy but pleasant trip, backpack only as far as Upper Green River Lake, camping either at the head or outlet end. Make a base camp here for day hikes into further lakes and valleys.

WHERE TO CAMP

The closer you get to the end of the Green River Lakes road, the heavier the campground use. Check at the Pinedale ranger station on the camping situation before you start.

Green River Lakes—23 units on a very pleasant forest loop near—but not on—the Lower Green River Lake. At the very end of the road. Full most of the time during the busy summer season. But spaces turn over almost every day. Piped water. Vault toilets. Open July through October.

Whiskey Grove—9 sites near the Green River about 30 miles from U.S. 187 on the Green River Road. Vault toilets. Piped water.

Newfork Lake—15 sites near New Fork lakes. Turn east off the Green River road about 15 miles from the highway. Campground in 5 miles. Vault toilets. Piped water.

Fremont Lake—52 sites along and above Fremont Lake, most with views of the lake. A good base camp near Pinedale if up-river camps are full. Piped water. Vault toilets. 7 miles northeast of Pinedale.

Where to Get Information

For information on the wilderness write:

District Forest Ranger
Pinedale Ranger District
Bridger-Teton National Forest
Pinedale, Wyo. 82941

COLORADO

rocky mountain national park

HORDES OF PEOPLE here. More than 2.5 million visit each year. But there's still beauty too.

Roads, such as the famed Trail Ridge road, will give you awing-but-distant looks at the mountains which tower, some of them, to 14,000 feet.

But for true beauty and much more privacy, try the trails.

To reach the area: From I-25, turn west at Loveland interchange onto U.S. 34, following the highway down the Big Thompson canyon to Estes Park. From Denver, drive northwest to Boulder taking U.S. 36 north. From I-70 to the south, drive west from Empire on U.S. 40, turning north again at Granby onto U.S. 34.

Some facilities in Rocky Mountain are open all year. But the summer camping season generally starts about mid-June with limited camping well into the fall. Brilliant color displays by the aspen here bring visitors into the park through October.

The park gets its heaviest use between July 15 and August 15 with campgrounds and trails crowded during all of that period. Use is heavy all week long but heaviest on weekends when Denver visitors join those already in the park.

Lowland trails generally open with the campgrounds in June. But many high country trails may not open until mid-July, or later, depending on the weather.

Daytime temperatures range to 85 degrees in July and August with nighttime temperatures ranging down to 35. August is the park's wettest month with an average of 2 inches of rain. June and July average only an inch. Afternoon thundershowers are common but of short duration from June through August.

September is a popular month for many people who visit the park. Although snow is not uncommon then, even at lower elevations, weather is generally clear, crisp and dry. Campgrounds are less crowded and most trails are open. Aspens start turning color usually by the middle of the month, depending on the frost.

The Park Service offers naturalist programs from June into September ranging from evening slide presentations at campgrounds and visitor centers to naturalist-conducted bird and beaver "walks". Schedules on all of the programs can be obtained at visitor centers.

The Service may in time close some roads, particularly in the Bear Lake area, if use continues to increase, establishing an inner-park bus system to move crowds from trailheads and viewpoints. Road and parking facilities in these areas are already overtaxed. Check at entrance stations.

WHERE TO DRIVE

Almost every road in this park is worth driving. Panoramas wherever you go.

Trail Ridge Road—The 40-mile trip from the Deer Ridge junction on the east side of the park to the Shadow Mountain National Recreation area on the southwest corner shouldn't be missed. Allow a minimum of two hours each way.

The highway, which climbs to 12,183 feet at the highest point twists its way through every life zone in the park. Formal vistas points along the way. And short nature trails too.

At Forest Canyon, for instance, a short walk leads to views 2000 feet down into a valley and across to peaks on the Continental Divide. Stop, too, at the Alpine Visitor Center.

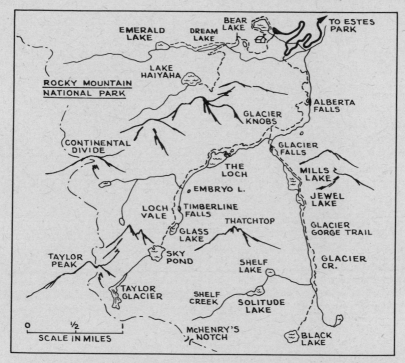

To make a loop trip, include a one-way drive on the Fall River road, a gravel motor road nature trail. Travel uphill on this road from the north side Deer Ridge junction to the Alpine Visitor Center. A guidebook explains features on the trip.

Bear Lake road—Drive 9 miles from the entrance station to a subalpine lake at the base of park's Front Range.

Turn south off the Ridge Road just west of the Beaver Meadow Entrance station. (If this road is closed, take a bus trip then.)

Look out here at peaks overlooking Glacier Creek and take time at the end of the road to walk around Bear Lake. An easy 1.5-mile trail.

WHERE TO HIKE

All it takes is a little effort here to get away from the crowds—even in the busiest time of the year. Hike just 2 miles and although you won't be alone you won't be standing elbow to elbow with fellow tourists either.

And two suggestions: First, be careful with your trash. These fragile areas aren't garbage dumps. Pack out what you carry in. And secondly, carry water. Heavy human use throughout this park may make some of the water unsafe to drink.

Emerald Lake—A 2-mile hike past two busy forested lakes to a handsome alpine one tucked away in a peak-topped gorge at 10,100 feet.

Find the trailhead to this and the Haiyaha trails (see below) at the end of the Bear Lake parking area. Walk toward the lake, turning left at the trail board. A paved path leads past the ranger station and then starts climbing slowly uphill to Nymph Lake, a lily pad-filled tarn, in half a mile.

Follow the main trail around the right side of the lake as it climbs again, first to views down on Nymph Lake and then to a ridge with another view, to the right, down on Bear Lake too, and on to a junction—Dream and Emerald lakes straight ahead; Haiyaha to the left.

The trail climbs now up the side of a pretty canyon to the outlet of Dream Lake, which truly deserves its name. Lots of big rock outcrops to sprawl on here—by yourself in the morning or with big crowds on a sunny afternoon.

To continue on to Emerald Lake, follow the trail along the right side of Dream Lake to the inlet where it now climbs sharply up one rock outcrop and then another to the outlet end of Emerald Lake.

Rest much longer here. And with more privacy any time of day. Rocks to sprawl on at the outlet or along the shore to the right. Eat lunch. Soak up the sun and, best of all, drink in the scene.

Lake Haiyaha—Pick out your own huge boulder here. There's more than enough for all. At the end of a 2-mile trail.

Find the trailhead at Bear Lake (see above) taking the trail to the left at the junction beyond Nymph Lake in a mile.

This trail is more developed than the Emerald Lake trail but it climbs persistently, nonetheless, reaching views down on Nymph Lake, Bear Lake and the Glacier creek valley in about a half-mile from the junction.

The trail, dropping slightly, finally ends at the lake in a welter of huge boulders. Pick your way carefully over and through them to the lake. It's truly Chaos Canyon here. Tumble on tumble. But the view? Halley Peak to the right and Otis to the left with scenery in between.

Mills Lake-Black Lake—For an easy trip walk 3.1 miles to Mills Lake. But for a strenuous adventure, hike on to Black Lake in a total of 5 miles.

Find the trailhead across the road from the Glacier Gorge parking area on the Bear Lake road about 7 miles from the Visitor Center. The trail starts off to the left.

The path crosses a creek and then starts climbing gradually to Alberta Falls (left of the trail) in about a half mile, continuing on to a junction with a trail to The Loch and Lake of Glass (see below) in another mile.

At the junction turn left following the trail first across a creek and then up and over a slab ridge reaching Mills Lake in another .7 miles. End your trip anywhere along the lake shore here. Or else cinch up your belt and continue past little Jewell Lake and on to Black.

Lake Haiyaha

Once you leave the end of Mills Lake, though, the real fun begins. From then on—"trail au naturel!" And nothing more. The path climbs rocks, skirts ledges and slogs through marshes. When the ground goes up, so does the trail. And when it drops, the trail does too.

And signs of man's work on this trail are almost nil. A cleared tree or two. Maybe a few sticks laid side-by-side in the mud. But little more.

So keep alert as you walk. Not that it's dangerous. You won't get lost. But you'll certainly miss a turn or two both coming and going. So two rules: Never cross the creek and always stay in the valley.

And near the end? Splendor, of course. First views from the meadows up at the glistening slab ridges between Arrowhead and McHenrys Peak. And then, finally, after you've climbed the last steep pitch, all you'd expect a mountain lake panorama to offer: Waterfalls sliding off cliffs, snow ridges, rock, marmots and air so fresh it startles the lungs.

Shady places to rest, around to the left. Otherwise, pick a boulder at the outlet and soak your feet.

The Loch and Lake of Glass—A 4-mile trail climbs past a pretty subalpine lake to a smaller but more spectacular one.

Find the trailhead across the road from the Glacier Gorge parking area (see above) following the trail to the left past Alberta Falls to a junction in about 1.8 miles. Keep right now, climbing to The Loch in another .7 miles. Rock islands here "floating" in a lake overawed by peaks.

Follow the trail to the right of the lake, climbing to a junction of a spur trail (right) to Andrews Glacier. Keep left, climbing into a steep meadow where the trail again goes nearly natural, grinding its way uphill through a maize of rock and then steeply up beside Timberline Falls to the last ledge below the lake. You'll need to use your hands here to get over the ledges. But no danger. Pick your way carefully. And slowly. Be assured: the end result's worthwhile.

On a windless day, just as advertised. A Lake of Glass. But even on a windy day, a pretty pond.

You'll have earned a rest here. But don't pride yourself too much. Many other hikers continue on a half-mile more to Sky Pond, the absolute end of the trail.

BACKPACKING OPPORTUNITIES

Persons hoping to make backpack trips in the park should probably defer finalizing plans until they reach the park.

The Park Service limits the number of persons permitted in every area and requires that all overnight hikers obtain permits and camp assignments. And the demand for permits often exceeds the number of sites available.

Permits cannot be obtained by mail. They are issued only in person at ranger stations and visitor centers. Rangers will, however, suggest alternatives if some areas are filled.

Backpackers are also urged to carry cooking stoves. Open fires are prohibited in some backcountry camps. The park has also closed many close-in lakes and trails to camping because of human impact problems.

WHERE TO CAMP

Nearly 600 campsites are available in the park, all of them open from late May through Labor Day. After Labor Day, inquire at Park Headquarters.

Bluntly, though, use here is extremely heavy. Campgrounds fill early every day during the peak season. Visitor centers and entrance stations have late information on camping possibilities but latecomers often are forced to camp outside the park either in National Forest camps or in commercial facilities at Estes Park.

Campgrounds off the Bear Lake road include:

Glacier Basin—190 campsites crowded into several lodgepole pine loops. 5 miles south of the entrance station road on the Bear Lake road. Flush toilets. Piped water. Sewage dump.

Moraine Park—260 sites, many of them tent-camper walk-in camps, on a series of forested loops. 1 mile west of the Moraine Park Visitor Center off the Bear Lake road and 3 miles from the entrance station. Flush toilets. Piped water. Sewage dump. Open all year. But no water and pit toilets in the winter.

Where to Get Information

For information on the park write:

Superintendent
Rocky Mountain National Park
Estes Park, Colorado 80517

the eagles nest

FROM LOWER CATARACT Lake in the northeast corner of the Gore-Eagles Nest Primitive area hike to either forested or alpine lakes near Eagles Nest mountain.

Again, no more than an introduction to this 61,000-acre area. There are 17 peaks here over 13,000 feet high and 33 over 12,000 feet. Elevations range from 8500 feet to 13,500 with the trails listed below climbing to more than 10,000 feet.

Heavy use here on weekends but during the week enjoy the back-country trails almost alone.

To reach the area: Drive north 19 miles from Dillon, Colorado, or south 12.3 miles from Kremmling on Colorado State Highway 9 to intersections with the Heeney road which goes around the west side of the Green Mountain Reservoir.

Find the spur road to Cataract Lake and the wilderness area off the Heeney road (from the south) 5 miles from the state highway and (from the north) 5.2 miles. The spur travels west ending just beyond the campground in about 2 miles.

Campgrounds here are open from mid-June until it snows in the fall as are most of the lower trails. High country trails, however, don't open until July, depending on the weather, remaining open generally through September.

Use is heaviest here on weekends between Memorial Day and Labor Day. The area gets some vacation use. Denver urbanites account for most of the visits.

Summer temperatures range into the 70s occasionally soaring to the 80s. Evening temperatures drop into the 40s with occasional lows in the 30s.

Afternoon thundershowers with light rains are common but of short duration. Long rainy periods are unusual here.

The Forest Service offers no special naturalist programs. Information on trails can be obtained at the District Ranger Station in Dillon.

WHERE TO DRIVE

Distant and only occasional views of the mountains from valley roads in this area. But one road does lead to a place where you can observe mountain birds.

Rock Creek Bird Nesting area—More than 80 species of birds including golden eagles, ptarmigans, magpies and sandpipers have been identified here.

Situated at between 9,500 and 10,000 feet elevation, this unique area has been set aside as a special habitat for nesting mountain birds.

To reach the area, take a 4-mile dirt road southwest up the Boss Mine road from the Blue River Campground located 10 miles north of Dillon on State Highway 9.

Get a checklist of birds from the Forest Service ranger stations at either Dillon or Kremmling.

The habitat here runs the gamut from streams, bogs and meadows to forest, cliffs and marshes. Nesting birds reach a peak in late June and July. But, please, don't disturb them. Although the area is open to the public, don't camp or drive on the meadows. Some species are extremely sensitive to the slightest disturbance.

WHERE TO HIKE

Trail junctions here are clearly marked and trail treads are easy to follow. But mileages on some signs may be as much as a half-mile off.

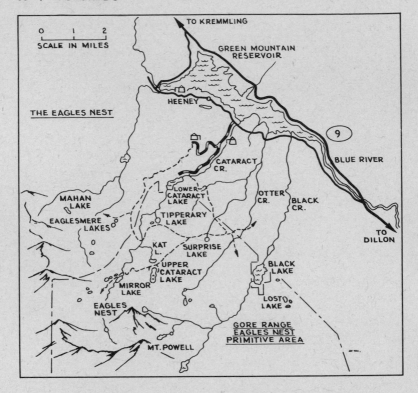

SCALE IN MILES
0 1 2

THE EAGLES NEST

TO KREMMLING

GREEN MOUNTAIN
RESERVOIR

HEENEY

CATARACT
CR.

BLUE RIVER

9

MAHAN
LAKE

EAGLESMERE
LAKES

LOWER
CATARACT
LAKE

TIPPERARY
LAKE

OTTER
CR.

BLACK
CR.

TO
DILLON

KAT
L.

SURPRISE
LAKE

UPPER
CATARACT
LAKE

BLACK
LAKE

MIRROR
LAKE

EAGLES
NEST

LOST
LAKE

MT. POWELL

GORE RANGE
EAGLES NEST
PRIMITIVE AREA

Hikers are urged to stay on the trails here, particularly in lower elevation forests. Landmarks are scarce and it's easy to get lost. So don't try to pre-guess trails. Few ever go where you think they're going anyway.

Upper Cataract Lake—Look up at Eagles Nest mountain from a clear blue lake in a crisp alpine setting. A 5.5 mile hike.

Find the trailhead off the south (left) side of a parking area less than a quarter-mile beyond the campground.

The trail drops from the road, crosses a bridge and then switchbacks up a grassy slope into aspen alternately climbing and coasting for the first mile.

At a creek crossing, however, the trail starts climbing stubbornly and persistently up a ridge for 1.5 miles to a junction with the Gore Range trail which runs through the foothills the full length of the wilderness.

Turn uphill, to the right, on the trail reaching Surprise Lake in less than a quarter mile. Lots of people here, particularly on weekends, both camping and picnicking. So trudge on, still uphill, for a long half-mile to a junction (left) with the upper lake trail.

The new trail climbs less steeply now through increasingly open forest, cresting ridge in 1.5 miles and starting downward again across open boulder and scree slopes. Vistas here down on small Kat Lake and up at surrounding peaks.

Find a trail junction between Kat and Upper Cataract lakes, turning left to Cataract. Less than a quarter-mile.

Camping and picnic spots where the trail first hits the lake. But continue across the outlet before ending your trip. Look out here back down the valley, clear to the flats near Kremmling, and upward at Eagles Nest.

The trail continues, if you have time, on to Mirror Lake in about 1.7 miles.

Eaglesmere Lakes—Hike less than 4 miles to a pair of quiet lakes tucked into forest almost—but not quite—out of view of Eagles Nest peak.

Find the trailhead off the end of a spur road to the right (north) just beyond the campground. The unmarked road ends in .3 mile at a campground loop. The trail starts off the end of the loop (the tread is clear) ducking into aspen almost immediately and climbing a ridge to views, in less than a mile, down on Lower Cataract Lake.

After gaining altitude above the lake, the trail winds away from the lake through groves alternately of aspen and spruce spaced between meadows. Cattle here. Watch, too, for elk.

At 3 miles, the trail reaches the north-south Gore Range trail. Turn right, following the trail north about a half mile over a ridge to another junction with a trail (left) to Eaglesmere lakes.

Reach the first lake in about a few hundred yards, hiking left to a narrow strip of land which separates the pair. Picnic or camp here. Other camping spots around both lakes.

No spectacular views here, only glimpses of Eagles Nest over the tops of trees.

Surprise-Tipperary Lake loop—Hike in on one trail and out on another, visiting two mountain lakes enroute. Roughly, a 10-mile loop.

Eagles Nest Peak looms over valley

Start out from the end of the spur road which leads north just beyond the campground (see Eaglesmere Lakes trail) climbing through meadows and groves of aspen and spruce to a junction with the Gore Range trail in about 3 miles.

Turn left this time (trail, right, to Eaglesmere) following the trail almost immediately to views down the valley over Lower Cataract Lake and as far out as the Green Mountain Reservoir.

The trail continues to drop now through, beside, over and around a series of rock outcrops, crossing Cataract creek in about 1 mile. Take a little time to explore the small cataracts here.

In another mile and a few more rocky ups and downs (watch for short spur paths to viewpoints over the valley) the trail reaches a junction with the Tipperary Lake trail. Drop to the left here reaching the lake in less than a quarter mile.

Dawdle as long as you want (many hikers backpack here, extending the loop trip over two days). Return to the main trail to continue south, climbing a little now to a junction with the Upper Cataract Lake trail. About 3 miles from the Gore Range-Eaglesmere junction.

Follow the main trail left, dropping downhill to Surprise Lake in another half-mile. Continue downhill again taking a trail, left, back to Lower Cataract Lake at a junction in a short quarter-mile. The trailhead on Lower Cataract Lake road is about 2.7 miles from Surprise lake.

From the parking area on the road, hike .3 miles up the spur road back to your car.

Cataract Falls loop—Stroll 1.5 miles around Lower Cataract Lake to views up Cataract Falls.

Find the trail at the end of the road beyond the campground. A five-minute walk leads to the lake, surrounded by pasture. Follow trails right or left toward the head of the lake and a bridge across the inlet. Views up here at the falls. Most spectacular in the spring. But worth viewing any time.

BACKPACK OPPORTUNITIES

Any of the day hikes listed here except, perhaps, Surprise Lake afford an opportunity for an overnight backpack trip. Surprise Lake is usually too crowded. As usual, the further you walk the fewer the people.

Take the trails as listed but allow yourself a few extra hours because of your load.

No permits required here. So the burden is on you to maintain your camping spot so others may find beauty here too.

WHERE TO CAMP

Camping facilities in the Cataract Lake area are limited. But oddly, they're seldom crowded except on weekends.

Overflow camping by permit for trailers and campers at state sites around the Green Mountain Reservoir.

Cataract Lake—8 sites on a small wooded loop near the end of the Cataract Lake road, 2 miles from the Heeney road. Pit toilets. Piped spring water.

Eaglesmere Lakes trailhead—A primitive camp at the end of an unmarked .3 mile spur road to the right just beyond the campground. Primarily a trailer-camper area. No water. Pit toilet.

Blue River—10 sites about 8 miles north of Dillon. Pit toilets. On the east side of the road. Camp here and drive to Cataract Lake or visit the Rock Creek bird nesting area.

Where to Get Information

For information, write:

District Ranger
Dillon Ranger Station
U.S. Forest Service
Dillon, Colorado 80435

the flat tops

A LOW-KEY SPECTACLE here. Different from anything else in this book.

High trails. Low trails. And flowers beyond belief. But an intimate country in a comfortable land. Nothing to shock you, really. Just lots to enjoy.

And mountains you'll want to come back to, for sure.

To reach the area: From U.S. I-70 across the middle of Colorado, drive north from Rifle about 41 miles to Meeker and then east from Meeker on State Highway 132 (the Trappers Lake road) to Trappers Lake in another 49 miles. Paved most of the way.

The lake lies on the northeast corner of the 118,000 acre Flat Tops Primitive area—a flat-topped plateau much of it at more than 10,000 feet elevation with mountains on top of that.

Campgrounds in the Trappers Lake area open about June 15 and remain open through mid-September, closing sometimes earlier if it snows.

Trails generally aren't open to travel before early July, or later, depending on the weather, closing with the first high-elevation snows in September.

Use is heaviest here through July and August with the greatest number of visitors on holidays. Weekend use is heavier than during the week with campsites available most of the time, Monday through Friday.

Campers here, however, seldom come for just a day or two. It's too far to travel for just an overnight stay.

Weather, as you'd expect at altitudes of 9000 feet and more, is cool all summer long. Daytime temperatures range in the mid and low 70s, with nights in the mid-30s.

Thundershowers are common on afternoons about every other day. But they pass quickly. Carry a rain jacket and keep on hiking.

Hikers are warned, however, about the danger of falling dead trees, particularly during wind storms. Spruce in this area was ravaged by a beetle in the late 1940s which killed all of the mature spruce on more than 300,000 acres on the Flat Tops Plateau. The dead snags still stand and many topple in every storm. So stay out of trees at such times if possible.

The Forest Service offers no naturalist programs here. Information, however, can be obtained at the ranger station in Meeker.

WHERE TO DRIVE

No roads to prowl once you've reached Trappers Lake and the edge of the Flat Tops. But the roads enroute make the trip there worthwhile.

North Fork-Trappers Lake road—No towering snow-capped peaks. No waterfalls. Simply a beautiful western Colorado mountain valley along a pretty river.

From Meeker, drive east first on highway 132 and the Trapper Lake road.

This, again, is a comfortable land. A place where man can find a little peace and a chance to see things quietly again.

Marvine-Phippsburg road—A gravel road that winds for 40 miles through scenic mountain backcountry from the Trappers Lake road to Phippsburg. Popular with Denver visitors bound for the lake.

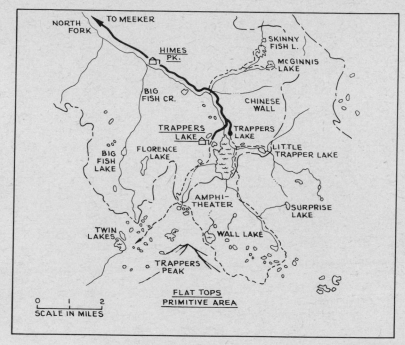

Turn north off the Trappers Lake road at Ripple Creek Pass about 42 miles from Meeker. Drive as far as you want. Vaughn Lake is 15 miles.

WHERE TO HIKE

Don't sample just one trail here.

Hike at least to the top of the Flat Tops above the Amphitheater and into the overflowing flower meadows along the trail to either McGinnis or Skinny Fish lakes.

Wall Lake—Climb out of forested valleys to the high, open rolling meadows atop the Flat Tops in the Flat Top Primitive Area. About 5 miles.

Find the trailhead off an unmarked parking area beyond the campgrounds, northwest of Trappers Lake. Drive past the entrance to the Shepherd's Rim camp loop about .2 mile, continuing straight ahead into an (unmarked) parking area as the road turns sharply left to a Trappers Lake trailhead. The trail starts from the west side of the parking area above a horse unloading ramp.

The trail—newly blazed—climbs into timber past a forested tarn and then above a small unnamed lake, both to the left. From the lake, the trail climbs through a grassy meadow and then through two flower meadows to a junction in about 1.5 miles with a trail from the east side of Trappers Lake.

From here on, the trail now alternately climbs and coasts as it makes its way over benches and through more flower meadows to the base of the Amphitheater wall, switchbacking the last half-mile up the wall to the top and the primitive area boundary. A total of 3.5 miles.

An entirely new world now. At 10,000 feet, rolling alpine meadows. Small patches of new spruce forest. And enough "mountains" to make it all look real.

Follow rutted trails to the left (east) passing four small unnamed lakes (to the right) and continuing on across the gently rolling fields to Wall Lake in another 1.2 miles.

Wall Lake, as you might expect, is literally "walled". Small granite cliffs around the far side. Places to camp here. But stay away from the bleached and tottering dead trees. They're likely to blow down.

Lush flowers in the meadows below the Amphitheater wall. Yellow, orange and blue ray flowers knee deep as you hike the lower trail. And patches of colorful Colorado columbine with their white cups and deep blue sepals as you go up the wall.

On the upper meadows, however, flowers vary in direct proportion to the sheep. Where the sheep have grazed, the flowers aren't. Where they haven't grazed, fields of color still.

Water may be unsafe to drink here, too, because of the sheep.

Skinny Fish and McGinnis lakes—Hike through a wild display of waist-high flowers to two lakes, each with its own unique personality. A half-mile hike to each lake from a trail junction in 2.5 miles.

Find the trailhead on the east side of the Trappers Lake road about 1 mile north of the resort junction. Parking just off the road.

The trail climbs across an open slope into groves of aspen and meadows to a junction in about a mile with the Lost Lake trail (to the left), continuing on through still more lush meadows to a second junction in another 1.5 miles with the two lake trails.

To reach Skinny Fish Lake, hike uphill from the junction to the

Flowers near Skinny Fish Lake

left as the trail switchbacks first through meadows and then into trees. From the earth-dam outlet of the lake, walk to the left around the lake to camping and picnic spots. Other camp sites visible across the lake.

To reach McGinnis Lake, drop downhill at the junction, to the right. This trail drops to a creek and then climbs through meadows and patches of trees to the outlet of the lake. The lake seems like little more than a pond when you first reach it. But continue on to the right and you'll find it all there. Colorful flower slopes and places to camp near the inlet.

The main part of the trail here crosses some of the lushest flower meadows listed in this book. Columbines, Sego lilies and lime-colored paintbrush at the start, changing into red paintbrush, wild roses and fields of hip-high yellow, blue and white ray flowers toward the end, with each meadow featuring its own particular color mix as the season progresses.

Deer here. And lots of chipmunks. And be sure to watch

downhill as you hike in for the many ponds beaver have built on Skinny Fish creek.

Little Trappers Lake—First take a long look at big Trappers Lake and then hike about a mile to Little Trappers tucked in a pretty forest setting just below the Chinese Wall.

Find the trailhead off the uphill (west) side of a parking area at the end of a spur road, which turns east off the campground road at the resort.

The trail climbs from the parking area to views of big Trappers Lake and the Amphitheater ridge in a quarter mile, dropping to the lake and following the east shore to a junction with the Little Trappers trail (left) in another half-mile. Watch for the junction after the trail passes, first, the boat rental cabin and then a log house above the Little Trappers outlet creek.

The trail to the little lake climbs sharply about a quarter mile to smaller Coffin Lake and then, turning right, makes its way, mostly through timber, to outlet of the lake. Flowers on small meadow slopes along the way.

Camping and picnic spots at the outlet or along the shore to the right.

BACKPACKING OPPORTUNITIES

Easy backpacking country, this, once you've climbed out of the valley into the high Flat Top plateau.

No permits are required here. For details on trail conditions check at the district ranger's office in Meeker.

For a very easy test backpack trip, hike to Little Trappers Lake or up to McGinnis or Skinny Fish lakes. (see Where to Hike). Camp spots at all three lakes.

Or backpack into Wall Lake, establishing a base camp for exploring other lakes in the wilderness area. Twin Lakes on top of the plateau is also a favorite place for many backpackers. People, but no crowds, on any of these trails. Yet.

WHERE TO CAMP

The Forest Service has developed a series of campground loops near Trappers Lake, each with a name of its own, although all are part of a single complex.

Trappers Lake—51 sites on a series of loops, none near Trappers Lake. Most in open new-growth spruce. All with views up at surrounding ridges. Piped water. Pit toilets. 49 miles from Meeker.

North Fork—47 sites in open forest. Pit toilets. Piped water. North of the road. About 34 miles from Meeker on the Trappers Lake road.

Marvine—23 sites near Marvine creek. Pit toilets. Water from creek. Turn (south) off the Trappers Lake road about 30 miles east of Meeker. Campground in 6 more miles.

Where to Get Information

For information on the Flat Tops, write:

District Ranger
Blanco Ranger District
White River National Forest
Meeker, Colorado 81641

maroon bells

BIG MOUNTAIN COUNTRY, this. Massive peaks and sweeping valleys. One picture panorama from the end of the road. But the instant grandeur ends with that: Better views and bigger vistas are reserved for those who hike.

And in the fall, add the glistening gold of aspens to every scene. Spectacular! No other word will do.

How to reach the area: Drive west from Aspen on State Highway 82, turning south onto the Maroon Bells road just outside of town near the stone Prince of Peace church. About 5 miles to the entrance station. 9.5 to the end of the road and lake.

The Maroon Bells lie near Aspen, one of the most popular ski resorts in the West. And even during the summer the small community crawls with tourists. But the mountains here don't reflect that rush. People, yes. Hikers, certainly. But they've come to see the mountains and not each other. A different scene. And nobody tries to sell the natural view.

The Maroon Bells-Snowmass wilderness, in which these peaks

lie, embraces 66,830 acres of mountains and high valleys that are almost wild worlds to themselves.

Peaks and ridges range from 12,000 to over 14,000 feet. The pair of Maroon peaks rise to 14,015 to 14,116 feet. And even the trails climb to 10,000 feet and above.

Some campgrounds in the Maroon valley are generally opened by Memorial Day and are kept open into early October. But the majority open about June 1 and remain in use through Labor Day.

Trails in the high country—and most of this country is high— sometimes open up in late May but often not until late June if the spring is cool. Trails generally remain open into late September and early October, again, depending on the weather.

The heavy use period in the valley starts Memorial Day and ends Labor Day with campground full throughout the week. The best time to avoid crowds and still enjoy the mountains is during September. Weather may turn unstable during the equinox. But the region also often enjoys sunny, crisp Indian summers late in the month. And, of course, there's fall color too.

Summer temperatures in the upper Maroon valley will range around 65 degrees during the day and in the upper 30s at night. Be warned, however, that it can snow here any month of the year.

Afternoon thundershowers with occasional hail are common. However, most last only a half to three-quarters of an hour.

Visitors are warned not to try climbing any of the mountains— even when they look easy—unless they've been trained to climb or are accompanied by someone who has. Rock on these mountains is notoriously "rotten" and likely to break away underfoot or when used as a handhold—with no notice at all.

No problems, though, on the trails. All are safe and all are well marked.

The Forest Service here offers no naturalist programs. Information about the mountains, however, can be obtained at the Aspen ranger station on the north side of the highway at the west end of town.

WHERE TO DRIVE

Almost every road near Aspen leads to an unusual vista of some sort.

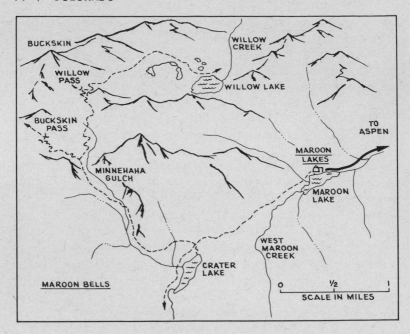

Independence Pass—Drive 21 miles east of Aspen on a narrow but paved road to one of the highest passes in the West at 12,095 feet.

Take state highway 82 east out of Aspen as it follows the Roaring Fork river higher and higher into the mountains, climbing, at the end, to well above timberline and constant vistas up one valley after another.

Ghost towns too along the way. Watch for the tumble-down cabins of the old mining town of Independence south of the highway about 17 miles from Aspen. Not much parking here. But if you stop don't destroy what you find.

At the top of the pass—the road continues east to a junction near Twin Lakes with U.S. 24—hike out trails both north and south of the pass to still higher viewpoints. Windy here. And chilly too, even in midsummer.

This is probably not a road to drive with a trailer or wide motor home, particularly if you're not used to mountains. Sections of this road are very narrow, so narrow in fact there is no centerline. Wide and long vehicles can be a hazard both to themselves and others. So park your trailer in Aspen. The pass is closed during the winter.

Ashcroft Ghost Town—Drive 12 miles up the Castle Creek road to an old mining, log-cabin ghost town which once boasted a population of 3500.

Several log cabins still stand almost intact here along with a high-front gambling hall and saloon.

This is an especially pretty drive in the fall when the valley aspens have turned to gold. To find the town, turn south off state highway 82 just west of Aspen near the stone church at a two-way junction which also includes the turnoff to the Maroon Bells. For Castle Creek turn sharply left. Maroon Bells more to the right. The road is paved.

The town prospered in the late 1880s with the operation of a nearby mine. When the mine failed, so did the town. By the end of World War I less than a dozen people remained.

Maroon Bells—No argument here. The most popular scenic drive in the Aspen area. Again, especially in the fall.

If you camp or hike here you'll make the trip automatically. But if you stay in Aspen drive 10 miles to the end of the Maroon valley road for a classic tourist-brochure view of the magnificent Maroon Bells.

Turn south off state highway 82 just west of town at the stone church. It's a two-way junction. Keep to the right. The road on the left goes to Ashcroft.

Park in the road-end parking lot and walk to the shore of Maroon Lake in five minutes for a water's edge look at the peaks. And hike on the north and west edge of the lake if you've got the time. An easy half-mile walk leads to a beaver dam and constantly changing vistas of the Bells.

WHERE TO HIKE

Trails here to meet every skill. Some to lakes. Some to alpine meadows and two to mountain passes.

Carry water on all the trails. Heavy human use and grazing sheep may make the water here unsafe to drink.

Crater Lake—No one should miss this walk.

Hike 1.6 miles from the trailhead of Maroon Lake to even more startling vistas of the Maroon Bells from Crater.

Find the trailhead off the end of the Maroon Bells road. It drops first down to the lake and then along the right shore before starting a persistent but not steep climb up to a saddle between the two lakes. Here the path climbs in and around boulders—the Maroon Bells are now back in view—dropping down to Crater Lake, and a junction (left) to the lake and (straight ahead) to Buckskin Pass.

A great place to wander a lake shore. The mountains here spring straight up from the lake more than 4000 feet.

No camping within a half-mile of the lake or along the trail.

Buckskin Pass—Hike nearly 5 miles through higher and higher alpine meadows to a classic pass at 12,400 feet.

Find the trailhead off the end of the Maroon Bells road following the trail first to Maroon Lake and then on toward Crater Lake (see above). But stay on the main trail, passing Crater Lake to the north.

Sheep at Maroon Bells

The trail climbs stubbornly through aspen and then spruce forest as it makes its way up Minnehaha Gulch.

After crossing Minnehaha Creek in about 1.7 miles the trail breaks into open meadows with 360 degree views now up at the surrounding mountains and back, on occasion, at Crater Lake. Maroon Lake, by now, is out of sight.

At 3.8 miles, watch for a junction with the trail (left) to Buckskin Pass and Snowmass Lake. You'll be able to see the switchbacks above you on the ridge.

Allow at least an hour to reach the pass in 1.1 miles. But it's worth every second of the climb. Enroute, ptarmigan, squabbling marmots, small birds feasting on bugs frozen in snow and, yes, even robins—at 12,000 feet.

But the pass itself is really where the action is. Pick a patch of grass and spend all the time you want looking first at Snowmass mountain and Snowmass Lake to the west and then back down at the meadows along Minnehaha creek which you just climbed. And, of course, out at the Maroon Bells which look entirely different now.

Here's what mountains are all about. No roads. No clearcuts. No towns. Only a single trail up and a single trail down. And tired but happy hikers working very hard to see it all.

If you're lucky you'll find lots of flowers on these slopes. But sheep bands are grazed here and once they pass—no flowers. In fact, meadows become instant but temporary barnyards, creeks turn into sewers and trails become a shamble of debris.

The destruction soon wears off. But the pleasures of the meadow will have been temporarily destroyed. And, yes, grazing is permitted in wilderness tracts.

Willow Lake—As an alternative to Buckskin Pass, hike beyond the meadow junction at 3.8 miles and continue straight ahead up to Willow Pass in another .8 mile. Views down another drainage here with Willow Lake downhill in another 1.7 miles. A popular overnight backpack goal.

BACKPACKING OPPORTUNITIES

Hikers planning backcountry trips should check at the Aspen ranger station about current regulations.

Backcountry camping is banned near some lakes. A half-mile

camping limit is enforced around Crater Lake. And camping at Snowmass is limited to five days.

A popular trip is one from Maroon Lake to Snowmass Lake via Buckskin pass—about 9 miles. Some groups extend the trip 8 miles more by splitting up. While one group hikes from Maroon Lake to the Snowmass campground, the other hikes from Snowmass campground to Maroon. The two parties generally meet at Snowmass Lake.

Others simply hike up the trail past Crater Lake and camp in clearings above Minnehaha creek.

WHERE TO CAMP

All of the campgrounds in Maroon valley are managed as a single unit from a central entrance station.

Camp spots are assigned, as campers enter the area. However, assignments can be changed if the camper finds another, vacant spot which he prefers.

Campers are seldom turned away here. The Forest Service has ample overflow facilities. But private campgrounds are available outside the forest (25 miles to Basalt).

Find the campground entrance station on the Maroon Lake road about 5 miles south of state highway 82. The campgrounds are spread out along the road, about one every mile, with Maroon Lake campground at the end.

Maroon Lake—59 sites on several loops well away from Maroon Lake but with views, nonetheless, of the Maroon Bells. Many sites in groves. Others out in the open. Vault toilets. Piped water. One of the valley's most popular camps.

East Maroon—14 sites near Maroon Creek. About 2 miles from the entrance station. Vault toilets. No water.

Silver Queen—6 sites about 1.3 miles from the entrance station. Trailer and camper sites only. No water. Vault toilet.

Silver Bell—8 sites a half mile from the entrance station. Vault toilet. No water.

Silver Bar—4 sites near the entrance station. Vault toilet. No water.

Where to Get Information

For information write:

District Ranger
Aspen Ranger District
White River National Forest
Aspen, Colorado 81611

ouray

HISTORY HERE. AND lots of it. But spectacular mountains and flower meadows too.

Ouray is a mining town that dates back into the late 1800s and which is still making money on its past. Lots of old buildings here just about as they were, and maybe even better.

But the mountains give the town its true flavor. "Switzerland of America" is the way the businessmen advertise the community. And they may be right.

And, oh yes: It's pronounced U-ray by the natives.

How to reach the area: From U.S. I-70 across the middle of Colorado drive south from Grand Junction to Montrose and then 37 miles on to Ouray.

The mountains here are part of the Uncompahgre National Forest and the Uncompahgre Primitive Area. Both are marked heavily by patented mining claims, with more than 16,000 acres of such private claims in the primitive area alone. It's these private holdings that account for all the road construction within the primitive tract.

Heaviest recreation use in this area occurs between Memorial Day and Labor Day with increasing use reported in September particularly by vacationers who wait until school opens to begin their travels.

The Forest Service's only campground near Ouray is generally open by Memorial Day and remains open until mid-October depending on the weather.

The campground gets its heaviest use on weekends and holidays. Even the commercial camping facilities in and near Ouray may be full then. But visitor levels seem to taper off a little between Tuesday and Thursday—although not very much.

Temperatures here during the summer may range into the 80s dropping at night into the 40s and sometimes even to freezing.

Afternoon thunderstorms with accompanying hail and snow are common in July and August. They seldom last very long, however, roaring into the valley and roaring out. Temperatures can drop suddenly after the storms creating the necessity for carrying light jackets in addition to rain gear when hiking in the mountains here.

Be alert also to the problem of acclimation to the elevation. Hikers may experience some problems with their breathing here. So take it easy until you've become used to the height.

Autumn can be particularly beautiful here after the aspens turn to gold. The city even schedules a "color week" in the last week of September to mark the occasion. Weather can be uncertain in the fall. But the area often enjoys an extended Indian summer after the mid-September equinox.

The Forest Service offers no naturalist-type programs here. However, Ouray businessmen present a nightly slide show in town. Inquire at the tourist information booth in the red caboose.

WHERE TO DRIVE

Red Mountain Pass—Natives call it the "Million Dollar Highway" because the road material is supposed to contain a million dollars worth of gold.

But the scenery is more impressive than the story.

Drive either to the top of the pass at 11,018 feet or all the way to Silverton, another mining town to the south. Vistas and views all the way.

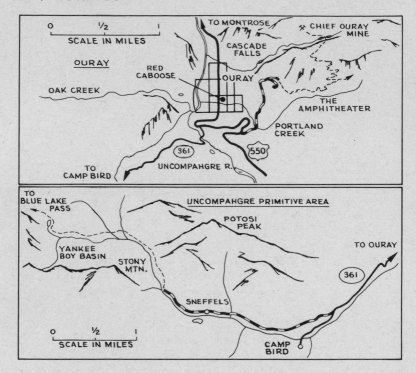

Evidence of heavy mining activity north of the pass. Orange, red and yellow tailing piles topped by dilapidated shacks and mining works on every turn.

From the top of the pass south, however, a whole new scene. The red and orange scars give way to green mountains now. And the streams run clear instead of orange.

Silverton in about 23 miles. Again, old buildings refurbished into a western town. Take a steam train here through the San Juan mountains to Durango. One of the few rail lines of its kind left in the country.

WHERE TO HIKE

Four-wheeled vehicle trails dominate this country. In fact, there may be more jeeps in Ouray than there are natives.

But there are still, thankfully, places here to walk. A few trails follow jeep roads, which aren't all that heavily used. And some go where no vehicles can travel at all.

And stay on trails. Don't try shortcuts. These precipitous mountains can be particularly deceiving. Each year, authorities are called to rescue some hiker who thought he'd found a "shorter way" and ended up stuck on a cliff.

And also stay out of mines. First, they are all on private land. And second, most of them are extremely dangerous. Many are from 30 to 70 years old.

Yankee Boy Basin—Hosts of blue and white columbine here, plus larkspur, paintbrush and lots of other flowers that change as spring moves through summer into fall.

And all plus waterfalls and mountain peaks, including Mount Sneffels at 14,150 feet.

You can hire a jeep and ride into this basin. But to truly appreciate its beauty, drive your own car part way, hiking the rest.

From Ouray, drive south from town on the main highway, turning right (west) in about a half-mile beyond the tourist caboose. The sign says Yankee Boy Basin.

Follow the gravel road at least 5 miles to Camp Bird, an active mining camp, on the left. The state highway ends there and a sign suggests that only four-wheeled vehicles proceed further.

But if you have a compact car or a pickup, drive another 2.5 miles, carefully, past the abandoned buildings of Sneffels to the end of the county road at a Forest Service sign.

If you decided to walk from Camp Bird—you'll certainly see much more if you do—hike up the road past an old mine shaft looking as you go into the deep, steep canyon formed by Sneffels Creek and across the canyon at occasional noisy waterfalls plunging off the canyon cliff.

At Sneffels—the road levels out here—take time to poke around the tumbledown dwelling on the right side of the road and to study the mining ruins across the creek to the south. A good place to wonder about mining laws that permit these private places in the midst of such spectacular public domain.

The "road" ends about a half-mile beyond Sneffels. From here on everybody walks except the jeep tourist. And again, walking is best.

Yankee Boy Basin

Once around the corner from Sneffels, the mountainsides literally explode with flowers and the streams blossom into waterfalls. And look uphill too at the silent wind-eroded rock gnomes that guard the ridges. No problem understanding why this basin is famous—nationwide.

Follow the road to the end in another 1.5 miles and if you still have time, follow a trail up to a small glacial Wrights Lake in another half mile.

Chief Ouray Mine and Upper Cascade Falls—A stiff 3-mile hike first to fantastic views down on Ouray, then past a pair of waterfalls and finally on to the mine.

Find the trailhead at the end of the upper road in the Amphitheater campground. A large display sign shows trails in the entire area.

Take the trail behind the sign to the right as it travels around a ridge to a junction with the old trail in about a quarter mile. Turn left here climbing on to a junction with the Chief Ouray Mine Trail in another mile.

From the junction (turn uphill to the left) the trail now switchbacks sharply 13 times up a ridge, climbing to first-views down on the Portland mine and across at the Amphitheater Ridge.

At the top of the switchbacks, the trail springs out to more spectacular views as it makes its way on ledges across the face of a cliff (no danger, though). Views here straight down from 10,000 feet onto Ouray almost 3,000 feet below!

About a quarter mile from the waterfalls, the trail climbs back into a valley passing between one waterfall above the trail and another below it.

Chief Ouray mine building beyond the falls. Again, this is on private land.

Return the same way you came but watch carefully for the campground spur trail after you rejoin the main trail. It cuts sharply to the right.

Good hiking shoes are a must on this trail. Some of it is steep with a few stretches little more than pencil marks on scree slopes. No danger. But no need to slip and slide as you walk, either.

Other trails—The Forest Service maintains several other trails in this area including two loops up and into the steep mountains west of Ouray.

Condition reports on these trails are prepared each year and posted in the Ouray tourist information center in the red caboose on main street. Ask to see the hand-written notebook where the notes are kept.

BACKPACKING OPPORTUNITIES

No backcountry permits are required in this vast area. Hiking is wherever you find it. And most of it is steep.

Many hikers climb from Yankee Boy Basin (see hikes) over Blue Lake Pass into the Blue Lakes below Mount Sneffels.

Another popular backpack destination is the Chicago Basin in the remote San Juan primitive area, south of Silverton. Take the steam train toward Durango, getting off at Needleton and hiking up Needle Creek to the old mining and ghost town area in the barren ridges there.

WHERE TO CAMP

Public facilities, as noted, are extremely limited here. So many campers, particularly trailer and camper owners, seek sites in the commercial campgrounds near the city.

Amphitheater—Only 30 sites on a forest loop on a mountainside above Ouray. Some with views down on the city. One loop closed to trailers. Full most of the time. Best time to find sites is early in the day. Contact the campground attendant about possible turn-over.

To reach the campground, drive south out of Ouray on U.S. 550 turning sharply left onto a paved mountain spur road on a highway switchback about 1.2 miles from Ouray. Use care here. The turn is very sharp. Campground in another .8 mile.

Pit toilets. Piped water. Cascade trailhead at the end of the main, upper campground road. Display sign.

Where to Get Information
For information on public areas around Ouray, write:

District Ranger
Ouray District
Uncompahgre National Forest
Montrose, Colorado 81401

mesa verde national park

LOOK BACK HERE and give new meaning to time.

In this nation, most of man's work can be measured in terms of only a century or two. But here is evidence of man two thousand years ago.

And don't jeer at the progress you see here. For in only 1300 years, these Indians moved from crude adobe structures on the mesa tops to the complicated apartments of stone beneath the cliffs.

And imagine the sounds of children in these cliffs and the silences that must have fallen when the men conducted rites within these kivas.

To reach the area: Drive east from Cortez, Colorado, or west from Durango on U.S. 160 to the park entrance 10 miles east of Cortez.

The park is open all-year round. But maximum services are available only during the heavy-use period from mid-June through Labor Day. All of the ruins which can be visited are open for inspection during that period. Naturalist programs are conducted

87

at full-scale levels. And buses operate into the recently opened Wetherill Mesa complex.

Use is heaviest here during the mid-week period with the lightest—but still heavy—use on weekends. The campground, however, is seldom full.

The park enjoys its best weather in May, September and October. But services and programs are limited during these periods. Some tours are offered either to the Spruce House or Cliff Palace ruin. At least one is kept open all the time.

But the Balcony House and Wetherill complex are always closed then. Food and other concession services are likewise curtailed and sometimes closed.

Summer temperatures here range several degrees cooler than those on the valley floor just outside the park. Daytime high temperatures average about 86 degrees in the July-August period with nighttime lows ranging about 57 degrees.

Almost all of the park's activities are naturalist oriented. Naturalists are on duty all of the time any of the ruins are open for inspection. They conduct trips to others and stage the familiar evening campfire programs.

During the summer, visitors can walk through Spruce Tree and Cliff Palace ruins. Visits to Balcony House are by ticket only. Tickets are issued on a first-come, first-served basis at the visitor center or museum.

Bus trips into the Wetherill Mesa section are also by free ticket only. But the number of tickets issued is limited. The 50-passenger buses make a 12-mile trip to the mesa where visitors transfer to mini-buses to tour ruins open in the area.

Although each ruin is slightly different, a tour of ruins in either the Chapin or Wetherill mesas will give a visitor a complete sampling of what these mesa and cliff dwellings have to offer. Allow at least one day for your visit here.

WHERE TO DRIVE

Scenic views from the park entrance road and views of ruins from loop roads in the Chapin Mesa area.

Park entrance road—Three formal overlooks between the entrance and the Navajo Hill Visitor Center afford views of mountain

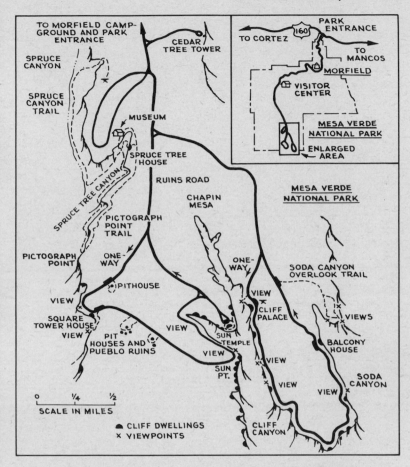

ranges surrounding the park and put the mesas in their proper geographic perspective.

From Mancos overlook—3.5 miles from the entrance look out easterly over the Mancos valley and at the La Plata mountains.

From the Montezuma overlook—6.7 miles from the entrance look over the Montezuma valley to the Ute mountains to the west, the San Miguel and Dolores peaks to the north and the Abajo and LaSalle mountains of Utah.

From park point—take a spur road to the right 10 miles south of the entrance for long-distance views of still more mountain ranges in New Mexico and in Northeast Arizona.

Ruin road loops—Two road loops south of the headquarters area lead to a series of overlooks with glimpses of as many ruins as you've got the time to see. Take binoculars and don't rush. At first glance all of these cliffs look simply like cliffs. But study them a while and ruin after ruin will reveal itself. Some small. Some large. In almost every crack.

WHERE TO HIKE

Hiking opportunities here are—understandably—extremely limited. A few trails near the Morfield Campground can be hiked without permission.

But no trail in the headquarters-ruin area can be hiked without permission from the Chief Ranger's office, near the museum. And the reason is obvious: It's the only way that the Park Service can protect these ruins from looting and destruction.

So always get a permit first. The penalties for not having one can be severe.

Knife Edge Trail—A 1.5 mile walk along a high old road to views over the Montezuma valley. A particularly good place to watch sunsets. Find the trail off the main campground road about three-fourths mile from the Morfield entrance junction. No permit required.

Prater Ridge—Hike a loop around a ridge with views most of the way. A 7.8 mile loop. Find the trail on the west side of the Morfield Campground. The trail climbs the east side of the ridge, loops around the top of the ridge and returns the same way.

Pictograph Trail—Strictly by permit. A 2.3 mile trail which drops into a canyon and then climbs past a modest set of pictographs to return to a forested trail on the rim.

Rangers will point out the trailhead when they issue your permit.

The trail drops first into Spruce Tree Canyon climbing below the edge of the rim for about a mile climbing upward past the pictographs and then more sharply to the rim. Views here across the canyon of Echo House. The trail returns through forest, away from the rim, to the museum.

Spruce Canyon Trail—Walk 2.1 miles through the bottom of Spruce Canyon from the museum to the picnic area on the Chapin Mesa loop road.

Rangers will point out the trailhead when they issue a permit.

Gain a sense here of the terrain in which these cliff dwellers lived and worked. The trail drops to the canyon bottom at the start, follows the canyon northward and then climbs sharply out of the canyon to the picnic area.

BACKPACKING OPPORTUNITIES

There are no backpacking opportunities in Mesa Verde National Park. Backpacking and overnight hiking are prohibited anywhere in the park. Hiking is restricted strictly to the few trails listed above. And, again, with reason: Protection of the artifacts to be found here.

WHERE TO CAMP

Campground facilities here are seldom filled even during summer rush periods. However, there are commercial camps outside the park and many trailer owners prefer to stay there rather than drive the climbing, twisting entrance road.

Morfield Campground—476 sites on a series of loops at 7800 feet elevation. Some sites for tents only. Others for tents and recreation vehicles. Some in wooded areas (no shade, but protection from wind). Others are in the open. Flush toilets. Piped water. Concession services nearby. 4 miles south of the entrance station.

Cliff Palace

Where to Get Information

For information on Mesa Verde write:

Superintendent
Mesa Verde National Park
Colorado, 81330

OTHER PROTECTED RUIN AREAS

Mesa Verde is only one of several protected ruin sites in the four-corner area of Colorado, Utah, Arizona and New Mexico. A number of national monuments have been created to protect other sites.

Each of the monuments is different from the others. Persons interested in studying ruins should visit several. Among the larger ones are:

Chaco Canyon—Fifteen major pueblos here and over 500 other prehistoric sites. The Pueblo Bonito with 830 rooms is the largest in the area.

Camping on 36 sites. Some restricted backcountry hiking on trails 1 to 5 miles long to ruins and vistas. Overnight backpacking is prohibited. In northwestern New Mexico off New Mexico highway 57.

Canyon de Chelly—Awesome canyons and ancient cliff dwelling—all amidst a present-day Indian culture.

Hike to only one ruin—a 1.5 mile trail to the famed White House Cliff dwelling. Views into the canyon from a road above it. Otherwise, all other travel in the canyon by vehicle or on foot must be done in the company of an Indian guide.

Camping at Cottonwood campground near the park headquarters. The monument is near Chinle, Arizona, southwest of Mesa Verde on State Highway 63.

Navajo—Cliff houses in towering red sandstone cliffs—two of which can only be reached by trail.

Register and hike 8 miles (one way) to the Keet Seel, largest cliff dwelling in Arizona. Or tour, with a ranger, the famed Betatakin ruins near the park headquarters.

Limited camping. 9 miles north of U.S. 160 about 22 miles southwest of Kayenta, Ariz.

Tuzigoot—A remnant of a town built by Indians between 1100 and 1400 A.D. Near Clarkdale, Arizona. No camping.

IDAHO

priest lake

NOT EVERY PART of the West can boast of towering mountains and precipitous valleys.

Mountain foothill country is scenic too. Low-key packages of subdued ridges, green forests, rolling hills and crystal lakes.

That's the Priest Lake Recreation Area and the Upper Priest Lake Scenic Area. Peaceful country. Beautiful too.

To reach the area: From Spokane, Wash., drive east on U.S. 2 to Priest River, Idaho, turning north onto Idaho State Highway 57. The Priest Lake Ranger Station in 31 miles.

The recreation and scenic areas are part of the Kaniksu National Forest which covers much of the forest in northern Idaho. Heavy logging here and grazing too. But recreation is playing an increasingly important role.

Some campgrounds open here in early May and remain open through late October depending on the weather. But all of the campgrounds are open during the heavy use period between July 4 and the last week in August.

The impact here is heaviest on weekends and holidays with the midweek period offering the least crowded facilities. September and October are also months in which campers can find lots of campground space, particularly in midweek. Fall fishing may increase weekend crowds.

Summer daytime temperatures run from the mid 80s to the 90s with nighttime temperatures dropping into the 60s. Autumn temperatures drop to the crisp side with frosts likely at least by October. The frosts, of course, bring bright autumn colors. The huckleberry bushes turn red and the tamarack yellow. Occasional thundershowers are reported here in summer. But the weather has more of a tendency to change slowly over longer periods of time.

No poisonous snakes or poisonous plants. But lots of mushrooms and huckleberries in the fall.

The Forest Service here conducts a modest summer naturalist program with daytime hikes on occasion into the Hanna Flat Scenic Area and evening programs at resorts and the Luby Bay Campground. Information on the programs is posted in the campgrounds.

WHERE TO DRIVE

Opportunities for finding vista points from roads here are limited. But the water-view opportunities are almost endless.

Bring your own boat or rent one at a local resort. Canoeing, too. But winds across the long lower lake tend to whip up a heavy chop almost every day making canoeing difficult except for an expert.

The Thorofare—Watch osprey dive here for fish in the crystal-clear stream which links Upper Priest Lake to the lower lake. Watch for moose, beaver, deer and lots of water birds, too. All within an unusual scenic area.

Find the Thorofare at the upper end of the larger lake, east of Tule Bay. The entrance is behind an artificial breakwater. Motorboats are permitted but they are warned not to create any wake while traversing the fragile stream.

Take your time here as the wide river winds its way easily through rich forests. Watch the tree tops for osprey nest and, if you're lucky, watch an osprey carry a fish home to its young.

No camping places on the Thorofare. But in the upper lake find

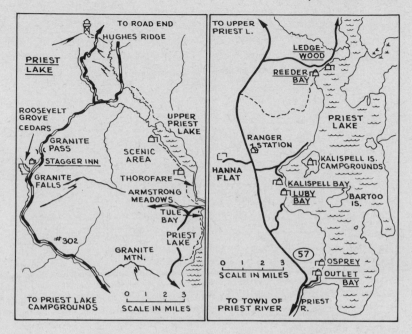

informal spots on sand beaches along the east side of the lake and two formal Forest Service campgrounds along the west shore.

Launch your canoe at the upper end of the lower lake or your power boat at a public camp or resort area to the south. Or rent a boat at a lower lake resort.

Lower Priest Lake—No formal water routes here at all. But explore the islands of Kalispell Bay in the south end of the big lake and prowl the west shore above Reeder Bay for informal places to picnic or camp along the shore.

Vistas, of course, constantly up at Chimney Rock and the Lions Head peaks of the Selkirk range to the east.

WHERE TO HIKE

Small trips lead to big places here.

Hike several of the trails in a day or spread the effort over several days. But sample them all, nevertheless. The true flavor of this area can be found no other way.

Upper Lake Trail—Hike 3 miles, or more, to the secretive upper lake on a quiet forest and meadow trail.

Find the clearly marked trailhead at the upper end of the large lake where the forest road ends at Tule Bay.

From the Reeder Bay campground, east of Nordman, drive north along the lake road 9 miles, turning right at the end, finding the trailhead (to the left) and a Forest Service dock and picnic area (to the right) in another .3 mile.

The trail leads to Armstrong Meadow in 2 miles, wending most of the way through heavy forest. From the meadow, the trail winds back into forest again until it reaches Plowbay Campground on the upper lake at the end of 3 miles.

Stay here. It's a pleasant site. Or else continue by trail on up the lake to the Navigation Campground. 3 miles more. The end of the trail. Oddly, these campgrounds—particularly in midweek—aren't busy. Boaters prefer undeveloped sites on the east side of the lake.

Upper Priest River—If you're traveling by boat take a few minutes—or an hour—to walk into the rich stand of western red cedar along the Upper Priest river. Trees here hundreds of years old, in an area not hiked by many.

Find the trailhead at the inlet end of the upper lake. Look carefully for a sign on the shore (sometimes shielded by trees) to the right (east) of the inlet in the very northeast corner of the lake. The trail continues up the river valley for several miles. Hike as far as you've time for.

Hughes Ridge Lookout—Drive 16 miles on forest road and then hike about a half-mile to an over-all view of the rolling hills in this area from a 45-foot lookout tower at 4200 feet.

Views here down on Upper Priest Lake, Hughes Meadow and the surrounding ridges. The tower is manned most summers. So visit with the lookout too.

Drive north from Nordman continuing onto a well-graded gravel forest road past the Roosevelt Grove of Ancient Cedars (3 miles). At a junction in another 2 miles, turn left onto a narrowing road toward Hughes Meadow and the Lookout, turning right at the next junction climbing 2 miles more through a clearcut on a narrower and narrower road. Not for low-slung passenger cars. Find the trail to the left after you've driven past, below the tower. The trail sign

Hughes Ridge Lookout

says a quarter-mile to the lookout. Make it a half-mile and take your time.

Roosevelt Grove of Ancient Cedars—No long trails here. In fact, the whole grove is hardly bigger than its name. But short walks take you, in one direction, to a pretty sloping waterfall and, in another direction, into a silent grove of majestic trees.

Find the grove off the road north of Nordman (see above) turning west down a spur road in about 3 miles.

Find Granite Falls off the campground road to the left in about 150 feet. The falls roars in the spring when the streams are full but tends to trickle in the fall. The water gushes down a sloping slab of rock.

To explore the cedars, keep right finding informal paths (or make your own) through waist-high fern, deeper and deeper into the grove. Trees here more than 800 years old. The grove was named for President Theodore Roosevelt.

Stay if you like in the small four-unit campground amidst the trees. Pit toilets. Water from the creek.

Hanna Flat Scenic Area—Walk a short nature trail here in a 20-acre grove of trees spared by a forest fire which swept most of this area in 1926. Get a plant brochure on the trail or at the ranger station.

To find the trail, turn west off the Nordman road about a quarter-mile south of the Priest Lake Ranger Station 4 miles from Nordman.

Old cedars again and a cross section of other area plants.

BACKPACKING OPPORTUNITIES

The Salmo River drainage near Canada, north of Priest Lake, and the ridges of the Selkirk range to the east of the lake are popular backpacking areas. Consult local rangers.

But within the recreation area, backpack to Upper Priest lake (see hikes) for an overnight stay at one of the campgrounds there. Or stay several days.

WHERE TO CAMP

Over 114 shore-based campsites here with 44 more in island camps in the middle of the lower lake.

In addition, undeveloped sites along both the lower and upper lake for boaters.

Campgrounds—both on the lake and on the islands—are most crowded on weekends. During the week, however, shore camps in particular remain about 85 percent full, with a vacant site somewhere if you look.

Campgrounds are listed here from the south end of the lake:

Outlet—23 sites, 1 mile from the highway on the lower lake. Turn east 25 miles north of Priest River. Flush toilets. Piped water. Beach.

Osprey—17 units near the lake just beyond Outlet camp. Modest beach. Pit toilets. Piped water.

Luby Bay—52 sites. Beach. Evening programs once a week. One of the more popular camps. Turn east off the Priest Lake road 28 miles from Priest River. 1 mile of gravel road. Flush toilets. Piped water.

Reeder Bay—19 sites near the water. Beach. At Nordman, 39 miles north of Priest River, turn east. Camp in 3 miles. Pit toilets. Piped water.

ISLAND CAMPS

These campgrounds can only be reached by boat. Campgrounds are signed. None has domestic water. Pit toilets.

Kalispell Island—Five campgrounds around the island: Schneider, 6 units; North Cove, 4 units; Silver, 9 units; Three Pines, 8 units and Rocky Point, 6 units.

UPPER LAKE BOAT OR HIKE-IN CAMPS

Plowboy—4 sites. Pit toilet. Water from the lake.

Navigation—5 sites. Water from the lake. Pit toilet.

Where to Get Information

For information on the Priest Lake area, write:
> District Ranger
> Priest Lake Ranger District
> U.S. Forest Service
> Rt. 5, Priest River, Idaho 83856

For information on other Idaho backcountry areas, write:
> Supervisor
> Idaho Panhandle National Forests
> Coeur d'Alene, Idaho 83814

hell's canyon
and seven devils

A CAULDRON OF wonders here. A scorching canyon and high barren peaks. All along the majestic Snake River between Oregon and Idaho, in the Hells Canyon-Seven Devils Scenic Area.

Hikes here are centered around Black Lake in the southwest corner of the scenic area and drives, along high ridges on the east side of Hells Canyon, north of the mining village of Cuprum.

How to reach the area: From I-80 across southern Idaho drive north on U.S. 95 to Council (or south on 95 from Lewiston). From Council drive northwest via forest road to the crossroads at Bear. Turn left (west) to Cuprum or continue northward to Black Lake— the longest backcountry drive in the book.

The Hells Canyon-Seven Devils Scenic Area embraces 130,000 acres on both sides of the Snake River canyon in Oregon and Idaho and in three national forests.

Elevations here range from 1300 feet at the bottom of the canyon to more than 9300 feet in the Seven Devils peaks.

Campgrounds and trails in the Black Lake area seldom open

before July 4 and generally remain open into October, depending on the weather, closing with the first snows.

Lower elevation camps at Lafferty and Huckleberry generally open in mid-May remaining open a little longer.

Roads on the rim of Hells Canyon above the Snake River can generally be driven from the first weeks in June on into October. But, here again, it all depends on the weather.

Busiest season is from Memorial Day to Labor Day with the heaviest use on weekends and holidays. No crowds, however, at any time.

Good tires are essential here. All of the roads in this back-country are gravel and some are extremely rough. And trailer owners are urged to leave their trailers at low-elevation campgrounds, taking day auto trips to the trailheads and views.

Rattlesnakes are common although seldom seen at elevations below 4000 feet. No snakes generally above that level.

Visitors are urged to stay on trails, particularly in the Hells Canyon area. This country is deceptively rough and—for a novice—dangerous.

All campers should probably check at the ranger station in Council on current fire conditions before entering the area. Fire permits are sometimes required here—even in campgrounds.

The Forest Service offers no naturalist programs in these remote areas. If you have questions, therefore, stop at the ranger station.

WHERE TO DRIVE

No paved-highway view drives in this part of the country at all. But fantastic vistas from gravel and dirt roads, which range from rough to rougher.

Hells Canyon Vistas—The Forest Service maintains a whole series of viewpoints atop the east rim of the Snake River Canyon north of the mining village of Cuprum—which means copper in Latin.

From Council drive west out of town on a paved road (it turns to gravel in 9 miles) toward Black Lake and Cuprum.

At the Bear junction in about 19 miles turn left (northwest) onto the Cuprum road passing through the mining town in about 8 miles.

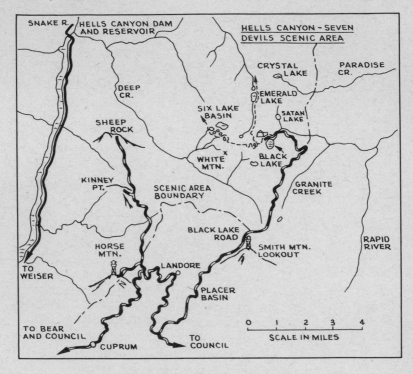

From Cuprum the road climbs past the mine works to a ridge above the canyon. Travel north to:

Horse Mountain Lookout—Vistas from 6887 feet out over Hells Canyon into the mountains of Oregon. No view of the river, however. Most spectacular in the spring when wild flowers are in bloom. The lookout tower here is usually manned.

Turn west onto the lookout spur road about 4.5 miles north of Cuprum.

Kinney Point—Walk out to a former lookout site on a big rock slab for still broader vistas—this one including the Snake River. Oregon mountains again. From 7126 feet. Find the viewpoint at the end of a spur road about 3.2 miles north of the Horse Mountain Lookout junction.

Sheep Rock—Drive 2 miles further along the edge of the ridge for the best vista of all. More precipitous views down into the canyon at the Snake and back over your shoulder toward the He Devil and She Devil peaks of the Seven Devils range. A nature walk here too.

Black Lake Road—This road can be a struggle. But still—ever changing scenery along the way.

North of Bear, the lake road climbs first through open grazing land, burned gold in late summer, into the greener and higher views of surrounding ridges near the Smith Mountain lookout 40 miles from Council.

Park off the road and walk to the lookout tower (a short quarter-mile) to vistas from 8000 feet embracing all of Bear valley, the rim of Hells Canyon and the Seven Devils peaks to the north. Watch for eagles too as they swoop across ridges and out over the forested valleys.

Landore and Decorah—A side trip between the Black Lake road and Cuprum leads past two old mining town sites.

Turn west off the Black Lake road about 1.25 miles north of the Bear campground junction, reaching Landore in 3.2 miles, Decorah in another mile and the Cuprum road in a total of 6 miles.

A brick chimney still stands to mark the mining smelter operation and town of Landore. Decorah, however, is marked only by sign.

The story has it that Decorah (a most appropriate name) was established by the professional ladies of Landore after they were driven out of that town by the miners' wives.

WHERE TO HIKE

All of the day-hike trips here start from Black Lake on the southeastern edge of the scenic area about 50 miles north of Council.

The road to the lake starts out on paved highway. It turns to gravel, however, in 9 miles and for the next 40 gets narrower and narrower, rougher and rougher and steeper and steeper becoming, finally, as it reaches the lake, little more than a two-track trail.

Certainly not a restful trip nor for anyone who gets tired of driving mile after mile at only 10 to 15 miles an hour.

But if you're looking for big vistas and constantly changing scenes, ending up at a pretty, remote mountain lake, it's worth all of the effort it takes.

No road, certainly, for a low-slung city passenger car. And if you're pulling a trailer leave it at one of the lower campgrounds.

Trails here are fairly well marked and all are easy to follow although some old mining paths can be distracting. If you find yourself at a mine site, explore it if you want, then retrace your steps. (Stay out of tunnels, they're all dangerous!)

Six Lakes Basin and Emerald Lake—Hike high above Black Lake to trails leading into two forested basins—one with six lakes and another with only one. 3 miles to Emerald Lake and 4 miles to Six Lakes Basin.

Find the trailhead up the entrance road about 25 yards from the Black Lake Campground. The trail starts uphill to the left (north) near a sign.

The path winds upward first through forest and then through a tumble of rock before climbing across open slopes, sometimes sharply, to a meadow tarn and junction in a long forest service 'le. Look back on Black Lake enroute.

From Six Lake Basin Trail

Use care in picking your way here. Several paths lead uphill to an old mining operation. (Explore old buildings and the remnants of a tramway if you have the time.) But the main trail tends uphill to the right, crossing a creek and then passing an old white bark pine with a square hole cut in it which once served, so local lore has it, as a postoffice for miners in this area.

From the meadow tarn, the trail to *Six Lakes Basins* switchbacks to the left across an open slope (you can see the trail from the tarn) to the top of an unnamed ridge—call it whatever you like once you've reached it.

The trail then drops over the ridge to the right traversing above Horse Pasture Basin to Joe's Gap in about another mile. From the gap, the trail now drops in a series of sharp switchbacks through scree and rock to the first of several lakes. Views to the northwest into the Wallowa mountains of Oregon.

Stop at the first lake if you like. A single campsite near the trail and lots of rocks to fish from. Otherwise, continue down the trail— all in timber now—past two other lakes and the end of the basin in another long mile. To find the other lakes, explore off the trail.

To hike from the meadow tarn to *Emerald Lake,*climb straight ahead to Purgatory Saddle in about a quarter-mile, following the trail downhill as it switchbacks very sharply to the lake in 2 miles. Views of the lake and Seven Devils along the way.

You'll have to wait until the return trip to find out why it was called Purgatory Saddle. The two miles now seem like 10.

Carry water.

BACKPACKING OPPORTUNITIES

Some of the best hiking in the Hells Canyon-Seven Devils area is reserved for backpackers, particularly in the heart of the Seven Devils themselves. These mountains can be explored only by trails, none of them short and none of them level.

From Riggins, Idaho, drive 18 miles west to the Seven Devils Campground near Seven Devils Lake. From here hike into several backcountry lake basins a day or two days away.

An 8-mile hike to the Bernard Lakes with a side trip to the lookout at Dry Diggins, and a three-day loop hike around the entire complex of He Devil, She Devil, Ogre and Belial peaks are among the more popular hikes here.

For information on this rugged country, write the district ranger at Riggins.

WHERE TO CAMP

In the Black Lake-Hells Canyon area camp at:

Lafferty—8 sites at 4600 feet in light timber on the west side of the Black Lake road about 20 miles from Council. Park your trailer here. Piped water. Pit toilets.

Huckleberry—8 sites on Bear Creek. In a wooded area about 30 miles north of Council. On a short spur road to the east of the main road. Pit toilets. Piped water.

Black Lake—8 sites near a pretty mountain lake. Some shaded. Some not. The most remote camp and the most difficult to reach. 50 miles from Council via rough road. Piped water. Pit toilets.

In the Seven Devils area west of Riggins camp at:

Seven Devils—9 sites in a pleasant wooded loop at the end of the road. 18 miles from Riggins. Pit toilets. Water at the nearby forest guard station.

Where to Get Information

For information on the Seven Devils area near Riggins, write:
District Ranger
Salmon River Ranger District
Nezperce National Forest
Riggins, Idaho 83549

For information on the Black Lake-Hells Canyon area which embraces two ranger districts write:
Supervisor
Payette National Forest
McCall, Idaho 83638

sawtooths

VAST SWEEPING VALLEYS below clusters of rugged, snow-capped peaks.

Hemingway country, this. And it's easy to see why: An extraordinary land of trout streams, spectacular lakes, glacial basins, timbered slopes, grassy meadows and, of course, tall peaks. All part of the new Sawtooth Recreation Area, north of Sun Valley and Ketchum, Idaho, where Ernest Hemingway wrote and died.

To reach the area: From I-80 across southern Idaho, drive north from Twin Falls on U.S. 93 to Sun Valley, Ketchum and Stanley.

The recreation area, created in 1972, embraces not only the 216,000 acre Sawtooth Wilderness but the scenic White Cloud and Boulder mountains to the east.

Grazing is permitted here and some logging too. But the principal use is recreation.

The "operating season" of the vast area is from June 15 through October 15 but the maximum season sometimes extends from as early as June 1 to November 15, depending on the weather.

High country trails some years do not open until early July, remaining open through October. Hikers may experience some unsettled weather, including snow, during the fall equinox. But after the equinox, Indian summers are common lasting often until the weather changes permanently for the worse late in October.

Heaviest use occurs during July and August with the lightest visitation during the middle of the week.

Summer daytime temperatures here will range around 70 degrees with nighttime temperatures dropping to about 35 degrees and down to 30 degrees on occasion.

The Forest Service here offers a variety of naturalist programs, including nature walks, wilderness day hikes and even auto tours from the Redfish area in addition to the evening motion picture and slide programs both at the Redfish and Stanley lake campgrounds.

Lightning storms are frequent here some years and infrequent in others. None of the storms, however, marches through the area with the afternoon regularity common in some other western areas.

WHERE TO DRIVE

Every road and highway here offers vista points of some sort. But there are a few places that no visitor should miss:

Stanley Lake—McGown peak here towers over Stanley Lake. Hundreds of different perspectives from the shore of the lake or from an overlook point on the road. Seek out the one that strikes you best.

Drive north from Stanley on Highway 21, turning left in 4 miles. The lake in 2 more miles.

Redfish Lake—Views deep into the Sawtooths here from the end of a glacial-basin lake that extends to the very edge of the wilderness. Easiest vistas from a picnic ground at the head of the lake. Others from campgrounds and nearby trails.

Drive south from Stanley about 5 miles turning right onto the Redfish Lake road. The lake in 2 miles.

Galena Overlook—Put the entire area in quick perspective here. Look back over Sawtooth valley and out at mountains as the highway climbs to a pass leading south to Ketchum. About 30 miles south of Stanley.

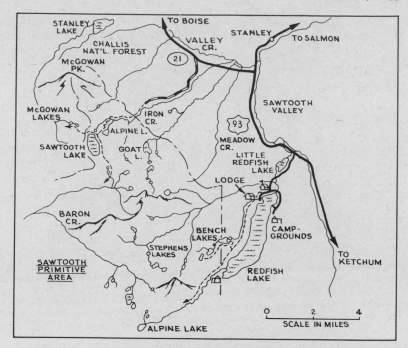

WHERE TO HIKE

Here, again, nothing more than a sampling—a hint—of the scenic wonders this area holds.

Sawtooth and Alpine lakes—Grandeur and spectacle here that must be seen to be appreciated. Classic mountains. Classic lakes. 4 miles to Alpine Lake, and 1 more mile to Sawtooth Lake.

Find the trailhead at the end of the road in a transfer camp at Iron Creek Campground. Drive north from Stanley 2 miles, turning left (southwesterly) onto the gravel Iron Creek Campground road. Trailhead in about 3.2 more miles.

The trail starts behind a large illustrated trailboard, ducking almost immediately into lodgepole pine. In a mile, cross the wilderness boundary, continuing in timber to a junction, in another mile, with a trail (right) to Stanley Lake.

Continue left (uphill) here as the trail starts switchbacking gradually but persistently, crossing Iron Creek and passing through a meadow before reaching Alpine Lake in another 2 miles.

Drop off the trail here to explore the lake which lies in a timbered bowl, surrounded by granite bluffs and watched over by a mountain peak. Limited camping at the east end.

From Alpine Lake, the trail now climbs in earnest switchbacking sharply up a ridge most of the last mile to Sawtooth Lake. Views now as you climb, back on Alpine Lake, out at the sawtoothed ridges of nearby mountains, and over the valley toward Stanley.

At the top of the ridge, the trail passes a pretty unnamed tarn (some camp places here), crosses the creek again and then climbs slightly to the first glimpses of Sawtooth Lake.

But don't stop now! The best is a little way on up the trail. Keep left around a bluff until, instantly, a classic view of mountains, lake and granite cliffs. Stop here for sure.

And if you still have time—and the ambition—return to the trail at the outlet end of the lake, hiking to the right still higher to McGown Lake in another mile in a still more alpine setting.

Although, frankly, Sawtooth Lake offers all the scene you'll need.

Lots of flowers enroute. At lower levels, Sego lilies. At higher levels, shooting stars, paintbrush and penstemon.

Bench Lakes—A string of individual wooded lakes tucked into a high valley above scenic Redfish Lake. 4-miles.

Find the trailhead west of the horse corral and east of the resort on the north side of the road. Watch for parking places and a sign.

The trail crosses behind and above the resort for about a quarter mile, climbing sharply then to the top of the forested moraine on the north side of the lake.

Once atop the moraine, the path climbs more gradually but just as persistently the rest of the way. Modest views down on Redfish in the first mile with the grandest views reserved for the third mile when the trail breaks out of timber into an old burn. 360-degree vistas here down on the entire lake and toward the rugged Grand Mogul and Chalkstone peaks at the head of the valley.

At the end of the third mile watch for a trail junction right (north) to the Bench Lakes. From the junction, the path dips slightly and then switchbacks up an open ridge, reentering timber again as it nears the first lake.

Hiker nears Sawtooth Lake

The trail first passes a small lily-pad lake and then moves westward to a second more heavily wooded and deeper lake guarded by two mountain peaks to the west.

A fisherman's trail continues around the left side of the second lake to two other upper lakes, another mile over windfalls and snags.

Carry water. None on the trail.

BACKPACKING OPPORTUNITIES

Opportunities for overnight and longer backpacking trips are almost unlimited in this wilderness area.

Among the more popular, however, are overnight hikes into Sawtooth Lake (see trails) and beyond Redfish Lake to Alpine Lake, 11 miles.

Also popular is a loop trail from Pettit Lake, south of the Redfish area, into Alice Lake (6 miles) or Twin Lakes (7 miles) and then on to Toxaway Lake (another 4.1 miles) and then back to Pettit Lake in another 7.2 miles. A 3-day trip.

Newcomers to this backcountry are urged to set short one-day goals to start with, at least. Trails here climb stiffly up and down. A five-mile trip sometimes can seem more like 10.

No permits are yet required here. However, restrictions are imposed on the size of groups. Groups are limited to 20 persons and any group of 10 or more must obtain a special permit.

WHERE TO CAMP

No dearth of camp spots here. The Forest Service maintains over 46 formal campgrounds within the recreation area and permits camping in hundreds of informal sites along highways, roads and rivers.

Listed here are only a few of the camps located in the Redfish-Stanley section of the recreation area.

Stanley Lake—39 sites on three separate campground loops. All oriented to the lake. Some near the water, but most above the lake. In lodgepole pine. Vault toilets. Piped water. Generally fills early in the day.

Redfish Lake—130 sites in a series of six separate campgrounds around the outlet end—both north and south. Many sites oriented to the lake. But many others in timber away from the water. One of the busiest and most popular campgrounds in the recreation area. Vault toilets. Piped water.

Iron Creek—12 sites on wooded loops near the trailhead to Sawtooth Lake. Piped water. Vault toilets.

Where to Get Information

For information on the recreation area and for reports on specific trails write:

Superintendent
Sawtooth National Recreation Area
U.S. Forest Service
Ketchum, Idaho 83340

craters of the moon

AN AWESOME LAND, here. Bleak. Severe. And harsh.

Certainly no place to spend a vacation. But if your travels lead you past this national monument, plan to spend at least a day.

Few better examples anywhere of what lava flows can do. Tube caves, craters, spatter cones, cascades and broken bridges amid frozen rivers of ropy and wrinkled pahoehoe (pa-hóay-hóay) and bristling, jagged lava known as aa (aḣah).

Not like the moon as we know it now, of course. But man hadn't reached the moon when this place was named. Still a prime example, though, of the primal forces that molded and shaped this planet earth.

How to reach the area: From U.S. I-80 across southern Idaho drive north on U.S. 93 from Twin Falls, turning right in 23 miles onto U.S. 26 toward Arco. From Idaho Falls, drive westerly on U.S. 20 to Arco and then west again on U.S. 20 and 26.

This monument covers more than 83 square miles of violent and almost barren land along the Great Rift which extends through the center of the monument into the Pioneer Mountains to the north. Lava has erupted from this rift, flowing over these plains for thousands of years, ceasing only about 2000 years ago. (And, perhaps, may even erupt again.)

Today, however, the black blanketed earth is starting again to spring slowly back to life as flowers, trees and finally sagebrush find root. A demonstration here, really, of both the tremendous destructive powers within the earth and the equally tremendous tenacity of the life on its surface.

Weatherwise, spring and fall are the best times to visit this monument. The weather is more moderate at those times. But the facilities of the area are not fully open except during the usual summer season. Campgrounds are generally in full operation from May through October, depending on weather conditions.

The weather here can be as harsh as the scenery in almost every season. Winds are often gusty during the day. And the sparse vegetation provides little shade. Hikers, therefore, should put on hats and shirts to protect themselves from the sun.

Summer daytime temperatures range into the mid-80s with extremes in the 90s. Nighttime lows range into the 50s dropping on occasion down to the 30s.

Good footwear is also important even on established trails. The lava is sharp and the sand extremely abrasive. Tennis shoes won't stand the gaff.

The Park Service conducts naturalist programs here consisting of daily guided walks to caves and craters and nighttime slide programs at the campground. Schedules are posted in campgrounds and the visitor center.

Visitors should be warned that there are no commercial facilities of any sort at or near the monument. The nearest store or gas station is 20 miles away. So if you plan to stay even for a night, come prepared.

WHERE TO DRIVE

A 7-mile loop drive passes most of the major features in this monument. However a true appreciation of all the features awaits the person who walks. For the lava here is more than something to look at. It's an environment that you must sense to know.

The loop road swings around the larger crater cones, affords a

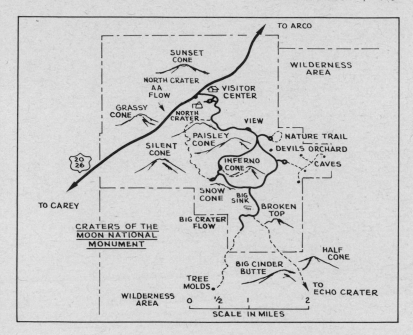

close-up view of spatter cones below Big Craters and, along a spur road to the tree mold trailhead, passes rivers of pahoehoe lava and lava cascades.

WHERE TO HIKE

You don't have to walk far here. But you most certainly should walk a little way on at least one trail to appreciate the fantastic violence which formed these craters, caves and cones.

Big Crater Loop—Start at the Spatter Cones parking area and hike 1.5 miles past the Big Craters to a second trailhead a half mile south of the campground entrance.

Find the trailhead to the right, uphill, from the Spatter Cones parking area, climbing switchbacks first up to an overview of the spatter cones and then back to the north along the rim of the Big Craters.

The trail climbs sharply up and down as it wends its way from one crater to the other and through the bottom of a third before

Lava Tree Molds

dropping down to the road again. Views near the end down on the visitor center complex and outward toward the Pioneer Mountains. Watch for rock cairns when the trail tread gets faint.

Tree Molds—Hike a mile into the wilderness to study the imprints of ancient trees cast into lava which buried them centuries ago.

Find the trail at the end of a spur road which leads south from the loop drive about a mile. The path is clear until you reach the tree-mold site along the west side of a cinder butte.

After passing the information sign, watch for posts near each of the separate molds. And be thoughtful here. Don't deface these molds. Let others enjoy them too.

Cave Trail—Hike over a turbulent lava flow to a series of room-like lava tube caves. Ice in some. Carry a flashlight if you plan to explore.

Find the trailhead at the end of a short spur road to the east from the main loop road. The trail leads off across a lava flat.

Each cave here is marked with a sign. If the trails aren't clear make your way carefully over the lava from one to the next. Indian Tunnel in a half mile. Beauty Cave in less than a mile.

Indian Tunnel, more than 830 feet long, is the largest and most popular cave. No light is needed here. Part of the ceiling has caved in.

Use care in entering every cave. Lava is extremely sharp. And hard.

Rift Trail—Leave all signs of roads—and often people—to appreciate fully the severe beauty and lonely harshness of the backcountry here.

Find the trail to the east of the spur road to the tree mold trail. Watch for sign. 4 miles to Echo Crater.

The trail here follows the Great Rift, from which most of this lava flowed, between a series of old buttes and cones. Every kind of lava display you can think of and plant life too. Go all the way. Or just a mile or so.

BACKPACKING OPPORTUNITIES

Very little backpacking here—even in the established wilderness area.

Although most of the backcountry caves, tree molds and cinder cones are identified on topographic maps a hiker must "navigate" this wilderness to find them. There are very few trails and no signs.

There's likewise very little water except in remote and hard-to-find waterholes. And very little wood. Hikers therefore must carry both water—at least a gallon a day—and cooking stoves.

And don't hike, if you can help it, at midday. It's much too hot. Hike mornings and evenings or during the spring and fall.

And register with monument officials before starting any trip.

WHERE TO CAMP

Camping here is limited to a single campground and there are no overflow public or commercial facilities nearby. Sites here generally fill early each afternoon during the peak of the summer season with the heaviest pressure on weekends and holidays.

And if you arrive and the campground is full, you must drive on to the next town 18 miles away.

Campground—51 sites on exposed loops. Few trees. Very little shade. Gusty winds. Flush toilets. Piped water.

Where to Get Information
For information on the monument, write:
Superintendent
Craters of the Moon National Monument
Box 29
Arco, Idaho 83213

high uintas

LOFTY MOUNTAIN COUNTRY this. At 10,000 feet, hundreds of lakes, meadows and even towering peaks. And all within a few miles of a spectacular road.

Nearly 10,000 people visit this area on a busy holiday or weekend from nearby Utah urban centers. And it only takes one trip there to understand why.

To reach the area: From Salt Lake City and Provo drive east to U.S. 189 and the quiet town of Kamas, turning east there onto State Highway 150. From I-80 across southern Wyoming turn south onto State Highway 150 at Evanston, Wyo.

Hot valleys in this part of Utah and Wyoming give way to cool, green mountains in less than 40 miles. This area borders the High Uinta Primitive Area, a wild, picturesque region containing the highest mountain range in Utah and hundreds of small lakes. And one of the most prominent east-west mountain ranges in the entire United States.

In this high region snow lasts late into spring and arrives early in the fall, creating one of the shortest summer seasons in the West.

The main highway through the area normally opens before July 1 and often closes by the third week in October due to snow.

The area occasionally enjoys a late fall season. But it can't be counted on. If you camp after Labor Day, as local officials put it: "Bring chains".

Summer temperatures, as you'd expect at such elevations, range from warm and warmer to cool and cooler. Daytime temperatures average in the 70s with an occasional hot day of about 80 degrees. Nighttime temperatures will average in the 40s with temperatures in higher areas sometimes dropping to freezing and snow is not uncommon in every month.

Lightning storms with hail are common here in July and August occurring mostly in the afternoon on the average of every other day. The storms, when they hit, however, only last an hour or so.

Visitors are warned about mosquitoes early and during the middle of summer. So bring lots of repellant. Warm jackets are always essential in the evening. And city hikers who arrive at these high elevations without a period of acclimatization may find themselves short of breath even on level trails until they get used to the altitude. Although the area is crowded with lakes only a few are suitable for large boats. Basically, this is canoe, kayak and raft country.

The Forest Service offers no formal naturalist programs in this area. Persons with questions can get information at the ranger station in Kamas.

WHERE TO DRIVE

Drive from dry brown valleys into a green subalpine forest along a 32-mile road from Kamas to Mirror Lake.

For the first 8 miles from Kamas, the road passes through a low-elevation area containing a cross-section of all of the plant life, except those of the desert, found throughout Utah.

The road then climbs to a series of viewpoints, first over the Provo River, then the outlet of the Duchesne water tunnel, Slate Gorge and the Provo River falls which, unfortunately, usually dries up in August.

Near Bald Mountain Pass at 10,700 feet the highway first switchbacks up to views toward the south from Bald Mountain

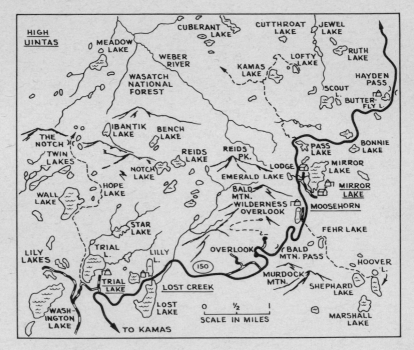

Overlook and then to the north from the Wilderness Area overlook.

From the pass, the road now skirts a whole series of lakes, reaching the last one—Butterfly Lake—beyond Mirror Lake near the head of the Highline Trail.

Make the drive midweek to avoid heavy weekend traffic.

WHERE TO HIKE

Find high lake, after high lake after high lake here—down almost every trail.

Most of the lakes can be reached by trail but a few require easy cross-country hikes. Pick a high landmark and take off to the lake of your choice.

Kamas and Lofty Lakes—Pretty meadows, lakes and even vistas from a trail that climbs to two lakes but looks down on several more.

Find the trail off a marked parking area on the west side of the highway just beyond Pass Lake about .7 miles north of the Mirror Lake Campground entrance.

The trail doesn't start directly into the forest. Instead, make your way, near the highway, back toward the outlet of Pass Lake watching for blazes on trees to the right (west) in maybe 50 yards.

The trail now starts westward, joining an old spur trail in a quarter mile and then continuing in another quarter-mile to a junction right (north) to the lakes. Holiday Park lies straight ahead.

From the junction, the trail drops downhill to a big meadow, following it for a quarter mile before climbing again, persistently this time, to a junction with the Cuberant Lake trail in a total of 2 miles.

Turn right uphill here climbing a stiff half-mile to the end of Kamas Lake, surrounded by forest and rock.

To continue on to Lofty Lake—which is exactly that —keep to the left, following the shore of Kamas Lake across the outlet and climbing then northerly, sharply at first, to a small meadow (watch for cairns) and then through a saddle to sudden views down on a host of other lakes—Cutthroat and Jewel to name only two—in a valley to the north.

If you've got time, drop down a fisherman's trail and explore these lakes. If you don't, continue on as the trail switchbacks now to a bench and across a meadow to Lofty Lake, all by itself atop this mountain-knoll, at 10,800 feet.

Bald Mountain—Hike 1.5 miles to a vista that takes in the entire countryside.

Find the trailhead at the end of the Bald Mountain Pass Trailhead and Picnic Area on a short spur road to the west of the highway about 29.5 miles from Kamas and 2 miles south of the Mirror Lake Campground entrance.

The trail, out in the open all of the time, starts westerly from the road, switchbacks up the mountain several times and then traverses first to the left and then back to the right climbing higher and higher to the best vistas at the top.

Look down to the northeast on Moosehorn and Mirror lakes and out to the southwest at Trial, Washington and Lost lakes and at mountains everywhere.

Best to hike here early in the morning to avoid the afternoon storms which often cloud the mountain.

Twin Lakes—Spend an afternoon here seeking out two pretty lakes just off a trail after hiking past several others.

Find the initial trailhead to Notch Mountain just beyond the Trial Lake Campground road. Turn off the highway, to the west, toward the campground in about 26 miles from Kamas or about 4 miles south of Bald Mountain pass. But rather than entering the campground in a few hundred feet, keep left, continuing below the Trail Lake outlet dam and watching for a trail sign on the right just as the road now turns sharply left, away from the lake. Park on the road.

The trail climbs to the west side of the lake, continuing up the lake behind some cabins and dropping back to the shore again before heading inland. Cross the Wall Lake outlet stream in about a half-mile.

The trail now climbs to Wall Lake, a reservoir-lake, turning right at the outlet. After passing an unnamed tarn (to your left) the trail climbs sharply up a rock bench to Hope Lake set amid slabs and rock. About 1 mile from Wall Lake.

From here, follow the trail toward The Notch, a distinct saddle

Twin Lakes

which you can see occasionally ahead and above you, climbing two ledge-benches to two small meadows and then to a third with a larger meadow extending off to the left for about a quarter mile, ending at a rock knoll.

Take a bearing on a mountain now and make your own trail down the middle of the meadow and around the left side of the knoll to arrive at the lower and smaller of the two Twin Lakes which lie, on the map, directly north of Wall Lake.

Find the larger crosscountry to the north from the lower lake.

Chances are you'll have both lakes all to yourself. Camp here if you like. Or just spend the afternoon soaking up the quiet beauty and solitude that's here.

Fehr-Shepard and Hoover Lakes—Three heavily forested lakes along a single trail in 2 miles. And you'll have to work a little.

Find the trailhead from a parking area across the road from the entrance to Moosehorn Campground. The path starts at a large sign, dropping to Fehr Lake in a quarter-mile and on to Shepard Lake in 1.5 and Hoover in a total of 2. The rocky path is down most of the way in and up all the way out.

The trail goes over two modest ridges to reach Fehr Lake, a popular fishing spot. From Fehr, the trail skirts the shore to the left, rounding the lake at the end and crossing the inlet. After climbing through a couple of meadows, the trail suddenly drops stiffly over a rocky ridge, past a little tarn to Shepard Lake. A view here up at Bald Mountain.

Here, again follow the trail along the lake to the left and then over a little ridge dropping sharply again to Hoover Lake.

Camp spots on all three lakes.

BACKPACKING OPPORTUNITIES

Hikers who plan trips into the High Uinta Primitive area should inquire about current permit and camping requirements.

Permits may be required in all backcountry areas with restriction also placed on the number of hikers allowed in some. Write to the headquarters of either the Ashley or Wasatch National Forests for details.

One of the more popular and relatively short trips into the primitive area is one to the Naturalist Basin, about 6.5 miles via the Highline Trail from the Mirror Lake highway.

The trail forks uphill from the Highline trail to more than a dozen lakes, some with trail access, some without. Go as far as you wish. This area and most of the lakes were named after French naturalists who once explored this country.

WHERE TO CAMP

Ample camping here at almost any elevation, particularly during the week.

The Forest Service has developed nearly 500 campsites in a series of campgrounds that start about 7 miles from Kamas and continue to near the Highline Trailhead. Moosehorn Campground just below Bald Mountain is the highest at 10,400 feet.

Listed here are some of the more popular camps in the lake basins around Bald Mountain.

Trial Lake—57 sites near Trial lake on a spur road off the Mirror Lake highway about 25.5 miles from Kamas. Vault toilets. Piped water.

Lily Lake—13 sites near Lily Lake about 26.5 miles from Kamas. Vault toilets. Piped water.

Lost Creek—36 sites on loops near Lost Lake about 30 miles from Kamas. Vault toilets. Piped water.

Moosehorn Lake—35 sites on wooded loops near Moosehorn Lake. Piped water. Vault toilets.

Mirror Lake—100 sites on loops off the far side of Mirror Lake. Some near the lake. Some not. A popular campground. Flush toilets. Piped water.

Where to Get Information

For information on the Mirror Lake area, write:
    District Ranger
    Kamas Ranger District

Wasatch National Forest
Kamas, Utah 84036

For information on the High Uintas Primitive Area, write:
Supervisor
Wasatch National Forest
4438 Federal Building
Salt Lake City, Utah 84111
or
Supervisor
Ashley National Forest
437 East Main St.
Vernal, Utah 84078

timpanogos mountain and caves

HIKE HIGH ON a mountain or deep into a cave. All in the same area.

Take scenic drives and hikes around the spectacular 11,750-foot Mount Timpanogos in the Timpanogos Scenic Area.

And explore unusual stalactite-ornamented caves in the Timpanogos Cave National Monument.

To reach the area: From I-15 south of Salt Lake and north of Provo, turn east on State Highway 80 following the highway first to the national monument and then into the scenic area around the Alpine Loop Highway to U.S. 189 in Provo Canyon.

TIMPANOGOS SCENIC AREA
MT. TIMPANOGOS

Camp in forests, hike to meadows or climb a mountain in this heavily used scenic area near two major Utah urban centers.

The season here, which centers almost exclusively around high trails on Mt. Timpanogos, doesn't generally open until early July after snows have melted, continuing through September depending, as always, on the weather. Unstable weather with snow is possible during the equinox in late September. But Indian summers here are not uncommon.

Campgrounds along the Alpine Loop Road on the edge of the scenic area generally open in June, closing in October.

Summer temperatures in the scenic area are always substantially cooler than in the valley urban centers. Daytime temperatures in the loop road area average about 85 to 90 degrees in the summer, with nighttime temperatures averaging about 55 to 60 degrees.

Temperatures drop as you climb higher on the mountain varying enormously at the summit where the thermometer can plunge from hot to near freezing in moments during an afternoon thunderstorm.

As indicated, use in this area is extremely heavy with most of it occurring on weekends and holidays as thousands of city dwellers pour into the forest.

During the week, however, visitor levels are usually much lighter although you can seldom hike or camp here without running into lots of people.

Traffic on the loop road around the scenic area follows the same use pattern—heavy on weekends and lighter during the week. But in the fall, when the aspens and maples turn color, traffic often reaches freeway proportions, bumper to bumper, even during the week.

The heavy use is causing severe management problems. And methods of controlling the use are under constant study.

Hikers here are urged particularly to avoid cross-cutting trails. Some trail slopes are extremely steep and erosion damage from cross-cutting is already severe. The thoughtless practice has also increased the danger of falling rock in several areas.

Hikers are also reminded to carry warm jackets or sweaters whenever hiking to the meadows or peaks—no matter how warm it is in the valley. Again, storms can bring severe drops in temperature anywhere on the mountain. Exposed ridges should be avoided in lightning storms.

The Forest Service in this area offers no naturalist programs. If you have questions inquire at the ranger station in Pleasant Grove.

WHERE TO DRIVE

The Alpine Loop Road around the east side of the mountain is one of the most popular "drives" in the Salt Lake area.

The 30-mile winding paved road links the American Fork

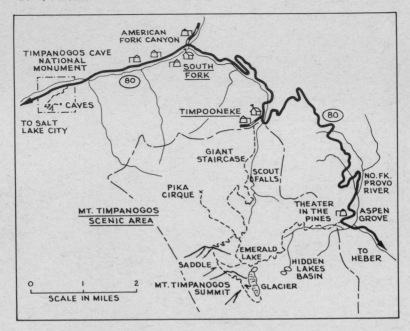

Canyon and Provo Canyons, climbing from about 5,000 feet at either end to more than 8,000 feet at the midpoint.

Vistas here of Mt. Timpanogos from every angle, deep canyons, waterfalls, valley views, meadows and, perhaps most spectacular of all—in autumn—the brilliant reds of the maples and golds of the aspen, everywhere you look.

Don't hurry. Avoid the weekends if you can. And don't try and haul your trailer. Park it in a campground and just drive your car.

WHERE TO HIKE

No easy trails here. It's a strenuous 10 miles to the top of Mt. Timpanogos and nearly 7 to the meadows around scenic Emerald Lake. And it's a climb of more than 4500 feet—no matter which way you go.

But—as always—the effort pays off: Vistas, meadows, flowers, waterfalls, alpine tarns and the grandeur of a truly massive and rugged mountain.

You can make this hike in any one of several ways: Hike up and back on either of two trails. Or make a loop trip—up one of the trails and down the other. You'll need two cars or else arrange to have someone meet you. Or just walk part way on either trail.

Allow a long day—and then some—if you plan to hike to the top of the mountain. Allow 6 to 7 hours, at least, if you just go to the Emerald Lake meadows and back.

Timpooneke Trail—The most gradual (and that's not saying much) with the least altitude gain (still 4500 feet) but offering the greatest variety of terrain (portions of this trail are actually flat). 6.5 miles to Emerald Lake. 9.1 to the peak.

To find the trailhead, turn off the Alpine loop highway about 6 miles from the Timpanogos Cave National Monument onto the Timpooneke Campground spur road. A trailhead parking area, to the left, in another quarter mile.

The trail here climbs persistently and often tediously up a staircase cirque to a meadow basin just north of the peak and then on to an even higher basin, cupping Emerald Lake.

The trail makes the climb in stiff spurts, switchbacking up ledges and crossing meadows, sometimes in timber and sometimes in meadows, and sometimes in the glaring sun and sometimes in shade.

When the trail crests the cirque at about 10,000 feet, it climbs on to a junction with a trail to Pika Cirque (keep left) and then to a second junction with trails leading two ways to Emerald Lake. Take the one that climbs to the right. The one straight ahead may look shorter, but it drops into a meadow and then has to climb back out again.

So follow the high trail around a barren rock slope to Emerald Basin or take a spur trail (right) midway leading to the top of the mountain. From here about 2.5 miles.

Flowers in profusion all along this trail. Lots of red paintbrush and bluebells. But the lighter shades seem to predominate. Even the penstemons on these slopes are pale and the columbine which grow so richly here are almost white.

And animals too. Deer at the lower levels. Grouse on the ridges and marmot scurrying in the rock at the top.

Water from streams along the lower levels but very little toward the end. Best to carry some.

Timpanogos Trail—Waterfall after waterfall here and vistas that never cease.

High on Mt. Timpanogos

Climb 3450 feet in 5.3 miles to the meadows of Emerald Lake. Climb 4900 in 8.3 miles to the top of the mountain.

Find this trail to the west of a parking loop at the Theater of the Pines picnic area about 6 miles by road from the Timpooneke Campground. The trail starts across a meadow to the west on a gravel path, beginning its climb to the head of this cirque after it crosses a bridge.

There's no counting the switchbacks you'll struggle up here. But always take the longest and flattest ones. These trails have been heavily eroded by thoughtless hikers who cut across the established trails. So pick your route with care. The longest way here is really the shortest.

Near the top of the cirque the trail climbs to a meadow, passing two little tarns—Hidden Lakes—and then circles upward to Emerald Lake at the base of a snowfield.

Stop here or continue, in about 3 miles, to the top. This final trail climbs steeply all the way. But the view from the top is unexcelled. The whole world. From the sprawling cities of the Great Salt Lake basin to all of the lakes and ridges to the east.

Water on this trail all the way to Emerald Lake. Lots and lots of waterfall. And one, about midway, that you can even walk under— for a shower.

BACKPACKING OPPORTUNITIES

Backpacking opportunities here are extremely limited. It's not forbidden in the peak area. But for purely management reason it's not encouraged. Heavy day use makes anything resembling privacy impossible. Water is limited and wood is nonexistent. So those who do backpack should carry drinking water and a cooking stove.

TIMPANOGOS CAVE NATIONAL MONUMENT

A cave, here, most certainly. And a beautiful one. But in addition, grand vistas of mountains and valleys too. For you cannot visit this cave without hiking first to the viewpoints more than 1000 feet above the valley floor.

The cave is open from May through October. But it can only be visited on formal, guided tours. Visitor use here is extremely heavy, often exceeding the capacity of the cave. So visitors should expect a wait before being able to start a tour. On weekends, when use is heaviest, waits of up to two hours are not uncommon. Tours are limited to 20 persons. Tickets can be purchased at the visitor center for a nominal fee, waived for children under 16.

Visitors to the cave are urged to wear sturdy shoes and bring jackets. Temperature in the cave is 43 degrees even in midsummer. Pets are not permitted on trails. Some backpack frames for carrying small children are available at the visitor center.

A cave tour takes about 3 hours and demands a 3.5 mile walk including a 1.5 mile uphill hike from the visitor center.

The paved trail climbs steadily and persistently the entire way. But rest stops offer an occasional opportunity to stop and enjoy the scenery which includes a look, at the top, out into the Utah Valley.

At the cave, visitors pass through a series of rooms to see such features as the Chocolate Falls, Father Time, Jewel Box and the Great Heart of Timpanogos. Helictites, small lace-like twisted and rolled stalactites, and hollow sodastraw stalactites are among the more interesting features of the cave.

Flash photographs are permitted.

Picnicking, but no camping, is allowed just down the road from the visitor center. Camping is in nearby National Forest campgrounds.

WHERE TO CAMP

The Forest Service has established nine campgrounds along the Alpine Loop Road to serve visitors to both the national monument and the scenic area.

Trash disposal facilities for all of the campgrounds are located in large city-type dumpsters at either end of the loop road. Campers are asked to carry their trash from the campsite to the dumpsters. There are no garbage cans in the campgrounds.

Campgrounds near Timpanogos Cave include:

House Rock—10 sites near the American Fork river. Some walk-in sites. Pit toilets. Piped water.

Grey Cliffs—5 sites across road from the river. Pit toilets. Piped water.

Little Mill—26 sites on a spur road across the river. Pit toilets. Piped water.

Higher elevation camps include:

Timpooneke—32 sites on aspen loops on a spur road west of the highway. At 7400 feet. Piped water. Pit toilets.

Mt. Timpanogos—27 sites. Near trailhead to Mt. Timpanogos trail. At 6800 feet. Piped water. Pit toilets.

Where to Get Information

For information on the Timpanogos Scenic area write:

> District Ranger
> Pleasant Grove Ranger District
> U.S. Forest Service
> P.O. Box 228
> Pleasant Grove, Utah 84062

For information on the Timpanogos Cave National Monument write:

> Superintendent
> Timpanogos Cave National Monument
> American Fork, Utah 84003

arches national park

RED ROCK, TOWERING slabs of balanced stone, gnomes and goblins eroded in cliffs.

All this and arches too. More than 90 of them still being formed— or tumbling down.

But stand here really more in awe of time. The sandstone from which all these features are still being carved was laid down more than 150 million years ago. Man in these terms seems little more than a passing fad.

How to reach the area: From I-70 across central Utah drive south from Crescent Junction toward Moab. Entrance to the park just 2 miles north of Moab.

Late August through October may be the best time to visit this park. Days are still warm then and evenings are cool. The crowds are gone and space is usually available in the campground. Formal naturalist programs, of course, will have been discontinued.

Use is heaviest here on Easter and Memorial Day weekends with the peak season extending from the two weeks before Easter through August. Campgrounds are usually full all during that period.

Local use from urban centers in Colorado and Utah is heaviest here in the spring, with tourists taking over most of the facilities in the summer.

Temperatures here in the summer range from warmer to hot, soaring as high some days as 110 and 115 degrees.

Daytime temperatures from late June through August average over 100 degrees, dropping to the mid-70s at night. Which means that if you plan to hike here in the summer, do so early in the morning or late in the afternoon.

Lightning storms, as elsewhere in the Southwest, are common in the summer and visitors are warned to keep off the exposed ridges and knobs of rock during any storm and to be alert for flash floods in the otherwise dry valleys after any storm.

Good footgear is essential in this park. The trails are rough and the rocks can be slippery. Rubber soles are a must.

The elevation—most of the land in the Arches is around 5000 feet—along with the heat pose hazards to persons unaccustomed to these conditions. Water should be carried on every hike. Experts say at least a gallon a day.

The Park Service presents naturalist programs each night from May into September at the campground. Persons camping in nearby commercial campgrounds are invited to attend. Rangers also conduct two-hour adventure hikes daily into some of the nameless canyons and arches of the Fiery Furnace section.

WHERE TO DRIVE

Driving opportunities here are limited almost exclusively to the paved road which starts at the Entrance Station and wends its way to the Devil's Garden in about 18 miles.

Spur roads lead into several special features from the main road. But a real appreciation of the park, as always, can only be obtained from trails which pass close to the features themselves.

Several dirt roads wind into remote parts of the park. Some of these roads are often closed. And others should not be driven without checking first at the Visitor Center. Conditions on these roads change almost daily with shifts in the weather.

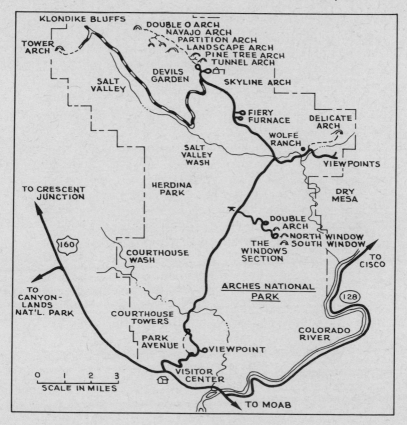

WHERE TO HIKE

Many of the most spectacular arches in the park can only be viewed from trails. But none of the trails is very long and all can be hiked with relative ease.

Plan hikes in the morning, however, to avoid midday heat.

Devil's Garden—Six arches—all different—along a single 2-mile trail that winds and climbs through a procession of red rock ribs.

Find the trailhead off the Devil's Garden parking lot just north of the campground. The trail, starting between ridges of rock, leads past the famed Landscape Arch in 1 mile and then past side trails to the Navajo and Partition arches, reaching the Double O Arch at the end of 2 miles.

The trail is heavily traveled to the famed Landscape Arch, a 291-foot span believed to be the longest natural stone arch in the world. (Spur paths lead to every conceivable view of the arch.)

From the Landscape Arch, however, trail use drops dramatically as the path now climbs quickly and sharply up a draw and then across a flat before working its way from rib-top by rib-top to the final arch.

Be alert here. The trail is marked almost exclusively now by cairns and occasional paint marks. So don't leave one mark or cairn until you have another in view.

And take time to look around as the trail climbs atop the spines. Some of the highest views in the park from here.

The Double O Arch at the end of the trial is precisely that—a wall with two modest arches eroded through it.

Returning, take the marked spur trails to the west to visit first, Navajo, and then Partition Arch, at the end of quarter-mile trails.

And take time to walk through the Navajo Arch into what seems like a Spanish courtyard, complete with olive tree. Don't wait, however, for a waiter to bring you wine.

Beyond Landscape Arch (as you return) turn east on another short spur trail to visit Tunnel and Pine Tree arches. Find Tunnel Arch a few hundred yards to the south, Pine Tree Arch a few hundred yards to the north.

Park Avenue—Walk just a mile—all downhill—to appreciate very quickly the overpowering grandeur of this park.

Find the trailhead off the South Park Avenue parking spur about 2 miles from the Entrance Station. Have someone meet you at the parking area, to the right, down the road in another mile.

The paved walk ends at a viewpoint. But the trail continues sharply downhill through the middle of the canyon.

Follow the tread here when you can find it. Otherwise, look for cairns. But it's impossible to get lost anyway. Just stay in the bottom of the gorge until you come out at the road.

Awesome views here up at the sculptured walls and balanced spires. And feel the heat reflected off both walls in the middle of the day, or better yet after the sun goes down.

Tower Arch—Follow arrow "blazes" across a barren valley to an arch hidden on a hillside and guarded by a grotto of goblins and towers.

To find the trail, drive 8 miles on a dirt and gravel road to the Klondike Bluff parking area. Take the first gravel road, downhill, off the main road, south of Devil's Garden. Follow signs.

At the parking loop, find the trailhead to the west. If there's no sign, look carefully for an 8-inch white arrow on a chest-high brown post along the bottom of the ridge.

The trail here is marked by such arrows spaced out across the desert every several hundred yards. When you reach one, search the horizon for another, never losing sight of one until you've found the other.

The trail—or way—climbs sharply up a ridge, drops across a valley and then makes its way, generally to the right, uphill into a maze of rock. Take care here in following the signs.

An adventure walk, for certain. And note why the arrow

Gnomes of Arches

markers are necessary here. It would be impossible to build a trail. Each new rain or windstorm would simply wipe it out.

And check with rangers before you start your drive. Summer storms occasionally make this road impassable. Probably not for low-slung city cars.

Delicate Arch—This is the park's most classic arch set, as it is, amid cliffs atop a dome of rock. 1.5 miles.

Find the trailhead about 2 miles from the main road on a spur, to the right, about 12 miles from the Entrance Station.

From the parking area, the trail passes an old ranch hut and then starts a gradual climb toward the arch. The trail, paved at first, soon traces a well-worn path in sandstone. Watch, too, for cairns. Views near the arch over the Colorado River gorge and the peaks of LaSal mountains.

The Windows—Take a series of very short walks here to several arches and a parade of other eroded rock displays.

Turn right off the main road about 9 miles from the entrance station. Arch loop in 3 miles.

Short trails lead to the spectacular Double Arch, North and South Windows and the Turret Arch in addition to other features. If you don't have time for anything else, walk here!

BACKPACKING OPPORTUNITIES

Backpack trips are possible here but they're rarely attempted. In the first place, most of the areas of the park are already accessible by road. And secondly, there are no backcountry hiking trails and very little water. But if you do decide to strike out, check with rangers before you start.

WHERE TO CAMP

Camping facilities in the monument are limited to a single campground about 18 miles from the entrance station.

Campers should check at the Visitor Center on the camping situation as they enter the park. The campground often fills early in the day.

There are, however, ample commercial camping facilities at

Moab just outside the park, as well as some other public facilities nearby. Information on these can be obtained at the Visitor Center.

Devil's Garden Campground—52 sites on both sides of a spur road. Hints of shade from small trees and ribs of rock on some sites. Most, however, are exposed. Valley views from several, too. Fire grills. But there's no wood whatsoever. Bring your own. Flush toilets. Piped water.

Where to Get Information

For information on the park write:
>   Superintendent
>   Arches National Park
>   Moab, Utah 84532

natural bridges
national monument

FIND A DIFFERENT beauty here, which was formed a different way.

While the arches to the north were carved almost solely by wind and rain, the sweeping bridges here were shaped first by the streams they all now span.

Glimpse them from the road. Or better yet, hike into the stream bottoms to truly appreciate the grandeur of this form of nature's work.

To reach the area: From I-70 across central Utah drive south past Moab to Blanding on U.S. 163, turning west on a new paved state highway 95.

This small national monument contains three of the most spectacular bridges in this part of Utah and prime examples of how such bridges form and develop. For here is a young bridge, thick and fat, and an older bridge, wearing thinner every year.

The visitor season here extends from April through November with the heaviest use in the spring between April and June when the flowers are in bloom, water flows in the canyon and the birds are migrating. Use is heaviest on weekends then, leveling out to week-around as the tourist season opens.

Summer temperatures here range from 85 to 90 degrees during the day, ranging as high as 104 degrees, with temperatures in the canyons 10 degrees higher. Evening temperatures drop into the cooler range.

Thunderstorms are common in this area during the summer and pose the monument's greatest hazard. Torrential flash floods often sweep down these canyons after upstream storms. And torrential is exactly what they are. Flood waters plunge downstream in a virtual wall sweeping everything and anything before them. And the skies may be absolutely blue at the time.

Park Service officials close these canyons whenever an upstream storm is seen. Heed those warnings. But if you're hiking in the canyon keep a lookout for storms in the upstream ridges. If you hear one, or see one, stop your hike and leave the canyon at once.

Visitors are urged to stay out of any Indian ruin they may run across in the monument. These sites are of incredible historic value and totally irreplaceable. And it's the same with pictographs to be seen on many of the canyon walls. These delicate drawings are only a single sand-grain thick. Touch them and the picture rubs off.

Observe what you find here. Enjoy what you see. But make certain others will be able to enjoy it after you leave.

The Park Service presents evening naturalist programs, beginning in April, which cover the history, geology and plant life of the monument.

WHERE TO DRIVE

Driving here is confined solely to the single loop road with viewpoints on it. Each of the bridges can be seen from the road. But you may have difficulty seeing them from afar in certain lights of the day when the shadows of the bridges blend in with the shadows of the cliffs. Look too for signs of cliff dwellings in the cracks of the canyons across from the road.

WHERE TO HIKE

Trails here lead to all of the bridges and down the streams between them. The paths, mostly on slabs of rock, are marked either with cairns or with painted (green) tracks of the big horn sheep.

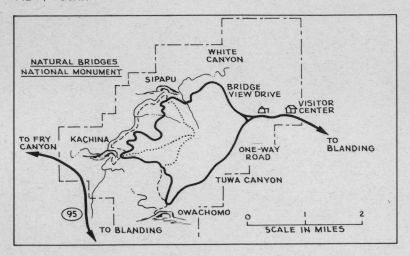

Hikers are urged to wear sturdy rubber soled shoes to avoid slipping on the slabs.

Hikers are also urged to carry water. These canyons can be extremely hot and there's no water on the trails. Protect yourself from the heat by wearing a hat and long-sleeve shirt.

Sipapu Bridge—Hike about half-mile, into the White Canyon to look up at a 269-foot span 220 feet high.

Find the trail off the monument loop road about 1.5 miles from the junction beyond the campground.

The trail, which starts off behind the sign, drops over a cliff on a stairway to a ledge tucked under a rock cliff. Walk around the ledge to vistas down-canyon and then return to the trail, mid-ledge, as it drops, sometimes by ladder, over rock faces to the bottom of the canyon and viewpoints below the bridge. A short but exciting walk.

Kachina Bridge—The youngest bridge here, more squat and fat than any of the others, but still spanning 206 feet in an arch 210 feet high.

Find this trail off a parking area about 4.2 miles from the junction beyond the campground.

The trail starts behind the sign, dropping down rock slabs (watch carefully for painted tracks and cairns) to the bottom of the canyon. The bridge gets higher and higher as you go.

Owachomo Bridge

Take time here also to explore sheltered "plunge basin" often full of water below a sometimes waterfall which can be seen by walking up Armstrong Canyon.

Owachomo Bridge—This isn't the largest but it's certainly the most delicate and startling of the bridges in this monument. It's also the most fragile and probably the oldest.

Hike about a quarter mile.

Find the trail off the loop road about 6.3 miles from the junction west of the campground.

Here again, the trail drops downhill into the canyon to the base of the bridge. Although this bridge only spans 180 feet and arches above the stream only 106 feet, it is the thinnest and narrowest of them all—only 9 feet thick and 27 feet wide.

White Canyon Trail—If you have the time here, spend an afternoon or morning hiking through White Canyon between Sipapu and Kachina bridges. A 3.5 to 4 mile walk.

The path here follows the stream bed most of the way, wending first to one side and then the other and sometimes even down the middle. You can't get lost here. But you may spend much of your time wading the stream, if it's flowing.

A good place here to appreciate both the history and natural wonders of this monument. Watch for Indian ruins on the cliffs, note the variety of bird and plant life as you walk the canyon, and observe too the signs of new arches and new bridges being etched out of canyon walls.

Check at the Visitor Center before taking this hike. And be alert to the danger of thunderstorms upstream.

BACKPACKING OPPORTUNITIES

There are no backpacking trails in this small monument.

WHERE TO CAMP

Camping here is pleasant, but very limited. And there are no commercial or formal public facilities nearby when the campground here fills. The nearest is 40 miles away. When the campground does fill, campers generally find space in undeveloped areas on nearby public lands.

Natural Bridge Campground—14 sites on a shady, forested loop. Pit toilets. Piped water at Visitor Center.

Where to Get Information

Information on the Natural Bridges National Monument can be obtained by writing:

> Superintendent
> Canyonlands National Park
> Moab, Utah 84532

bryce canyon national park

KINGS, QUEENS, WISEMEN and castles here in a royal rock display along the side of a multi-hued plateau.

Wind and rain were the sculptors of these shapes. Some have formal names. Others you can name yourself.

And a pleasant place to visit in midsummer too. Temperatures on this plateau are much cooler than in the valleys down below.

How to reach the area: From I-70 across central Utah, turn south at Salina onto U.S. 89, turning east on State Highway 12 seven miles south of Panguitch. Or from Zion National Park, turn north on U.S. 89 from State Highway 15.

This long and narrow park embraces about 56 square miles along the east rim of the Paunsaugunt Plateau in central Utah. Elevations in the park range from near 8000 to over 9000 feet with the edge of the plateau towering nearly 2000 feet above the floor of the valley to the east. All of the park's famed erosion features are located below the plateau rim.

The park season begins in April with roads and campgrounds opening from then on as weather permits and use demands and it continues through October with the park enjoying some of its best camping weather from Labor Day on.

Park visitation is heaviest from mid-June to Labor Day with use midweek as heavy as it is on weekends. Naturalist programs which include campfire talks and guided walks are conducted by park rangers during that period. After Labor Day the programs are generally discontinued. But campgrounds and roads remain open and visitors can prowl canyon trails now almost by themselves.

Despite scorching temperatures in nearby valleys, daytime summer temperatures in the park range in the 80s during July dropping to the 70s in August. Nighttime temperatures during the summer drop to the mid-40s.

Afternoon thundershowers here are common but generally of short duration. July and August are the park's wettest summer months. But even then the rainfall is light and inclement weather seldom lasts more than a day or two.

Hikers in the park are urged to wear sturdy shoes. Although all of the trails are well-maintained they are occasionally rocky and sometimes muddy. Hikers should also make concessions to the elevation here until they've acclimatized themselves. At elevations here of between 8000 and 9000 feet some persons may find themselves short of breath, even on level trails.

WHERE TO DRIVE

The park's main road, which winds 20 miles along the top of the plateau from the entrance station to a deadend at Rainbow Point, takes drivers past a complete sampling of the many sculptured wonders here.

The road, which climbs almost 1000 feet during the trip, offers no continuous views of the canyon but it does pass a series of 12 viewpoints along the way. Stop at them all. Short trails lead from many of the points to bigger and better vistas. Walk them all.

Part of the road is closed each winter being maintained then only as far as Paria View.

WHERE TO HIKE

Lots of short trails here. But a number of interesting longer ones too.

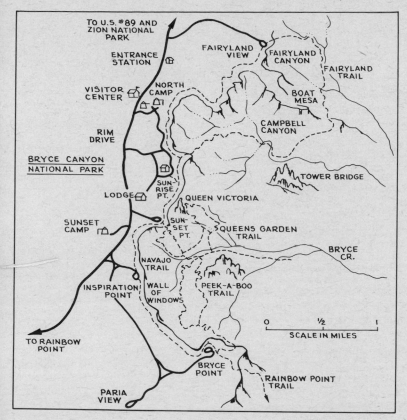

Hike from any of several vista points down into the canyon to appreciate close-up the variety and wonder of this place.

But remember, if you walk down you must also walk back up. Some of these trails drop as much as 1000 feet. Patience, however, is all that's really required on any of these trails. None of them are steep and all are graded evenly and gradually.

And use care not to kick rocks over the edge of the trail. Many of these paths switchback directly over trails below. And don't shortcut either. Erosion in this area is rapid and difficult to control.

Fairyland—A complete cross-section of the canyon here. Through eroded cliffs to a canyon floor.

To start at the highest point so that you can walk out at the lowest, take the trail from the North Campground ending your trip

Along the Fairyland Trail

in 5.5 miles at the Fairyland Viewpoint. To complete your loop, hike another 2.5 miles from the viewpoint along the rim back to camp.

To find the trail walk to the canyon rim from the campground turning to the right (south) following the rim to a junction of the Fairyland Loop trail in about a quarter mile.

At the junction turn downhill following the trail first into Campbell Canyon and then to a junction with the Tower Bridge spur in about 1.5 miles. To see the bridge, turn right 200 feet, returning to the main trail.

From the junction, climb then a series of twisting switchbacks over a ridge below Boat Mesa to drop into Fairyland Canyon before climbing, again, to the rim at the Fairyland viewpoint.

The trail starts at 8000 feet, drops to 7250 near the Tower Bridge junction, climbs again to 7500 feet, drops once more to 7150 feet in Fairyland Canyon and then climbs to the rim at 7804 feet.

Vistas along the way of every size. Broad views of sweeping valleys and mountains to the east. Smaller ones of endless rock figures parading on the cliffs. And closeup glimpses of single snarls of twisted weathered wood. Deer tracks in the canyon and flowers too.

Guidebooks point out such features as Oastler Castle, Crescent Castle and the Palace of the Fairy Queen. But don't limit yourself to those. Name a few of your own. There are more than enough to go around.

Queen's Garden-Navajo loops—Take these trails separately or put them together to hike past some of the more popular rock figures in the park.

Separately, the Queen's Garden trail drops .8 mile from Sunrise Point and the Navajo trail makes a 1.5 mile loop from Sunset Point.

To put them together start at Sunset Point on the Navajo Loop hiking through the canyon to the Queen's Garden trail returning to the rim at Sunrise Point. About 2.7 miles.

From Sunset Point follow the main trail downhill taking either one of the Navajo loops spurs at a junction in about 100 yards. Both spurs drop in a series of switchbacks to a junction at the bottom, passing a series of erosion features given names to fit their seeming shapes.

At the junction in about .7 mile, turn north onto an .8 mile connecting trail that leads to the Queen's Garden trail. At the Queen's Garden junction take time (turn left) to see Queen Victoria posing against the sky and then climb upward on another series of switchbacks to Sunrise Point.

Turn left here following the rim trail back to Sunset Point. An almost level half mile.

A cross-section of colors here—pinks, reds, oranges and grays, all below a brilliant blue sky. Plus vistas, of course, out into the valley and even a short tunnel or two.

These are easy uphill and downhill trails. So take your time and enjoy!

Others—The nearly level *Rim Trail* winds along the edge of the rim from the Fairyland viewpoint to Bryce Point offering a leisurely opportunity for ever-changing views into the canyon. Start in the middle or at either end, walking as far as you want. A good place to watch the sun rise.

From Bryce Point take the Peekaboo loop (about 3 miles) or hike to the Hatshop (a 4-mile roundtrip) toward Rainbow Point.

BACKPACKING OPPORTUNITIES

The Park Service here requires hikers to obtain permits before taking any overnight trips into the canyon. Backcountry camping is restricted to assigned campsites at park water points. Camps at other points are prohibited.

Backpacking here is confined to the 22.6-mile under-the-rim trail which extends from Bryce Point to Rainbow Point. Hikers can make the entire trip over a two or three day period or take a series of shorter hikes from spur trails between the two points. No loop hikes here. So make arrangements before you start for transportation back to where you began.

The park trails climb occasionally into the cliffs for closeup views of rock formations. But most of the time they wind along canyons with views up at the changing eroded forms.

WHERE TO CAMP

The Park Service has developed more than 200 sites in two campgrounds within the park, and keeps some of them open from May through October.

Campgrounds here are usually full every night during the peak season in July and August. Campers who are turned away can find ample facilities in nearby commercial camps.

North Campground—110 sites on a series of wooded loops near but not on the canyon rim. Just east of the Visitor Center. A tent camp with trailer pull-through sites. Flush toilets. Piped water.

Sunset Campground—115 sites on timbered loops on the west side of the main park road. 1 mile south of the Visitor Center. Last to open in the spring. Flush toilets. Piped water.

Where to Get Information

For information on Bryce Canyon write:
Superintendent
Bryce Canyon National Park
Bryce Canyon, Utah, 84717

zion national park

THEY LOOK LIKE mountains when you first see them. Towering pinnacles. Rugged crests. Some of them, even, with mountain names like Deertrap, Three Patriarchs and Towers of the Virgins. And waterfalls, too, gushing off the cliffs in the spring.

But at Zion they're really not mountains at all, only the high vertical cliffs of one of the most colorful and spectacular canyons in the West. You simply look up here, rather than down.

To reach the area: From I-15 which crosses Utah north-to-south, turn east on Utah State Highway 15 south of Cedar City. Or from U.S. 89, turn west onto the same highway at the Mt. Carmel Junction north of Kanab.

This park embraces a total of 230 square miles. But only a small part of it in the Zion Canyon is generally visited by the public. That's the area reviewed here.

Some campsites in the canyon are kept open all year. But the heaviest use here occurs between mid-May and Labor Day.

High trails do not open generally until March, remaining open through November, depending on the weather. Canyon trails are open all year. Naturalist programs, including campfire talks and guided hikes are conducted throughout the visitor season from May through September.

One of the best times to visit the park is during the spring beginning in March. Flowers are in bloom then. Most of the waterfalls are pluming full. And the weather is at its best. But if you plan to hike into the park's famed "Narrows", however, late June, late September and early October are the best times to come.

Summer temperatures in the canyon range from warm to warmer averaging in the high 90s and low 100s with the highest ever recorded at 115 degrees. Nighttime temperatures drop to a comfortable 50 to 60 degrees.

Thunderstorms are common here in July and August, roaring over the park quickly, swelling streams and turning dry waterfalls back on again. They pose few hazards except to hikers on exposed ridges and in deep canyons where flash floods can force hikers to high rocks until the water subsides.

Hikers here are urged always to carry water and protect themselves from the glaring sun and heat. Streams here often dry up in the summer. And the smooth rock faces can create an oven-effect in canyons which heightens the impact of the heat.

And don't leave the trails unless you know what you're doing. This is deceivingly precipitous country chopped up with treacherous canyons even on the plateaus. And be careful too about knocking rocks off any high trails. Many of these trails switchback directly over hikers below. And never hike at night. Darkness settles in these canyons suddenly and often totally. So if you become trapped by darkness simply wait it out.

WHERE TO DRIVE

Fortunately, the only way to see this park, even in part, is to get out of your car. First, all of the scenery is above you. And second, all of the close-up features must be walked to, albeit on short and fairly level trails.

Canyon Overlook—Walk a half-mile, climbing about 163 feet, to a high vista point overlooking Zion Canyon and out at the surrounding cliffs, ridges and "mountains".

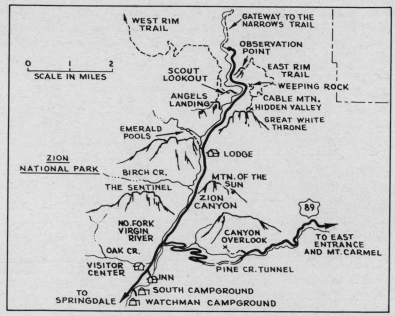

Find the trail at the east end of the Zion-Mt. Carmel tunnel. Park on the south side of the road, crossing the highway to the trailhead.

The trail starts up steps and then winds along a ledge beneath a cliff before reaching the viewpoint. Breathtaking here, really.

Weeping Rock—Duck under a dripping wall into one of the most refreshing spots in the park on a hot day.

Find the trail off a parking area east of the park road about 4.5 miles north of the Zion junction.

The trail crosses a bridge (in the spring watch suckers here trying to migrate upstream by holding themselves to the rock with their mouths) then climb steadily to the face of a cliff where water drips over a viewpoint. Lush greenery along with a constant cooling spray.

Gateway to the Narrows—Walk a level mile here to a glimpse down the Zion Narrows and up (after rains or in the spring) at a number of wispy waterfalls.

Find the trail off a large parking loop at the end of the road, 6.5 miles north of the Zion junction.

The trail here follows the river past a lush display of cliff-draped greenery supported by seeps of water from the canyon wall. Rich displays of shooting stars, columbines, fern, monkey flowers and mosses.

From the end of the paved trail walk a little way into the canyon itself if low water permits. Keep an eye and ear peeled, however, for possible storms.

WHERE TO HIKE

The full variety of the spectacle offered in this canyon can only be appreciated by hiking the longer trails which climb, often strenuously, through an ever-changing world of vista and plant.

Hidden Canyon—Climb a mile from a hot and crowded big canyon into a cool and uncrowded small one.

Find the trailhead out of the Weeping Rock parking area (see drives). The trail starts across the bridge. Straight ahead.

The path, paved most of the way, switchbacks immediately up the East Rim trail about .6 miles to the Hidden Canyon junction. Turn right here and follow the trail still higher as it climbs out across the face of a cliff before ducking in to the canyon entrance. Vertical views here—really—down to the canyon floor.

The formal trail ends at the canyon opening. But pick your way up the narrow stream bed as far as you'd like. The canyon ends in about another mile with a small natural bridge in the right bank about a half-mile from the entrance.

A hidden world here all of its own. Cool. Quiet and still wild.

Observation Point—There's no doubt, once you reach this point, that Zion is a canyon. Climb 3.6 miles (it'll seem much longer) from the canyon floor to the very top of the plateau for vistas that really never seem to end. One of the highest points in this part of the park.

Find the trailhead at the Weeping Wall parking area (see drives and Hidden Canyon). After crossing the bridge, the trail switchbacks up the side of Echo Canyon before ducking about halfway into a pretty narrow gorge.

Find respite here both from the sun and the constant effort of climbing. Water here occasionally. And take time to admire the slice-like slot that the stream has cut for itself in this solid rock.

Hidden Canyon

From the gorge, the trail lunges out to a barren ridge switch-backing tediously up a trail blasted out of solid rock. Just below the rim, the trail traverses a ledge for about a half mile, topping the plateau to reach the Point in another quarter mile.

Vertical views of the entire valley here from 6509 feet, 2200 feet above the valley floor.

And be sure to note the changing plant life as the trail makes its climb. It starts out amid plants of the moist valley, climbing next into desert and finally out into a mesa world that supports forests of Ponderosa pine.

Emerald Pool—Climb to two small pools below towering cliffs with waterfalls added in the spring. About 1.5 miles.

Find the trailhead across a bridge over the Virgin River from a parking area opposite the Zion Lodge.

The trail bears right along the river and then climbs gradually but persistently to the first pool in about a mile. Follow the trail here around a ledge behind a waterfall, climbing upward then to the top of the falls. The trail here drops to the second pool through boulders (follow the chain) in another .3 mile.

In spring, a spectacular falls streams off the face of the cliff above the upper pool. Cool showers when wind fans the spray.

BACKPACKING OPPORTUNITIES

Backcountry use in Zion has not been heavy but it is increasing every year. The number of trails to remote areas is limited and water is extremely rare.

Hikers, who are required to register, should consult with rangers on trail conditions and on water locations before planning any extended trip.

The Narrows—This popular backcountry river-bottom trail winds its way 15 miles—and more—down a canyon so narrow that in some places the sun never reaches the bottom.

Start at several points at the north end of the canyon and hike out at the Temple of Sinawava at the upper end of the canyon road. The trail is not recommended in July, August and early September due to river flood conditions. The best time to hike it is in late June, late September and early October when the water is low. Register before you start. Good shoes are essential.

West Rim—Hike a strenuous 13 miles from the bottom of Zion Canyon up the West Rim trail to Potato Hollow. Hike all the way or stop at established water points enroute.

Deep canyons and high plateaus. Some of the most spectacular country in the park. Camping is barred in some of the lower canyons. Register before you start.

WHERE TO CAMP

A few campground loops are kept open in this park the year around with others being put in service as use demands. Most of the time, even during the rush season, campers can find sites within the park. There are also large commercial camping facilities nearby.

Some sites on these campgrounds are located in trees, including an old orchard. Many, however, are in open grass areas.

South Campground—145 sites on a series of loops. Store nearby. Flush toilets. Piped water.

Watchman Campground—228 units some of them near the Virgin river. Others on a hillside. Flush toilets. Piped water.

Where to Get Information

For details about Zion write:

    Superintendent
    Zion National Park
    Springdale, Utah 84767

ARIZONA

grand canyon national park

EVERYBODY KNOWS ABOUT Grand Canyon, right?

Pictures of it in books. Pictures on TV. Articles in magazines almost every year. And in newspapers too.

There certainly can be no surprise here. No surprises at all.

And tragically, some people actually think that's true.

But the fact is, nobody but nobody knows anything about Grand Canyon until they've walked to the edge of its rim. And then, all they think they know goes up in one big gasp.

For no matter how many pictures you've seen, or how many books you have read, nothing prepares you for the canyon itself.

It's simply bigger than real. No words, no pictures tell the story at all.

Hike here if you possibly can. Drive if you have no other choice. But see it for certain.

How to reach the area: To reach the South Rim, which is all that is covered here, drive north from Flagstaff on U.S. 180. From U.S. 89, turn west just south of Cameron onto State Highway 64, driving to the Desert View entrance.

The best time—but not necessarily the most popular time—to visit Grand Canyon is probably in the spring and fall.

During the park's rush season from mid-May through Labor Day, the park is literally overrun with people. Roads and trails are crowded. Traffic jams are not uncommon. Campgrounds are filled. Vista points overflow. And even the weather is at its hottest with daytime temperatures at the rim around 80 to 90 degrees and, at the bottom of the canyon, over 100 degrees.

But from mid-March to mid-May and from Labor Day until mid-November, all that changes. Some of the naturalist programs which include talks and guided walks will have been discontinued. And most of the elaborate commercial activities will have been curtailed. But almost all of the people will have gone home and a visitor can then see and enjoy the canyon without the constant hassle of crowds.

The weather is also cooler during the early and late season. Daytime temperatures will range then from the 60s into the upper 70s at the rim with nighttime temperatures dropping to the 30s and 40s.

At the bottom of the canyon, daytime temperatures will have dropped below the 90s with nighttime temperatures running in the 50 to 60-degree range.

And the weather is also relatively drier in the spring and fall, although precipitation in the early spring and late fall can sometimes end up as snow.

Thundershowers are common over the canyon from early July until the end of August. Although these storms can produce torrential downpours in local areas, they rarely last more than a half hour or so, usually ceasing completely by nightfall.

Heat is the greatest single hazard in the park, particularly to hikers. And no one should hike into the canyon without carrying water and lots of it. A gallon per person per day is the rule. Proper clothing is essential too.

The Arabs always protect their bodies from the sun and hikers here should do the same. Wide-brimmed hats, light, long-sleeved shirts and light, full-length trousers are recommended as protection from sunburn and heat stroke. Walls of the canyon often capture and reflect heat sending temperatures as high as 120 degrees.

Good shoes are likewise important. The trails here all climb

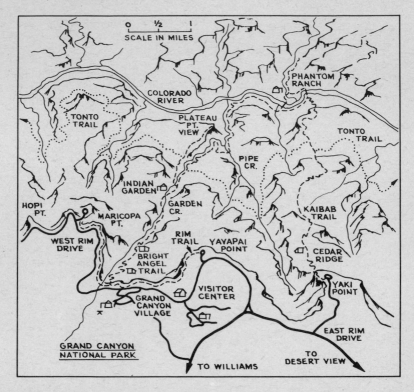

sharply and persistently. Sandals, saddle shoes and cowboy boots won't do the job.

Again, this South Rim section of the park is one of the busiest in the entire national park system. In an effort to ease the traffic congestion, the Park Service may institute special free bus service in the Grand Canyon village area. Some roads may be closed and visitors may be required to park and take the busses in order to visit sites along the West rim. The busses are to be scheduled about every 15 to 20 minutes.

WHERE TO HIKE

There's no doubt that Grand Canyon looks big from the rim. It's got to be one of the biggest views around.

But to truly appreciate the canyon's scale you must hike into it. Its size then becomes far more than just a visual thing. It takes on a physical dimension you can actually feel in terms of tired muscles and sweat.

From the top of the canyon all you can do is look down. But from below the rim you can also look up and it's from this point that the whole scene becomes bigger than big.

There are only two trails—the Bright Angel and the Kaibab—that can be hiked without a special permit. Some take one trail to the bottom or part way and return the same way. Others take one trail down, generally the Kaibab, and the other trail out, spending one day or more.

Listed here are two shorter hikes—one on each trail—that will give you a feeling for the canyon without killing you in the process.

Plateau Point—Drop 3100 feet in 6 miles to a vista point where you can look up at the towering rim and down another 1400 feet into the roiling Colorado river below.

A cross-section of the entire canyon here—steep trails, an oasis midway, a sample of a mid-level plateau, and a wild turbulence of rocky cliffs.

Find the trailhead off the canyon rim just west of the Bright Angel Lodge. It's the only trail that goes downhill.

Immediately after dropping over the rim and through an arch, the trail starts a series of switchbacks that don't end for another 3 miles.

In about 1.5 miles the trail passes the first of two resthouses, (shade but no water here) continuing—still downward—to the second rest house at about 3 miles.

From the second resthouse, the trail continues to drop for another half-mile finally tapering off slightly as it wends its way through heavier desert growth to Indian Gardens. Shade trees here, actually. Water and a campground (see backpacking). Restrooms too. Stop here for sure, as if anyone needs to ask.

To continue on to the river pick up the main trail on the east side of the campground as it drops more sharply now losing 1400 feet in just 3.5 miles.

To reach Plateau Point, find a section of the Tonto trail across the creek bed to the west at the lower end of the campground, following it across the plateau to a junction with the Plateau Point spur in about three-quarters mile. Turn right reaching the point in another three-quarters mile.

Storm at Plateau Point

And give yourself lots of time here. Vistas up, down and all around. To the south, the sheer walls of the canyon you just climbed down. To the north and below you the raging river that caused it all. And around you, a desert scene completely unlike that on the rim.

Return the same way you came. But expect to take about twice as long.

Cedar Ridge—An exciting sample of the special spectacle to be found on the Kaibab Trail.

Find the trail at the end of a short spur road which leads west off the Yaki Point road about .7 mile north of the East Rim Drive.

The trail, which starts from the north side of a parking area, drops first below the rim and then works its way northward before switchbacking down to a formal rest area with a pit toilet in about 1.5 miles.

Constant vistas here as the trail winds down an exposed ridge first on one side and then the other.

Return from the formal rest area or continue another 3.5 miles to the Tipoff, where the trail starts its final drop to the river, or 6 miles to the river itself.

Rim Trail—You won't gain the sense of the canyon here that you'll gain on the other trails, but at least you'll avoid some—but not all—of the crowds.

This paved trail starts at Maricopa Point on the West Rim road and continues eastward along the rim about 4 miles to Yavapi Point Museum. Start from any number of places in between by simply making your way to the rim and walking in either direction as far as you want.

BACKPACKING OPPORTUNITIES

Backpackers who stay on the Kaibab and Bright Angel trails can hike without permits. But they must get campground reservations if they plan to remain in the canyon overnight.

The number of hikers permitted at any of the four campgrounds is limited. Reservations can be made by mail, in person or by telephone but hikers holding reservations must appear in person to get their final camping permit.

Hikers taking overnight trips on these trails can camp at Bright Angel campground, 75-person limit; Indian Gardens, 75 limit; Cottonwood, 50-person limit and Roaring Springs, 25-person limit. Hikers can also stay at a guest ranch at the bottom of the canyon. Reservations, however, must be made in advance.

Backpackers who plan to hike on other than these two trails must register at the Visitor Center before beginning their trips.

There are a number of unmaintained trails throughout the canyon which are best described in a booklet, "Inner Canyon Hiking", that can be obtained by mail or at the Visitor Center for a nominal charge.

All backpackers into the canyon are urged to carry as little as possible—except water. Hikers should carry at least a gallon of water a day for each person. Tents are generally unnecessary here. It seldom rains at night. And a light blanket will do in place of a sleeping bag. Canned foods are preferred here over dehydrated foods favored on other trails because of the lack of water. And pack out all trash.

WHERE TO CAMP

Campgrounds here usually fill before noon on every day during the peak season. The best bet, therefore, is to make a prior reservation through the Park Service-American Express reservation system before leaving home.

No one is permitted to camp in the park except at campgrounds. And overflow facilities are limited to a National Forest Service campground 6 miles south of the park and two commercial facilities about 30 miles away.

Mather Campground—320 sites in pleasant pine forest. In the Grand Canyon Village area. Flush toilets. Piped water.

Desert View—50 sites in forested area near the east entrance. Piped water. Pit toilets. Stores facilities nearby.

Where to Get Information

For information about the park write:
> Superintendent
> Grand Canyon National Park
> Grand Canyon, Arizona 86023

saguaro and organ pipe cactus national monuments

NOT EVERY SPECTACLE in the West includes high cool mountains and crystal lakes.

There are deserts there too. Sprawling, parched and hot. But interesting nonetheless with their own wildlife, their own plants and their own particular kind of scenery. And certainly as much a part of the nation's heritage as any mountain range.

Sampled here are just two such desert areas—The Saguaro National Monument near Tucson and Organ Pipe Cactus National Monument near the Mexican border.

SAGUARO NATIONAL MONUMENT

It's named for just one type of cactus which grows in both parts of this two-section monument. But it's known for the vast variety of other plants which grow here too.

A cross-section, really, of the type of desert country found in central Arizona.

And it is pronounced: Sah-wa-ro.

To reach the area: Find the headquarters and Visitor Center in the Rincon mountain section of the monument east of Tucson at the end of the Old Spanish Trail road. To reach the monument's information station in the Tucson mountain section, drive west from Tucson on West Speedway Blvd. about 15 miles from the freeway.

This is desert country, strictly. And the best time—if not the only time—to visit it is during the fall-winter-spring season.

June, July and August are times to stay home. For temperatures here in the summer range constantly in the upper 90s and 100-degree range. Fall-to-spring temperatures, however, range from the low 70s in the daytime in mid-winter to sometimes near-freezing at night. And it rains less then too. Summer rainfall is heaviest in the thunderstorm season from July through September.

And time your visit during the midweek periods, particularly if you plan any backcountry hikes. Weekend use is particularly heavy by nearby urban hikers.

The monument here offers naturalist-conducted walks in the winter and maintains nature trails off the Bajada Loop drive in the Tucson mountain sector and the Cactus Forest drive in the headquarters area. A museum display at the Visitor Center also tells the plant, animal and geologic story of the monument.

Wildflowers bloom here generally in March and April and again in August. But the displays depend entirely on the right combination of rain, sunlight and temperature making them impossible to predict.

Cacti seem to bloom with greater regularity. However, even they will be found blossoming in some areas and not in others at a given moment.

Most cactus bloom here in the March-April-May period with each variety blossoming in its own time. The Saguaro cactus generally blossom in May to June and the Barrel Cactus during August through September.

WHERE TO DRIVE

For overviews of this area and glimpse of desert plant life drive either the Bajada Loop road in the Tucson mountain section or the Cactus Forest drive in the Rincon mountain-headquarters area.

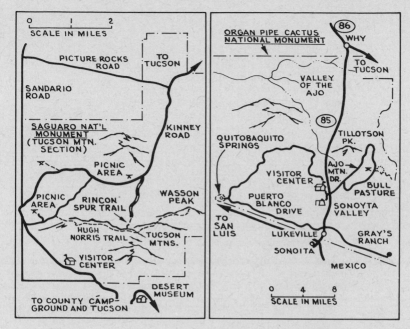

Bajada Loop—This 9-mile drive loops through a dense stand of saguaro cactus to views over the cotton fields of the Avra valley and out to the Silverbeel mountains.

Drive west from the Tucson mountain information center, passing a nature trail in about a mile and an overlook trail in 2 miles. Take time to walk them both. Keep left at junctions to return to the information center.

Cactus Forest Loop—This paved drive loops 9 miles through another stand of saguaros past vistas, this time, of the Rincon mountains, Tucson mountains, Tucson and types of rock which make up this region.

Find the road east of the Visitor Center complex. Take time to walk the nature trails here too.

WHERE TO HIKE

Best day-hiking trails in the monument are located in the Tucson mountain section, west of Tucson.

Here in less than 5 miles a hiker can walk through a forest of the monument's namesake cactus and along high ridges to look for miles across the flat desert plains.

Carry water. And hike only during the fall-winter-spring part of the year. Summer temperatures here soar near 100 degrees.

Hugh Norris Trail—Hike part way or all the way to Wasson Peak at 4687 feet through samples of high desert terrain and plant life.

Find the trailhead off the east side of the Hohokam road about three-quarters mile from the Kinney road junction north of the information center.

The trail switchbacks up a ridge through a heavy stand of desert plants and then traverses along the north side of the mountain ridge, reaching a junction with a spur trail from the north in 2.7 miles and a junction with a steep trail to the top of Wasson Peak in another 1.8 miles. The peak in .3-mile more.

Most views along this section of the trail look to the north and west. But find occasional vistas to the south over Tucson when the trail nears the top of the ridge. 360-degree views from the top of the mountain.

Flowers here in season. And be sure and note the slat-like woody skeletons of dead saguaro and the lace-like framework remains of other cactus in the area.

BACKPACKING OPPORTUNITIES

Backpacking opportunities in this monument are concentrated in the eastern Rincon mountain section on 65 miles of trail.

The Tanque Verde Ridge trail and the Douglas Spring trail lead to six remote camps in the mountains. Camping, however, is restricted to established sites and the number of permits is limited in each camp. Hikers can obtain permits at the Visitor Center. All are issued on a first-come, first-served basis. No permits are issued by mail.

The best time to hike here is during the midweek in the fall-winter-spring season. Heaviest use occurs on weekends.

Information on trails and backcountry camps can be obtained at Monument headquarters.

WHERE TO CAMP

There are no camping facilities in either section of the Saguaro National Monument. Visitors to the Tucson mountain section, however, can find camping sites in a Pima county park. There are also commercial campgrounds in Tucson.

Palo Verde Campground—115 campsites on a large loop 2.5 miles from the Arizona Sonora Desert Museum south of the monument information center. County operated. Flush toilets. Piped water. Primarily a camper truck and trailer site.

ORGAN PIPES CACTUS NATIONAL MONUMENT

Much more here than a winter camping center. Although that's what many seem to use it as.

Camp certainly. And enjoy the sun. But spend your time prowling the formal backcountry loop roads and the monument's few trails to understand and appreciate what a desert really is.

Life here actually in abundance when you consider the severity of the environment.

To reach the area: From Tucson drive west on State Highway 86, turning south at Why, Arizona, onto Highway 85.

Quitobaquito Springs

This monument, sprawling over 516 square miles contains prime examples of three different types of southwestern desert—the Sonora desert to the south, the California desert to the west, and the Upland Arizona desert of the east.

The monument's "season" here generally extends from November through April with the busiest period between January and mid-April and peaks during the Christmas holiday, on Washington's birthday, Easter and Thanksgiving.

But one of the best periods to visit the park may be in late April and May. Crowds are gone then. Temperatures remain generally pleasant and flowers, particularly the cactus, are still in season.

Temperatures during the winter season range generally from the upper 60s to the low 70s, dropping at night into the upper 30s and 40s.

In summer, however, the thermometer often climbs to the intolerable levels, for all but desert buffs. Temperatures then range continually over 100 degrees during the day with nighttime temperatures in the 70s.

Rains are also lightest during the winter season. Afternoon thundershowers are common in July, August and September.

The wildflower season here can run from ordinary to spectacular, depending on yearly weather conditions. The season usually begins in March lasting into July, depending on rainfall, temperatures, etc.

Cactus generally start blooming in February with some species continuing through September. The organ pipe for which the monument is named generally blooms from May through July.

Interpretive programs are conducted in the monument from January through March with evening campfire programs, nature strolls, birds observation sessions and auto caravans.

WHERE TO DRIVE

The Park Service has developed two formal loop drives here which lead deep into the desert country and prime examples of both the plant life and the mountains in the monument.

Puerto Blanco Drive—This 51-mile drive in the western section of the monument sweeps through the La Abra plains into the Puerto Blanco mountains with views enroute of the Ajo and Bates mountains, and the Quitobaquito and Cipriano hills. Picnic areas and a trail to Quitobaquito springs.

Ajo Mountain Drive—This 21-mile loop skirts the Diablo Mountains to bring closeup views of the Ajo range. See too the 36-foot arch above Arch Canyon. Picnic areas and trail to Bull Pasture.

WHERE TO HIKE

Day-hike opportunities on formal trails here are relatively limited. However, visitors can wander through the desert almost anywhere in the monument without getting lost.

Bull Pasture—Climb 1.7 miles onto a high plateau overlooking a grassy basin where ranchers once grazed bulls.

Find the trail off the Ajo Mountain Drive about 11 miles from the highway. The trail starts on the east side of the road across from a picnic area. The trail winds first up onto the side of a ridge before ducking into Estes Canyon and climbing sharply up the side of the canyon past wrinkled, wind-eroded cliffs to a windy plateau on top. You'll have climbed 1000 feet.

Stop at the top for views back down at the road and over the Bull Pasture. Take time too to prowl the area for flowers in season. Bring your lunch.

On the way back down, turn right at a junction in about a half-mile, following a spur trail downhill into the bottom of the canyon. A different world here entirely. Follow the trail sometimes down the dry stream bed (watch for cairns) as it winds back to the road. Add a half-mile to the trip this way.

Quitobaquito Springs—No lengthy or strenuous walk here. But unless you leave your car and follow the trail you'll never appreciate an oasis.

Find the trail around the small pond and explore the springs to the right (north) up a short draw.

An entirely different world of plants here. Not cooler, certainly. But unbelievably lush and green. Water birds here too, many of them in mid-migration. Over 180 species have been identified.

BACKPACKING OPPORTUNITIES

There is no formal backcountry trail system in this monument but overnight cross-country trips, particularly into the mountain areas, are possible. Registration and permits are required.

Hikers should be warned, however, that there is no drinking water unless that found in potholes is boiled. Carry a stove. No natural wood can be burned here. Fire permits are also required.

For information on possible trips and mountain climbing opportunities write for a hiking and mountaineering guide.

WHERE TO CAMP

Camping here is primarily oriented to trailer and truck campers who visit the monument as part of a winter tour of the southwest. However, some sites are designated for tents.

Overflow commercial camping facilities can be found in nearby Lukeville.

Organ Pipe Campground—208 sites on a series of high loops in a desert setting. No shade. Piped water. Flush toilets.

Where to Get Information

For information on Saguaro National Monument write:

    Superintendent
    Saguaro National Monument
    Box 17210
    Tucson, Arizona 85710

For information on Organ Pipe Cactus National Monument write:

    Superintendent
    Organ Pipe Cactus National Monument
    Box 38
    Ajo, Arizona 85321

WASHINGTON

mount baker

GLISTENING WHITE PEAKS against rich green slopes.

Mount Baker, northernmost volcano in the Cascade range, dominates the countryside here. But it's now a solo show.

Add the spectacular Mt. Shuksan to the east and the high ridges of the Skagit range to the north to make the picture complete.

To reach the area: From I-5, north and south through western Washington, turn east at Bellingham onto State Highway 542 driving to Glacier and the Heather Meadow Recreation area near the Mt. Baker lodge.

This high mountain country around the 10,750-foot snowheaped volcano is part of the Mt. Baker National Forest which borders Canada and the North Cascades National Park.

Campgrounds in this region open late in May remaining open through October, weather permitting. But the high hiking country is generally not clear of snow until early July—sometimes even later—remaining open until the snows return, generally in October.

Weather can be wet here, as it is throughout the Northwest, through May and June with July and August the driest months of the year—sometimes. Rains generally return in mid-September. However, Indian summers are not uncommon.

Summer temperatures throughout this area range on the cool side day and night. Daytime highs in the valleys average in the mid and low 70s with nighttime temperatures dropping to the high 40s.

Thunderstorms are rare here even in the summer. However lower elevations are often socked in with morning fogs. And rainy weather, when it comes, generally hangs around for a day or two.

Biting bugs may be a nuisance around some of the high lakes early in summer. But repellant is generally sufficient to keep them away.

Hikers, particularly those unfamiliar with the ways of mountains, are urged to stay off steep snow fields which sometimes persist on trails through late summer. If a steep slope is covered with snow it is wiser to turn back than risk injury in a fall.

And when hiking in these mountains always carry a jacket and rain gear. Storms can come up suddenly here plunging temperatures to near freezing levels.

Good hiking shoes are essential too. All the trails listed here are easy to follow but sections of them can be rocky, muddy and steep.

The Forest Service here offers no naturalist programs. Persons needing information can obtain it at the Glacier Ranger station.

WHERE TO DRIVE

Mt. Baker and Mt. Shuksan command views from roads and highways here with glimpses of other peaks reserved for hikers.

Glacier Creek road—Drive up a winding, climbing logging road to a vista point at 4000 feet where Mt. Baker fills the entire eastern sky.

Drive east past the Glacier ranger station about a half-mile, turning right (south) onto the Glacier Creek road, No. 3904, following the gradually narrowing logging road 9 miles to a viewpoint at the end of a series of switchbacks.

A pleasant evening drive. Watch the sunset change the colors on Baker's glaciers. And if you make the trip in the fall be sure to check the salmon run up Thompson creek under a bridge about a mile from the highway.

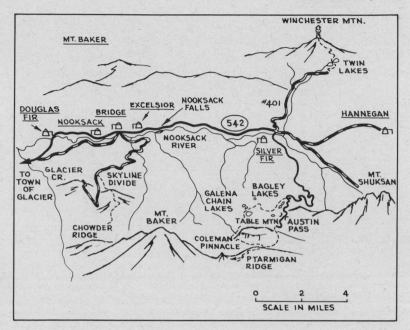

Heather Meadows—Mt. Shuksan stars here along with the heather meadows. But you can find views of Mt. Baker too.

From Glacier follow the state highway past the Silver Fir Campground and then sharply uphill as it switchbacks to the Heather Meadow Recreation area. Some ski structures mar the summer scene here. But find classic pictures of Mt. Shuksan over the small Picture Lake near the road in the middle of the meadows area.

For similar vistas of Baker, continue on up the road (it turns to gravel now) driving beyond the ski-lift complex about 2 miles. This road, never open before July, may be closed by snow some years until late fall. If it is, get out and walk.

To see Mt. Baker, walk out well-worn tourist paths from the end of the road until you find the view that suits you best of the big volcanic peak. Reflections in a tarn or two.

WHERE TO HIKE

Prime hiking country this. And covered here are only a handful of the more popular trails.

Before starting any of these hikes, however, check on trail conditions at the Glacier ranger station. Some may be clogged with snow all year. And trailheads may change as the result of logging activity.

Skyline Divide—Hike 2 miles or longer, if you like, to a high ridge with a sky-full of Mt. Baker, Mt. Shuksan and and the forest ridges to the north.

Drive east from Glacier ranger station about three-quarters mile turning south onto the Glacier Creek road and then east again in about 100 feet onto the Deadhorse road, No. 3907.

Find the trailhead in 14 miles. Parking on the right side of the road. Trail uphill to the left.

The trail climbs through timber for 2 miles with only occasional views out over the valley. But at the end of the climb—total vistas from an alpine ridge.

Pick a gawking spot for lunch or spend an hour or so hiking out along the ridge as it climbs and then drops its way toward Mt. Baker. Quit when you're tired or run out of trail.

Winchester Lookout—Hike past two pretty alpine lakes to a lookout building at 6521 feet with 360-degree views into Canada, out toward Puget Sound and of all the mountains in this corner of the north Cascades. +.5 miles.

This is strictly a check-then-take-it trip. Before you start this hike, stop at the Glacier ranger station to ask about the road and trail which sometimes never open until late fall, and some years not even then.

To find the trail, turn north off the paved highway east of Glacier in about 12 miles, following a twisting, climbing old mining road another 5 to the Tomyhoi trailhead. Park here and walk 2.5 miles up an old road to Twin Lakes.

The lookout trail starts northerly between the two lakes, branching uphill (to the left) in about a quarter mile and then switchbacking across steep open slopes to the top.

If there's snow on this trail do not attempt to cross it. Either make your way around it, if that's possible, or simply turn back.

Lots of flowers in season. And allow yourself at least a half-hour just to soak up the scene.

Chain Lakes—Walk 2 miles through heather meadows to a basin of mountain lakes including one with icebergs in it.

Twin Lakes from Manchester Peak

To find the trail, drive east from Glacier to Heather Meadows Recreation area (see drives) continuing on to the end of the gravel over Austin Pass to Kulshan Ridge. Some years the last part of this road may be packed with snow. So drive as far as you can and then walk.

Find the trail at the end of the parking area as it traverses, on the level, along the steep side of Table Mountain toward the west.

In about a mile, turn right (trail ahead continues to Ptarmigan Ridge) crossing an alpine saddle to drop then sharply downhill past little Mazama Lake and then on (to the right) toward Iceberg Lake. No real icebergs here of course. But large hunks of snow often float on this lake—just like icebergs—all summer long.

Stop here or continue on to the left to visit Arbuthnot and Hayes lakes.

Return the same way you came (the easiest route) or continue north on a more rigorous trail over another saddle, down into Bagley lake basin and then back up again to Kulshan ridge.

For a variation of this trip, take the trail to Ptarmigan Ridge rather than the lakes at the junction in the first mile.

The path here drops into a valley and then climbs to a heather ridge, winding higher and higher as far as you safely want to go.

BACKPACKING OPPORTUNITIES

No limit here to the opportunities for overnight hikes. You can start with the day hikes, listed above. Or strike out on almost any trail you drive by with the most spectacular scenery, as always, reserved for those willing to work the hardest and walk the farthest.

Popular backcountry hikes here include those leading into the North Cascades National Park from the end of the Hannegan road, No. 402, east of Glacier. (Continue east beyond the highway maintenance station rather than following the paved road (right) up hill.)

The trail leaves national forest land and enters the national park beyond Hannegan Pass, dropping then either into the Chilliwack river valley or climbing out on an alpine ridge past small lakes and a lookout for almost 10 miles.

Hikers must obtain a backcountry use permit from the National Park Service. Campfires are banned above timberline, so pack a stove. Permits can be obtained in this area at the Glacier ranger station.

WHERE TO CAMP

All of the campgrounds in the forest north of Mt. Baker are located in the valley along the North Fork of the Nooksack river. Campgrounds open as the snow melts in the spring and can be used until snow falls in autumn. The usual season extends from mid-June through October.

Douglas Fir—36 sites, some near the river. Others on a forested loop above it. Pit toilets. Piped water. 2 miles east of Glacier.

Nooksack—16 units, generally away from the river. Pit toilets. Piped water. 4 miles from Glacier.

Excelsior—9 units on a gravel bar. Pit toilets. Water from creek. 7 miles from Glacier.

Silver Fir—31 units on loops in a timbered flat near the river. A popular camp. Pit toilets. Piped water. 13 miles from Glacier. Closest camp to Heather Meadows.

Where to Get Information

For information on this district of the Mount Baker National Forest write:

> District Ranger
> Glacier Ranger District
> Mount Baker National Forest
> Glacier, Wash. 98244

orcas island and moran state park

MAY SOUND A little incongruous to take a boat to an island and then camp in a forest.

But that's the way it works out here—and all for the better.

The island is Orcas Island in the middle of the spectacular San Juan group in northern Puget Sound. And the campgrounds are in Moran State Park, tucked into the middle of the island, without any access to the sea.

You can find vistas of the surrounding water and islands atop Mt. Constitution. But, otherwise, it's strictly a pleasant, peaceful forest scene of trails, waterfalls, lakes and lots of deer.

How to reach the area: Directions alone simply won't do here. For getting there—via ferry—is one of the highlights of the trip.

From I-5 along the western side of Washington state, turn west at Mount Vernon, driving to the Washington State Ferry terminal outside (west) of the fishing and port town of Anacortes.

Here drive your vehicle aboard a Washington State ferry and spend the next hour or more—depending on the ferry you take—winding through the scenic San Juan islands, stopping at some, passing others.

At Orcas, drive off the ferry and on to Moran State Park, following signs, in about 14 miles.

A couple of suggestions: Avoid weekend trips if you can, either coming or going. Ferry traffic is heaviest then even though ferries depart about once every two hours, during the summer.

Second, always arrive at the ferry terminal, again either coming or going, in plenty of time. Occasionally the last persons in line have to wait for the next ferry.

And consider also the possibility of stopping at one or more of the islands as part of your trip. The state ferry system offers stop-over privileges which permit such visits without any increase in fare.

For information on ferry schedules, stop-over privileges and costs check with the system (see Where to Get Information) before you leave home.

Although some camp sites are kept open at the state park all year, the regular camping season opens April 1 and continues into September. The park's busiest season, of course, is during the school vacation period with the heaviest impacts on weekends and holidays. Use is lightest midweek. But even then campgrounds can be full.

Park officials post a "full" sign at the Anacortes ferry terminal whenever campgrounds are filled.

This chain of islands, located as it is in the rain shadow of the Olympic mountains to the southwest, generally gets more sunshine and less rain then points elsewhere on Puget Sound.

The average summer daytime temperature here varies from 65 degrees near the water to 70 and 75 degrees inland with maximums seldom over 90 degrees. Nighttime minimums range near 50 degrees.

Rainfall levels taper off in May and June with July and August the driest months. Rains generally resume in October and continue through the winter.

Campers here face few problems. There are no poisonous snakes or bears. Trails are all relatively easy to follow. Even the water in the lakes is warm enough to swim in.

The state park offers no naturalist programs. Persons can get information, however, from park rangers.

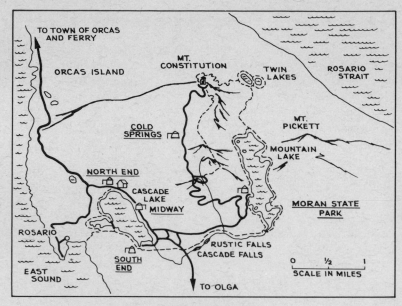

WHERE TO DRIVE

Even exploring by auto can be rewarding here. Drive to the top of Mt. Constitution, the highest point in the island chain, and then wander island backroads to small towns and water-vista points.

One warning: There are no public saltwater beaches on this island. All of the waterfront is privately owned.

Mount Constitution—The road only climbs 2400 feet, but the view—wow! All of the San Juan islands plus the big coastal mountains too.

Take the paved road into Moran State Park, past Cascade Lake, following it uphill to the top of the mountain and its distinctive stone tower, 6 miles from the park entrance.

Climb the tower to see Vancouver Island to the west, snow-crested Mt. Baker to the east, Mt. Rainier to the south, the Olympic mountains to the southwest and islands all the way around.

And make the trip more than once if you stay in the park. Great sunrises. Better sunsets. And grand views all day long.

The Island—No directions here. Simply point your car down any road.

But be sure to seek out the villages of Olga, East Sound, West Sound, Deer Harbor and even Doe Bay. Some of these places consist of little more than a store or cluster of sleepy buildings. But all are interesting.

Life is different here, you'll find. Clocks seem to run slower and longer. And the people do too.

Evening Drive—From the Cascade campground drive out of the park to the west just about dusk. Fawns, does and antlered bucks roam openly in the meadows there as the sun goes down. Watch for deer too within the park. They may be watching you even when you're not watching them.

WHERE TO HIKE

You'll have to remind yourself you're on an island. Glimpse of the surrounding water from high points. But otherwise, the paths wind through rich forest—just like on the mainland.

Cascade and Rustic falls—Start at one island lake, hike past two delicate waterfalls to a second lake. About 3 miles.

Find the trail between the road and Mountain Lake on the south side of Mountain Lake Campground.

The trail follows the shore of the lake across Cascade Creek, then drops downhill first on one side of the creek and then the other past rotting sections of old wire-wrapped wooden flume.

Find the two waterfalls to the left of the trail about half way. You'll hear them both. Rustic Falls first. Cascade Falls second. Both run their fullest in the spring.

Beyond Cascade Falls, the trail crosses the road. Bear to the right, down the road, watching for the trail downhill to your left. A number of way trails lead to Cascade Lake after you see it through the trees.

Twin Lakes—Two ways here to reach a pair of lakes: One way from a mountain top, the other from a larger lake.

From Mt. Constitution drop to the lakes in 1.5 miles. From Mountain Lake, hike slightly upward for 2.1 miles. Or, go all the way from Mt. Constitution to Mountain Lake—passing Twin Lakes enroute. About 3.5 miles.

Find the trail from Mt. Constitution off the downhill side of the vehicle turnaround loop below the tower. The path first drops across a series of open ledges with occasional views out as far as Mt. Rainier, switchbacking downhill into forest and on to the lakes. Keep right at two junctions on the way.

To reach the lakes from Mountain Lake, find the trail along the lake shore north of the campground. The path follows the lake for more than a mile, turning inland beyond the second creek crossing, arriving at Twin Lakes in another mile.

Easy trails loop both lakes. Loiter awhile before returning.

Cascade Lake trail—An ideal evening stroll of less than a mile part way around pretty Cascade Lake.

Find the trail along the lake off the end of the road into the South End campground in the southwest corner of the lake. The trail climbs along a rocky slope, across an outlet bridge, continuing along the lake on a bluff dropping in front of the ranger's house to reach a picnic area. Return the same way.

Waiting San Juan Island ferry

BACKPACKING OPPORTUNITIES

No overnight backpacking is permitted in the park. Camping is restricted to established roadside campgrounds.

WHERE TO CAMP

All of the public camping on this island is confined to four campgrounds within the state park. There are also several commercial camps on the island. Best time to camp is probably midweek. Use is heaviest on weekends and major holidays.

A state fee is charged for all campsites.

North End—50 sites on pleasant forest loops across the road from Cascade Lake. Flush toilets. Piped water.

Midway—57 sites on both sides of the park road with about 17 of them oriented to Cascade Lake. Others on wooded loops. Flush toilets. Piped water.

South End—17 sites in open timbered area along the shore on the southwest end of Cascade Lake. A popular camp. Flush toilets. Piped water.

Mountain Lake—18 sites on a small neck of land jutting into Mountain Lake. A quiet camp away from the main road. Flush toilet. Piped water.

Where to Get Information

For information on Moran State Park, write:

  Chief Ranger
  Moran State Park
  Eastsound, Wash. 98245

For information on island ferry schedules, write:

  Headquarters
  Washington State Ferries
  Seattle Ferry Terminal
  Seattle, Wash. 98104

north cascades

HOW CAN YOU capture an area like this with words? Or even on film?

The truth is, you can't.

You can sample it a little here and there. Visit this lake or stand in awe of that peak or another ridge.

But to dramatize the whole area in just a paragraph or two—impossible. It must be seen to be believed. And even then, in years, not days.

So it's little more than nibbles that is proffered here. Small tastes—that's all—of a pass or two, some lakes and vistas, here and there.

To reach the area: From I-5, north and south through western Washington, turn east at Burlington onto the North Cascade Highway (State 20) reaching Marblemount (a park ranger station here) in 56 miles and Washington Pass in 113 miles.

More than 1050 square miles of some of the most rugged and spectacular mountains in the West are protected here in a federal system of parks and recreation areas.

The North Cascades National Park in two units embraces most of the high mountain country between the Canadian border and Lake Chelan—an area containing over 150 glaciers and hundreds of peaks, lakes and streams.

Two national recreation areas protect the upper part of Lake Chelan and all of the Ross Lake-Skagit River lands surrounding the Seattle City Light power complex there.

Sampled here, however, are only two small parts of the entire region—a section on the Cascade River and another on either side of the North Cascade Highway which bisects the area east to west.

Low elevation recreation facilities in the park and recreation areas generally open in mid-April remaining open until mid-October. High country trails and camps, including the highway, however, seldom open before June and often not until early July, closing with the first snows in late September, or October.

Rain can be expected on the west slopes through June each summer tapering off in July and August which are generally the driest months of the year.

Use here is heaviest on weekends and holidays when urban campers and hikers from the Seattle and Puget Sound region rush to the mountains in droves. So plan your trip here in midweek if you can. Less crowds. More campsites. More room on the trails.

Average summer maximum temperatures in these mountains range from 75 degrees in the lower elevations to the lower 60s at higher levels with nighttime temperatures ranging in the 40s.

Above 4000 feet, minimum temperatures may occasionally drop below freezing, even in midsummer. In general, temperatures in these mountains drop about 3 degrees in every 1000-foot gain in elevation.

Summer lightning storms, so common in the Southwest, are rare here. However, fog is common, blotting out trails some days, making travel almost impossible. And there are no "passing showers" here either. When the weather turns it generally stays "turned" for several days.

Hikers are urged to carry extra warm clothes and rain gear on any hike—even for just a day. Storms can come up rapidly in these mountains posing dangers to the unprepared. Good shoes, as always, are a must. Roots, rocks and mud are not uncommon on these trails.

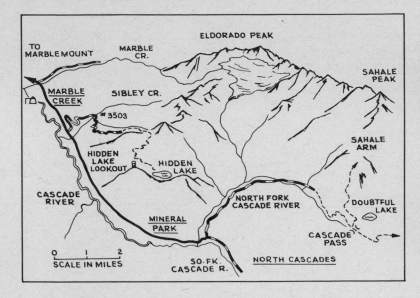

The Park Service presents evening naturalist programs at the Colonial Creek Campground and also schedules naturalist-led walks. Schedules are posted in campgrounds.

WHERE TO DRIVE

Drive over two mountain passes through some of the most spectacular scenery in Washington state.

Find both passes in the middle section of the North Cascade Highway. The road starts from I-5 along Puget Sound and ends on the east side of the Cascade range at Okanogan on the Columbia River.

But the most spectacular portion lies along the 88-mile section between Marblemount, on the west side of the range, and Winthrop, a made-over western town, on the east.

The highway from the west wends first along the Skagit River through a narrow mountain gorge to Diablo Lake and Ross Lake. Views from formal overlooks out over both lakes and up at Colonial and Pyramid peaks.

From above Ross Dam, the road now winds up Granite Creek reaching Rainy Pass in 52.3 miles and Washington Pass in about

57 miles from Newhalem, center of Seattle City Light's power operations here.

At Washington Pass take a short spur road north off the highway to a formal overlook. Views here down Early Winters Creek to Silver Star Mountain. Early Winter Spire and towering Liberty Bell mountain are just across the road.

From the pass, either return or continue on to Winthrop, a redone western town with wooden sidewalks, false store fronts and all.

The road is open generally from June through October, depending on the weather.

WHERE TO HIKE

Some trails listed here follow level valleys. But most climb persistently to reach lush meadows, chill lakes and vistas filled with snow-topped mountains.

Cascade Pass—Glaciers here wherever you look. Heather meadows. Rugged peaks. A 3.5 mile hike, But make it during the week if you possibly can. Weekend use here is heavy beyond belief.

To find the trail drive east from Marblemount on the Cascade River road (cross the Skagit River bridge) to its end at a trailhead parking lot in about 25 miles.

The gravel road follows the Cascade river most of the way, climbing steeply and sometimes very roughly the last several miles. Use care in driving here. No trailers, certainly.

From the parking lot, the trail switchbacks gradually up a timbered slope climbing out into open meadows toward the end on a long traverse across the head of the valley to the pass itself.

If you have time, continue up a steeper trail to the north to the top of Sahale Arm. Better vistas here, of course, including views down on Doubtful Lake. Drop to the lake if you want. But better yet stroll along the top of the ridge as far as you care to. Eventually a glimpse of Glacier Peak.

Alpine country here for real. Plus flowers too. Red columbines, paintbrush, penstemons. Bring a flower book and make a list.

But no camping or fires at the pass or on Sahale Arm. Heavy day use already endangers these meadows. And carry water. Streams here may be contaminated—by people, again.

Ridge above Hidden Lake

Hidden Lake—Cross rock-strewn heather meadows to top a Cascade crest and view a hidden lake. A 3.5-mile hike.

Find the trail at the end of logging road 4.2 miles from the Cascade River road. Drive east from Marblemount on the river road, turning uphill to the north on road No. 3503 about 1.5 miles beyond the Marble Creek Campground.

The trail starts in a clearcut, climbing then through timber for about a mile before breaking out into open meadows.

Once in the meadows, the trail climbs first up the side of a ridge, traversing to the right through boulders and heather before turning sharply uphill toward the top of the ridge and views down on Hidden Lake.

All of this trail is in National Forest land. Park boundary follows the crest.

Avoid steep snow here. Turn back if the way is completely blocked.

High vistas of the valley as you climb, but find the biggest view at the very top—a literal wall of glaciered Cascade peaks from north to south.

To reach the lake, scramble downhill over rough, steep talus slopes. There's also an old lookout building on a hearby hill.

Thunder Arm—No climbing here. Just a gentle pleasant stroll along a creek-and-forest trail.

Find this trail out of Colonial Creek Campground at the end of the campground road south of the North Cascades Highway. It's well signed.

The trail starts along the Thunder Arm of Diablo Lake, crossing Thunder Creek in about a mile and then winding gradually up and down along the east side of the creek through lush forest, reaching Middle Camp in about 5.5 miles.

Lake Trails—A handful of short trails lead from the North Cascade Highway into three pretty mountain lakes.

From Rainy Pass, about 5 miles *west* of Washington Pass (see drives) hike less than a mile south of the highway to *Rainy Lake* on a wheelchair grade trail to watch a waterfall plume off cliffs. Or, from the same point, avoid the crowds on weekends in particular by hiking 3.3 miles up a steeper trail to *Lake Ann* in a pleasant mountain cirque.

To hike to *Cutthroat Lake,* surrounded on three sides by rugged peaks, hike 2 miles from the end of a 1-mile spur road west off the highway about 4.5 miles *east* of Washington Pass.

WHERE TO CAMP

To camp near the Cascade Pass and Hidden Lake trails stay in Forest Service campgrounds along the Cascade River.

Marble Creek—28 units, some along the river, others back on a quiet forest loop. A very pleasant camp. Pit toilets. 9 miles from Marblemount.

Mineral Park—22 units on forest sites on both sides of the North Fork of the Cascade River. Some oriented to the river. Two walk-in sites. 17 miles from Marblemount.

To camp in the North Cascade National Park along the North Cascade Highway:

Goodell Creek—26 sites between the highway and the Skagit River. Toilets. Piped water. Just west of Newhalem.

Colonial Creek—167 sites on both sides of the North Cascade Highway. Near but not on Thunder Arm of Diablo Lake. Boat launching. Some walk-in sites. Flush toilets. Piped water. 10 miles east of Newhalem.

BACKPACKING OPPORTUNITIES

There are more than 340 miles of backcountry trails in these park and recreation areas.

Hikers must obtain backcountry use permits whenever they plan overnight trips. Get them at park or forest service ranger stations. Camping in designated areas only. No open fires permitted in subalpine areas, so carry stoves.

Some of the day hikes (above) can be turned into overnight hikes if permits are obtained. But longer hikes are possible down almost every trail. The Pacific Crest trail traverses a portion of the area.

Where to Get Information

To get information on the North Cascades National Park and the Ross Lake and Lake Chelan National Recreation areas, write:

> Superintendent
> North Cascades National Park
> Sedro Woolley, Wash. 98284

To get information on national forest facilities in this area, write:

> District Ranger
> Baker River Ranger District
> Mount Baker National Forest
> Concrete, Wash. 98237

the stillaguamish

LAKES BY THE dozen, ice caves, a beautiful river and, of course, lots of snow-capped peaks.

This is one of the most popular mountain recreation areas in the Puget Sound region. Extremely busy on weekends. But a visitor can still enjoy the region during the week.

And an excellent sample of the more subdued beauties of the foothill valleys of the Cascade range.

To reach the area: Drive first to Granite Falls and then east to the village of Verlot. To get to Granite Falls, turn north off U.S. 2 east of Everett onto State Highway 9, turning east again in about 6 miles onto State Highway 92, reaching Granite Falls in about 9 more miles.

Recreation in the Verlot area centers along the south fork of the Stillaguamish River in Mount Baker National Forest.

It's an old but not rich gold mining region and some persons still pan for gold in some of the creeks. Logging also continues here. So if you drive backroads during the week watch out for logging trucks.

Campgrounds in this valley generally open about Memorial Day remaining open through October, depending as always on the weather.

Summer use in this area is extremely heavy, particularly on weekends and holidays when urban dwellers flock to the valley in droves. Even the trails are clogged with people then.

During the week however, use drops substantially. A few local families vacation here during the week but by and large campground spaces are always available and trails again become nearly private affairs.

The weather here follows the usual Puget Sound pattern of rains into June with the best weather of the year during July and August. Rains return again in mid-September, but the region often enjoys a late Indian summer, sometimes into October.

Daytime temperatures in the valley will range in the low and mid-70s with nighttime temperatures dropping to the cool upper 40s. Higher elevations will be uniformly cooler. Even though valley campgrounds may open in late May, some trails on these ridges may not open before late June and even early July.

Hikers and campers face no particular problems here. Carry extra warm clothing and rain gear and, of course, stay on trails. Low elevation forests on this side of the Cascades are strictly not for wandering. Undergrowth is dense and trails can easily be lost sight of.

The Forest Service here offers no formal naturalist programs. If you have questions, stop at the Ranger Station in Verlot.

WHERE TO DRIVE

The main attraction here is the valley and the winding Stillaguamish River. But side roads lead to spectacular views.

Mt. Pilchuck State Park—The road leads to a winter ski area but the summer views shouldn't be missed.

Drive east from the Verlot Ranger Station, turning south in about a mile, following a paved road 8 miles to a ski area parking lot.

Vistas enroute over the valley. But from the top, views all the way out to Puget Sound and east and north at peaks above the river.

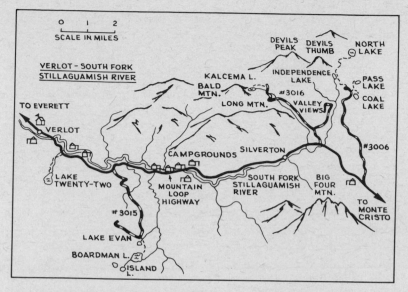

Big Four—Commanding vistas of Big Four mountain at the upper end of the river valley.

From Verlot drive east past the old mining town of Silverton, turning north onto the Deer Creek road in about a mile. Turn right at a "T" junction in another mile and drive as far as you can. The road ends in a high logged-off area.

Vistas here across the valley at Big Four Mountain and other mountains in this section of the Cascade range.

Monte Cristo—More mountain views, these from a small forest camp near the old mining camp-turned-resort of Monte Cristo.

From Verlot drive east to Barlow Pass at the end of the paved road, continuing east toward Monte Cristo for about 4 miles, taking a short, steep and narrow spur road uphill to the left near the end to reach a forest camp.

Stop here to look up at an entire circle of snow-capped peaks which surround this small but scenic basin.

WHERE TO HIKE

Trails here—all of them short—to mountain lakes galore. And ice caves too.

Lake Twenty-Two—Hike through a lush natural area past several small waterfalls to a very popular lake. 2.4 miles.

Find the trail on the south side of the highway about 2.4 miles east of Verlot just beyond Twenty-Two creek.

The trail climbs steadily uphill through groves of cedar reaching the outlet end of the lake. Picnic spots on the north shore. A snowfield to the south.

Boardman Lake—Hike past one small lake to reach another. About 1 mile.

To reach the trail, turn south from the highway onto the Schweitzer Creek road about 2 miles east of the Gold Basin Campground. At a junction in about 2.8 miles, keep left finding the trailhead off the left side of the road in about another 2 miles where the road makes a sharp switchback to the right.

The path first passes little Evans Lake, a weedy tarn, and then continues on to Boardman Lake at the end of a mile. At the lake, hike to the right for picnic spots.

Independence Lake—It's only a three-quarter-mile walk. But it leads to a quiet little lake nestled in forest with a meadow all its own.

To find the trail turn north off the highway just beyond the Big Four Campground road about 15 miles from Verlot, driving to the end of the road. Trail on the right.

The path starts in a clearcut and then drops to a stream before climbing sharply up to the outlet of the lake. Follow the trail around the lake to the left to a small quiet meadow at the other end.

Kalcema Lake—You'll only have to hike a half-mile here, unfortunately, to reach a pretty mountain-guarded lake. And it's unfortunate because the trail is such a pleasant one.

To find the trail, turn south off the valley road about a mile east of Silverton, turning left at the "T" junction in about a mile. The trail starts from the uphill (left) side of the road from a small parking area in about another 3 miles.

The trail climbs easily through open timber to picnic spots along the lake. Particularly pleasant in the fall.

Ice Caves—Exactly that: Caves eroded out of an almost permanent ice and snow field by warmer creeks.

To find this trail, drive 15 miles east of Verlot turning south off the highway to a parking lot in the Big Four area. The trail leads directly south from the parking area, crossing a bridge and then climbing through forest to high rocky ledges almost directly below Big Four peak.

The caves and snowfield are tucked into the always-shaded base of the mountain. Do not enter the caves. And don't try to walk above them. You could fall through!

BACKPACKING OPPORTUNITIES

Although most of the trail destinations in this valley are only a day away, many of them still afford opportunities for overnight backpacking trips.

No permits are required in this area. However, again, hikers are urged to protect the area by confining fires to old fire sites and by packing out their trash.

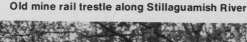

Old mine rail trestle along Stillaguamish River

Two of the more popular overnight goals here include one into the high Goat Flat meadows below Three Fingers peak and another up Mount Dickerman. Both lie north of the valley.

These places can be overrun on weekends. The number of cars parked at trailheads will give you an idea of the situation. Check at the Verlot ranger station for other alternatives.

WHERE TO CAMP

The Forest Service has developed a host of camping facilities along the river. All of them are extremely pleasant. But they're also heavily used, particularly on summer weekends and holidays when even the undeveloped spots along the road are filled.

Additional campgrounds can also be found east or north of Barlow Pass. There is one commercial camp facility west of Verlot.

Turlo—19 sites across from the Verlot Ranger Station. Some sites near the river. Pit toilets. Piped water.

Verlot—24 sites some for tenters only. Flush toilets. Piped water. Just east of the ranger station.

Gold Basin—67 sites. A few near the river but most on pleasant forested loops. Largest campground along the river. 3 miles from Verlot. Pit toilets. Piped water.

Boardman Camp—7 sites along the river. 6 miles from Verlot. Pit toilets. Water from river.

Red Bridge—11 sites in a forested area. 8 miles from Verlot. Pit toilet.

River Bar—6 sites for trailers on a gravel river bar. Across the road from Red Bridge Campground. Pit toilets.

Where to Get Information

To get information on the Verlot area write:
>   District Ranger
>   Verlot Ranger District
>   Mt. Baker National Forest
>   Granite Falls, Wash. 98252

hurricane ridge

ALPINE MEADOWS HERE precisely as they ought to be: Flowers, hillsides of them. Vistas, huge. With whistling marmots, deer, hawks, chipmunks and golden eagles too.

This isn't the place to rush in and rush right out. You can drive to these wonders. But you should stand among them to really believe they're true.

To reach the area: At Port Angeles, on the north side of the Olympic peninsula on U.S. 101, turn south on State Highway 111 in the middle of the city, passing the Visitor Center of Olympic National Park on the edge of town and driving on to the park entrance in about 5 miles. Hurricane Ridge in another 12 miles.

Hurricane Ridge is situated on the north side of Olympic National Park in one of the few places where a visitor can drive on a paved road to see the full spectacle of peninsula's inland mountains.

Although these mountains are less than 8,000 feet high every major peak is heaped with snow with more than 60 active glaciers in the heartland of the park.

199

Some campgrounds and trails at lower elevations remain open, in part at least, all year round with camps and trails at higher elevations opening as the snow melts every spring.

The highest trails, however, seldom open before late June or early July depending on the weather.

Good camping and hiking here usually continue into the early part of September. But be prepared for some instability in the weather after that. Early snow storms can be dangerous.

If you have a choice, plan to visit the park in the off season, or at least in the middle of the week. Use is heaviest here from Memorial Day to Labor Day and on weekends and holidays.

May, June, July and August are months with the least rainfall in this section of the park with rains returning in September and continuing through April.

Temperatures in this part of the Olympics vary with elevation. At Port Angeles, summer daytime temperatures range in the lower 70s with nighttime minimums of around 50 degrees. Those averages drop about 3 degrees a thousand feet as you climb into the mountains.

Hikers here should follow all the usual precautions for hiking in the Pacific Northwest. Always carry extra warm clothes and rain gear, regardless of the weather when you start. Storms can come up suddenly here. And the greatest hazard on the exposed ridges of the park is the danger of being chilled in a sudden combination of wind and rain. And wear good shoes, of course.

The Park Service conducts regular summer naturalist programs from late June through Labor Day. These include campfire talks and guided walks. Details are posted in each campground.

WHERE TO DRIVE

Drive from sea level to alpine meadows at more than 5000 feet. And give yourself lots of time to enjoy what you see.

Hurricane Ridge Road—Look first over the Straits of Juan de Fuca and then deep into the snow-clad heart of the Olympics.

Start your drive from Port Angeles, turning south off U.S. 101 onto State Highway 111 near the center of town.

The road passes the park Visitor Center at the edge of the city and then climbs inland to the park entrance and Heart o' the Hills Campground.

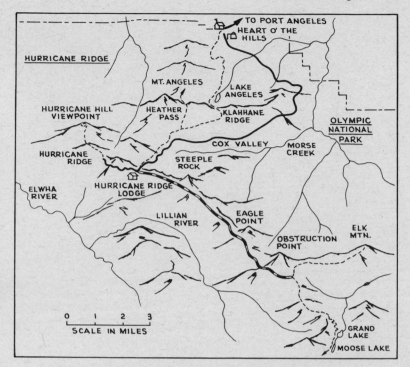

HURRICANE RIDGE

TO PORT ANGELES
HEART O' THE HILLS

MT. ANGELES

LAKE ANGELES

HURRICANE HILL VIEWPOINT

HEATHER PASS

KLAHHANE RIDGE

OLYMPIC NATIONAL PARK

COX VALLEY

MORSE CREEK

HURRICANE RIDGE

STEEPLE ROCK

ELWHA RIVER

HURRICANE RIDGE LODGE

LILLIAN RIVER

EAGLE POINT

ELK MTN.

OBSTRUCTION POINT

GRAND LAKE

MOOSE LAKE

0 1 2 3
SCALE IN MILES

From the entrance the road climbs sharply first to high views over the straits, the city, Vancouver Island, and the distant San Juan Island and then on to vistas of the Olympics themselves.

And don't end your trip at Hurricane Ridge Lodge. Drive another 1.2 miles to the end of the road. Mt. Olympus here and the entire Bailey range. Plus flowers as the snow retreats with a blooming peak in mid-July.

Obstruction Point—Variations here on a theme from Hurricane Ridge.

From Hurricane Ridge drive another 8 miles via a narrow but well-graded gravel road to still more viewpoints, more meadows and probably a little more privacy.

From Hurricane Lodge drive *back* toward Port Angeles turning downhill on a narrow gravel road in a few hundred yards.

The road looks extremely narrow at first but it gets a little wider as it goes, winding its way along a ridge past a spire at Eagle Rock, ending just below Obstruction Peak at about 6000 feet.

Pure alpine country this. Gnarled trees to start with. Then sweeping almost tundra-like flower meadows at the end. Same mountains. New view. From higher up.

WHERE TO HIKE

All of the mountain meadows here can be "seen" from a car window. But to truly appreciate the cool fresh air, the delicate scent of all the plants, the wet dew and the busy songs of the meadow birds, get out of your vehicle and walk.

And please stay on the trails. These fragile flower meadows cannot survive a trampling crowd.

Hurricane Hill—This may be the easiest hike here, and also one of the most spectacular.

Hike about 1.5 miles to vistas circling from the Strait of Juan de Fuca, which links Puget Sound to the Pacific Ocean, around to the snow-capped Olympics to the south.

Find the paved trail at the end of the Hurricane Ridge road, beyond the lodge and picnic area. The trail climbs uphill through meadows along a ridge to a circle-walk at the top. Markers here identify both plants and scenes.

Heart o' the Hills—Seems a little unlikely but you can still hike through high meadows on a trail that goes downhill.

Hike 10 miles from Hurricane Ridge at 5200 feet to the trail's end near Heart o' the Hills Campground at 1800 feet.

Find the trail uphill off the Hurricane Ridge road east of the lodge. It's signed. Someone will have to leave you there and pick you up at the other end.

The trail, paved to start with, climbs gradually at first up and around ridges to the east finally leveling out above the road and reaching a junction with the steep Switchback Trail from the road in about 2 miles.

Keep straight ahead, switchbacking now up to the pass and a junction with the Lake Angeles-Heather Park trails. Turn right, toward the lake, hiking along Klahhane Ridge for about 1.5 miles before dropping down into forest and the lake at about 6.5 miles.

Fog in high country

From then on, it's down some more through timber to the end of the trail near the campground.

And don't hustle. Take a day and spend lots of time being awed by views.

Obstruction Point—You can hike down to two lakes (4 miles) if you have the time. But if alpine scenery's your thing, just stay on the ridge.

From the end of the Obstruction Point road hike either south toward Grand and Moose Lake, or east toward Deer Park.

The trail to Deer Park (in almost 8 miles) climbs across tundra-like meadows, to the east and left of the parking area, toward Elk Mountain, dropping in about 4 miles to a high saddle between Elk and Maiden peaks. Stop here, dawdle awhile and return.

The trail to the lakes starts south of the parking area, winds across a flat open ridge past a series of small tarns. Stroll as far as you want, but find full views of Mt. Olympus in less than 2 miles as the trail drops eastward over the ridge to the two lakes.

BACKPACKING OPPORTUNITIES

Backcountry hiking in Olympic National Park is limited only by how far you want to go and how long you've got to stay. For your choice of terrain here is endless: Seashores, if you like. Rich rain forests. Alpine meadows. Along rushing rivers or atop mountain ridges. Take your pick. More than 500 miles of trail!

No permits are yet required in this park. Heavy use, however, is becoming a problem and hikers are urged to help protect the backcountry by limiting fires, controlling human waste and packing out all trash.

And we'll make no trip suggestions here. Check with rangers. Study maps. And buy any of the several good backcountry guides published for this park alone.

WHERE TO CAMP

Although there are many campgrounds throughout Olympic National Park, only one serves the immediate Hurricane Ridge area at Heart o' the Hills.

In case this campground is full inquire of park rangers about other camps along the north side of the park.

Heart o' the Hills—105 sites on several very pleasant loops in a lush forest setting. Flush toilets. Piped water. 5.4 miles from Port Angeles.

Where to Get Information

For information on this and other sections of the park write:
> Superintendent
> Olympic National Park
> 600 East Park Avenue
> Port Angeles, Wash. 98362

olympic ocean beaches

HUNDREDS OF PLACES here to prowl tide pools, play tag with surf, hunt for rare Japanese fishing floats, find driftwood, or, if you'd rather, simply wrap yourself in vacation thoughts.

More than a dozen short trails lead to as many wild ocean beaches along the Pacific Ocean in Olympic National Park.

To reach the area: Take U.S. 101 either north from Hoquiam and Aberdeen, Wash., or west from Port Angeles, driving toward the logging town of Forks.

From Forks drive west about 14 miles to La Push and Rialto Beach or south to Kalaloch in about 33 miles.

Most of Olympic National Park embraces high, snow-capped peaks and rich rain forest valleys. But the far west side includes about 50 miles of wild ocean beaches which stretch from Cape Alava, the westernmost point in the conterminous United States, to the Quinault Indian Reservation at Queets.

Central sections of the beach near the Indian village of La Push and the southern stretch near the beach-bluff campground of Kalalock offer easiest access to the shore.

Most of the beach trails and campgrounds here are open the year around. Only the inland trails are closed by snow in the winter. Weather ranges from extremely wet, particularly in the winter, (more than 140 inches of rain fall here yearly) to spectacularly sunny and mild in midsummer.

Daytime summer temperatures average in the upper 60s with nighttime temperatures down to about 50 degrees. In the winter, temperatures range from the upper 40s during the day to about 36 degrees at night.

Hikers here need to be aware of the tremendous power of ocean surf. Each year some visitor is hurt or killed by a wave-rolled driftwood log or pulled from a rock by an unexpected wave. Don't try to round headlands awash with surf and never remain in drift piles once the tide moves in.

The National Park Service conducts naturalist programs at Kalaloch and Mora Campgrounds. They include the usual campfire programs and nature walks. Check schedules in the campgrounds.

WHERE TO DRIVE

For views of the ocean and beaches from roads in this area, drive north from Kalaloch along a short stretch of highway exposed to the ocean; or out to La Push getting views of the surf and offshore islands from roads in the town itself; or, from the picnic parking area at Rialto Beach.

WHERE TO HIKE

For the easiest hiking along the ocean, seek out trails near Rialto beach beyond Mora Campground, outside the Indian village of La Push, or along the highway both north and south of Kalaloch.

Rialto Beach—Walk through a tunnel here carved through a small island by the sea or prowl a curved beach constantly thundering with surf.

To drive to Rialto Beach, turn west off U.S. 101 about 2 miles north of Forks, following signs to the beach and Mora Campground. About 13 miles.

To reach *Arch Rock* hike north along the beach from the Rialto

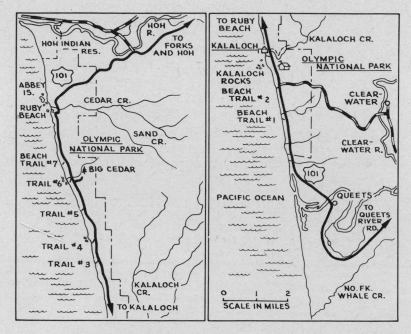

Beach parking area, crossing Ellen Creek in about a mile and finding the arch island in another half mile. Walk through it at low tide. Look through it at high. And don't rush your trip. Leave time to explore nearby low-tide rocks for iron debris and anchor chains from long-wrecked ships.

To explore an island and beach, hike south from the parking area along a sandspit toward *James Island* in the Quileute Indian Reservation. Sometimes you can cross to the island on very low tides. But hurry back or you could be trapped by the incoming tide. Check the tide schedule before you leave.

La Push beaches—Hike to three differing ocean beaches from the road leading to La Push.

To reach La Push turn west off U.S. 101 about 2 miles north of Forks (see Rialto) following signs to the village in about 14 miles. All trails here lead from the highway *before* it reaches the town.

To reach *First Beach,* find a parking area off a spur road near the Beach #1 sign at the edge of town.

Watch whales and sea birds from the curving beach that extends from the lighthouse in La Push to the first rock headland south of the village.

Find the signed trail to *Second Beach* on the ocean side of the road just uphill from the village. The trail winds an easy .6 mile through rain forest to the beach. Hike south to your own private lunch or viewing spot.

Find the trailhead to *Third Beach* about 1.5 miles east of the village. Park on the south side of the road. The trail starts with gravel but ends in mud.

To find a waterfall plunging from a cliff into the sea, hike south on this beach another mile.

Kalaloch—Six short trails, both north and south of the Kalaloch Campground, lead to sand beaches where fishermen net smelt, to quiet coves crowded with seastacks, or to long strands of sandy beach rowed with driftwood.

To reach Kalaloch Campground drive 35 miles south from Forks on U.S. 101.

To hike to *Ruby Beach,* find the trail on the ocean side of Highway 101 about 8.5 miles north of Kalaloch campground where the highway turns sharply inland.

This northernmost trail on the Kalaloch strip leads to a small bay filled with spectacular spray-washed rock islands, all close to shore.

At the beach, hike south to caves carved in the rock cliffs. Or wade the creek to the north and hike a long, sandy beach to an Indian village on the Hoh River. 3 miles.

Find trails to *Beaches #1 and #2* south of the Kalaloch Campground. Beach #1 in about 2 miles, Beach #2 in 1. Short trails lead to driftwood-heaped strips of sandy beach highlighted some years by huge eroded stumps embedded at the water's edge.

Trail to *Beach #3* leaves the highway north of Kalaloch in about 3 miles. Watch for sign. Trail drops over a bluff to another sandy beach, this one watched over by wind-bowed cedars clinging to the brow of a cliff.

The *Beach #4* trail leads from a parking area west of the road about 4 miles north of the camp. Gray sand here, pounded by a constant surf and framed by rock outcroppings filled with tidepools teaming with life. Fishermen net smelt here.

Note the small holes which seem drilled in rocks where the trail crosses a stream to the beach. Holes were bored—and some are still occupied—by piddock clams.

Take your lunch, watch the gulls and look out at the lighthouse at Destruction Island. In the fog, listen to the island's deep-throated horn. All from the end of a short trail to *Beach #6*, south of Ruby Beach. It's signed.

Rain Forest Trails—No trip to this area would be complete without visiting the rain forest trails on the Hoh River south of Forks.

To find the trails, drive to the Hoh Rain Forest Visitor Center about 19 miles east of Highway 101. Drive south from Forks to the Hoh road junction in 14 miles.

A three-quarter-mile trail from the Visitor Center leads through *Hall of Mosses,* a classic example of rain forest foliage and lush undergrowth. The 1.5 mile *Spruce Trail* winds along the Hoh river through groves of Sitka spruce and maples. Watch for elk here in the winter.

Low tide at Rialto Beach

BACKPACKING OPPORTUNITIES

If you have time, spend a weekend or a week exploring sections of the ocean wilderness beach strip both north and south of La Push.

Hike north from Rialto Beach to Cape Alava and Lake Ozette or south from Third Beach to the Hoh River on trails that occasionally duck inland around headlands but most of the time simply follow the ocean shoreline. About 15 miles each way.

Check with rangers before starting on any hike and review tide tables for incoming tides. Some headlands on both trails cannot be rounded on any tide. Camping in shelters (usually full) or along the beach, well back from the high-tide line.

Trail permits available at trailheads and ranger stations. Pack out your trash.

WHERE TO CAMP

Two campgrounds here serve the ocean beach camper. Overflow camping in nearby rain forest camps.

Mora—91 tent and trailer sites on very pleasant forested loops. Away from the ocean. 12 miles from U.S. 101 by paved road. Flush toilets. Piped water. Some loops open in winter.

Kalaloch—180 sites on a bluff overlooking the Pacific. Some sites (usually taken) look out directly on the beach. But most are on sheltered, timbered loops. An extremely popular campground. Often full. Open in the winter. On U.S. 101. Flush toilets. Piped water.

Where to Get Information

For more information on the beach and rain forest area write:
Superintendent
Olympic National Park
600 East Park Avenue
Port Angeles, Wash. 98362

mount rainier national park

OTHER PEAKS RISE around Puget Sound in every direction. But Mount Rainier overawes them all.

To residents here it's simply "the mountain". The horizon hallmark of every perfect day. The most magnificent and spectacular feature on the entire rim of the sky.

And it would be impossible to cover all of its wonders in one small section of this book. For every side affords surprises of its own.

So sampled here are the delicacies of just one part—the Sunrise-White River section—in the northeast corner of the park.

To reach the area: From Enumclaw, Wash., southeast of Seattle, drive southeasterly on State Highway 410 to the White River entrance of Mount Rainier National Park.

Although the park only covers 378 square miles, it embraces one of the most spectacular volcanic peaks in the entire world. Rising 14,410 feet, the mountain towers more than 8000 feet over the surrounding peaks of the Cascade range and shoulders more glaciers than any other single mountain in the conterminious United States.

The camping season here generally runs from early June through late October with one campground on the south side of the mountain open all year round.

Use is heaviest from Memorial Day through Labor Day with the greatest impacts on weekends and holidays, which means that if you have a choice, camp and hike here in the middle of the week.

Fall camping is also popular, albeit sometimes cool. Mornings then can be crispy, even frosty. But crowds will have disappeared and the spectacle of fall will have replaced the flower colors of the spring.

Weather around the mountain is almost impossible to predict. It's so large it creates its own. Statistically, however, July and August are the driest and sunniest months in the park with rains and clouds tapering off and on in June and September.

Even in the summer, however, the mountain is often socked in with low drizzling clouds for days at a time, blotting out all vistas and chilling the landscape. Hikers should be particularly aware of these weather changes, always carrying extra warm clothing and rain gear even on day-only hikes.

Summer daytime temperatures in the White River campground will average about 72 degrees dropping to the 50 degree range at night. Temperatures at Sunrise will be substantially lower.

Dangers in this park are few. But hikers and campers should be warned about steep snow and attempts to hike onto glaciers. Glaciers should only be explored if you are equipped and trained for glacier travel. All of the glaciers on Rainier are live, moving rivers of ice with gaping crevasses, often hidden under thin layers of snow.

And each summer hikers are injured and sometimes killed while attempting to "slide" on the steep snow fields which sometimes end on rocks.

The Park Service conducts a variety of naturalist programs here each summer in the mid-June-Labor Day period including campfire slide shows and talks, and guided walks to flower meadows, ice caves and other park features. Programs are posted in campgrounds.

WHERE TO DRIVE

You can "see" Mount Rainier from the freeway in Seattle. But to truly appreciate it by car, drive the high roads around and near it.

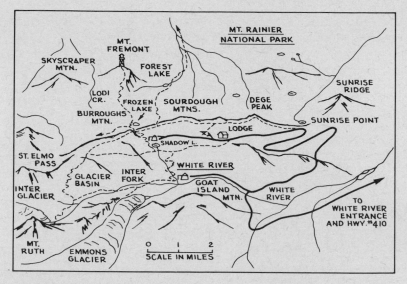

Sunrise road—Start with sweeping flower meadows, add a huge glacier-filled valley and then top it all off with towering Mt. Rainier and you've got Sunrise.

From the White River Entrance Station drive 15 miles up a paved switchback road which starts in tall forest and then climbs into alpine country.

Stop at Sunrise Point (6100 feet) en route. In addition here to Mount Rainier look north to Mount Baker and Glacier Peak and south to Mt. Adams, Mt. Hood and Mount St. Helens.

Tipsoo Lake—A reflected view of the mountain, this time in little lakes atop Chinook Pass on the east side of the park.

Follow Highway 410 from Enumclaw past the White River entrance road, turning east at the top of Cayuse Pass, driving to the crest of the Cascades at the pass.

Stop at the picnic area and walk east around Tipsoo Lake for reflected views of Rainier. For slightly different reflected glimpses of the peak seek out small tarns hidden on a bench above the highway on the south side of the road.

Stevens Canyon Road—A great summer drive but a fantastic one in the fall: Hillsides laced with autumn color topped with a frosted Mount Rainier.

Follow Highway 410 past the White River entrance to Cayuse Pass, continuing straight ahead at the pass onto State Highway 123 to the Stevens Canyon Entrance road, about 11 miles beyond the pass.

Turn west here driving about 21 miles up a winding, climbing road to Paradise. This road opens in mid-June. But it's at its best in the fall when the huckleberries and vine maples turn to brilliant reds and yellows.

WHERE TO HIKE

Just because you've seen one view of Mount Rainier doesn't mean you've seen them all.

This mountain puts on a new face at every turn. Sometimes this color. Sometimes that. Sometimes framed in forest green. At other times in granite gray. Towering occasionally over streams or more spectacularly above glaciers and waterfalls.

Trails here offer just a few of these faces. Sample them all and then decide which face you like.

Emmons Glacier—Look up at Rainier and its companion spire, Little Tahoma, over a boulder strewn and heavily crevassed Emmons Glacier, largest in the park.

Find the trail out of the far end of the White River Campground off the main campground road just before it loops back above the river.

The trail starts out along the interfork of the White River, turning left at a junction in about 1.5 miles, crossing the creek and climbing to the glacial moraine.

Hike up the moraine as far as the path goes, looking down at the huge boulders and debris scattered atop this moving field of ice. Scientists speculate that some of these rocks were thrown there as late as 1963 when a big slab broke off Little Tahoma and plummeted down the ice.

And stay off the glacier, even here. Glacier walking is dangerous unless you are mountaineer trained and equipped. So just listen to the glacier groan and snap and drop an occasional boulder.

Glacier Basin—A green heather basin tucked into a tight cirque with Rainier, as always, towering overhead.

Mount Rainier from Tipsoo tarn

To find this trail start at the White River Campground (see above) continuing straight ahead at the junction in about 1.5 miles. The trail follows the creek, climbing to the basin in about 3.5 miles. Climbing paths continue higher from the basin.

Note the old machinery left from a now-defunct mining operation. A small part of the park here is still privately owned.

Sourdough Ridge—One long crescendo here with a cymbal crashing vista at the top.

Find the trail (you can see it clearly from the road) uphill out of the Sunrise picnic area (to the right out of the parking area beyond the lodge).

Follow the trail straight up the meadow, turning right (east) at the top and following it high above the road. In about 2 miles turn uphill another quarter-mile—more steeply now—to the top of Dege Peak. Return either the way you came or down to Sunrise Point in just 1 mile, providing you've arranged for transportation.

Vistas here along the trail out at the mountain, Emmons Glacier and the White River valley. But from Dege Peak! (The cymbal crash goes here!) All of the mountains of the North Cascades, the Olympic range, the smog covered foothill of Puget Sound, and never tiresomely, of course, Rainier across the entire southern sky.

Fremont Lookout—As if there isn't enough to see. Add this to your list.

Find this trail uphill from the Sunrise picnic area (see above) turning *left* this time at the top of the meadow. The trail climbs sharply then up the ridge past a junction with a trail (right) to Forest Lake and then drops down around the side of Frozen Lake. Bear north around the lake past spur trails to Burroughs Mountain and Berkley Park heading due north on the lookout trail. A 2.8 mile hike.

Again, new views of the same old mountain. Rainier this time over Burroughs Mountain with vistas to the north over Grand Park. Carry water. And binoculars too.

And whistle at the marmots as you pass.

BACKPACKING OPPORTUNITIES

More than 300 miles of trail climb through valleys and over ridges in this great park. And all of them lead to exciting meadows, lakes, forests, waterfalls, glaciers and, of course, new glimpses of Mount Rainier.

The Park Service, however, controls backcountry overnight camping in the park through a reservation system, limiting—out of necessity—the number of persons who can camp at any one backcountry site.

Reservations can be made either in person or by mail. But final permits must be picked up in person at the park. If the campsites you desire you already booked, park rangers will suggest alternative areas.

There are few "favorite hikes" here. Every trail is busy. The most popular, however, is probably the famed 90-mile Wonderland Trail which circles the entire mountain. It can be hiked in 10 days to two weeks—the longer the better—or in small sections. Backcountry camping here, again, by reservation only.

WHERE TO CAMP

The Park Service maintains a number of campgrounds throughout the park. Those listed here, however, are confined to the northeast corner.

Campers can also find facilities outside the park in National Forest Service campgrounds along the White River and Highway 410.

Campgrounds within the park include:

White River—125 sites on a series of pleasant forested loops above the White River. Some with views of Mt. Rainier. 5 miles from the White River entrance. Flush toilets. Piped water.

Sunrise—63 sites in an open alpine setting in a basin below the Sunrise Visitor Center at 6403 feet. No views of the mountain from the campground. One of the few camps in the northwest above timberline. 15 miles from the entrance station. Flush toilets. Piped water.

Campgrounds maintained by the Forest Service include:

The Dalles—46 sites on forest loops near the river. 25 miles from Enumclaw. Pit toilets. Piped water.

Silver Springs—44 units also along the river. 31 miles from Enumclaw. Pit toilets. Piped water.

Where to Get Information

For information on Mount Rainier National Park write,
Superintendent
Mount Rainier National Park
Longmire, Wash. 98397

mount st. helens

WHEN IT COMES to perfect symmetry in mountains, artists seem to do a better job than nature.

But at Mount St. Helens, nature wins the prize, constructing in centuries of violence an almost perfect snow-topped volcanic cone.

And then, in an act of ultimate vanity, she added a crystal lake to reflect it in.

How to reach the area: From I-5, north of Portland, Ore., turn east at Castle Rock, Wash., onto State Highway 505, driving on to Spirit Lake in about 46 miles.

Mount St. Helens (9677 feet) is one of the three major volcanoes in southwestern Washington state, sharing the skyline with Mt. Rainier to the north and Mt. Adams to the west.

The mountain is part of Gifford Pinchot National Forest which embraces most of the federal forest land in this part of the state.

All of the St. Helens camping and hiking features outlined here center around facilities on the north side of the mountain at Spirit Lake (3200 feet).

The season here, because of the elevation, is generally shorter than in most other areas of the state. Campgrounds around the lake sometimes don't open until early July with trails often remaining clogged with snow even later. The season generally, however, extends from late June until early October, ending with the first snows.

Summer daytime temperatures here will range in the low 70s with nighttime temperatures dropping into the mid-40s and even lower at higher elevations.

Rains are not uncommon. The mountain almost seems to manufacture its own. July and August, however, are the driest months with rain levels generally increasing during September and October. However, good weather is not uncommon during those two months.

Persons who hike here, particularly on the mountain itself, are urged to carry extra warm clothing and rain gear and keep an eye cocked for changes in the weather. Clouds can blanket the mountain quickly and unexpectedly at any time. The white-outs pose little hazard to persons on trails. The tread remains easy to follow. But anyone on an open mountain slope may face a problem in finding his way.

No hiker should attempt to climb this mountain or explore its glaciers without proper training. These slopes are deceivingly steep and the glaciers which look so benign are laced with treacherous crevasses and cracks.

Hikers should also show concern here for the delicacy of the terrain. Plant life on the high meadows of the mountain in many places is less than 200 years old. The volcano erupted its last time in the 1800s coating the peak and countryside with pop-corn pumice. And one skuff of a foot here can destroy life for another 200 years.

And be sure to test this pumice: It floats! Find a dry piece of any size and drop it into the lake.

The Forest Service conducts naturalist programs at the Spirit Lake Campground during the summer. It also operates a full-time visitor information office near the campground.

WHERE TO DRIVE

The roads around Spirit Lake serve up a number of introductory views of Mount St. Helens. But for one of the best (all of the better

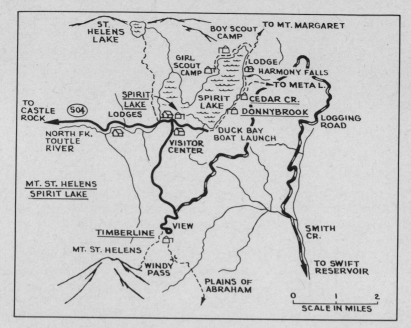

ones, of course, are reserved for hikers) drive beyond the campground to a loop vista point high on the side of the mountain at about 4100 feet.

Turn right at the visitor information station. Vista point in 4 miles.

St. Helens here towers in proper classic form over alpine meadows, rock outcrops and snow.

For other views and a glimpse of clearcut logging operations turn left (east) off the paved road onto forest road No. 100 driving to a viewpoint in 3 miles from the visitor center. This road is often closed during the week because of the intense logging operation. But from the crest of the ridge look out into the heavily logged valley to observe the impact of clearcut techniques.

WHERE TO HIKE

Follow trails to high meadows, mountain vistas and even a lake.

Plains of Abraham—Cross pumice slopes and hike over a windy pass to prowl a barren world of volcanic violence.

Find the trail uphill from the vista parking loop 4 miles south of

Spirit Lake. There are lots of paths here so bear off to the left making your way to a trail which you can see through a saddle between the mountain and a ridge to the east. Windy Pass (4800 feet) in a mile.

From the pass, drop down into the Plains of Abraham, an almost flat plateau strewn with fallen boulders and weird lava shapes but still colored with wildflowers in profusion.

Stay on established paths if you can. These tender slopes can barely withstand natural forces much less the tramping of hikers.

Glacier View—Hike through high alpine meadows to look at a glacier and Mt. Rainier too.

To reach this trail, drive from Spirit Lake to the vista point parking lot and then hike from the southwest corner of the lot to a climbers campground in about 250 yards.

From the campground take a climber's trail which leads clearly uphill to a meadow ridge with increasing spectacular views back down on Spirit Lake and out toward Mt. Rainier—and up, of course, at St. Helens.

In about a mile, the path reaches a point above the snout of Forsyth Glacier. Stop here. Don't climb down onto the glacier or proceed further up the mountain unless you're equipped to climb and trained.

But do look at and listen closely to the ice below you. This is a living glacier still grinding away at the mountain. Spend a few minutes waiting for it to crack, pop and bounce rocks down the ice. The lower part of the glacier's snout looks deceivingly like the ground. But it's actually ice buried under glacial debris.

From the glacier wend your way back downhill, this time more leisurely, taking side trips out over the rolling meadows to soak up the tremendous views.

Harmony Falls—A bonus hike: First Mount St. Helens towering and reflected in Spirit Lake and next, a pretty waterfall.

Find the trail along the east shore of Spirit Lake beyond the boat launching ramp at the end of the road past the visitor information station.

The trail wends easily north above the lake past two small campgrounds (see Where to Camp) to Harmony Falls Lodge in 2.5 miles.

Find the waterfall uphill behind the lodge. But first take time to drop down to the lake and look back at Mount St. Helens. You'll have seen this view someplace else for certain. It's in almost every mountain book.

Return the same way you came.

St. Helens Lake—You won't escape the crowds entirely here. But you will escape the mountain.

Find the trailhead about three-quarters of a mile west of the Information Center where the highway crosses the Spirit Lake outlet. The trail starts northwest of the bridge, circling around the outlet and then climbing sometimes easily and sometimes sharply toward the forested lake in about 3.5 miles. Again, no views of Mount St. Helens from the lake. But hints of solitude. Camping along the east shore.

BACKPACKING OPPORTUNITIES

Overnight backpacking opportunities here center mostly around mountains north of St. Helens and Spirit Lake.

One trail to Mt. Margaret loops into the backcountry from one

Western camping

point and out again at another, with high vistas and lakes along the way.

The other winds its way further north to Grizzly Lake and a basin laced with other lakes.

Again, hike here if you can during the week. Scooters are still permitted on some of these trails and their use is largely confined to weekends.

No backcountry permits are required here.

WHERE TO CAMP

Camping here centers largely around the Spirit Lake campground. However, the Forest Service also maintains three small camps on the lake shore. These camps can be reached either by boat or trail, with boaters and water skiers taking them over most weekends.

Spirit Lake—124 sites on timbered loops, some near the lake but most in trees. Crowded on weekends and holidays. No views of St. Helens. Flush toilets. Piped water.

Timberline—10 sites in a subalpine climbers' camp just below timberline above Spirit Lake. Views of the mountain. Generally used by climbing groups. Pit toilets. Piped water. To reach the campground, drive to the vista point parking lot 4 miles uphill from Spirit Lake hiking into the camp area about 250 yards from the road.

Donnybrook—12 units on the east shore of Spirit Lake. A trail or boat camp. Pit toilets. Hike a mile from the Duck Bay boat launch area.

Cedar Creek—12 units on the east shore of the lake. Boat or hiker camp. Find camp .3 miles north of Donnybrook. Pit toilet.

Bear Cove—11 units on north side of the lake. A boat-only camp. No trail. Pit toilets.

Where to Get Information

For information on the Spirit Lake area, write:
    District Ranger
    St. Helens Ranger Station
    Cougar, Wash. 98616

mount adams

IT'S MORE THAN size that earns this mountain's mention here.

High it certainly is. At 12,307 feet it dominates this corner of the Cascade mountain range.

But the huge peak's alpine meadows may be its most spectacular attraction. More than 480 different species of wildflowers grow on the slopes of the Bird Creek Meadows covered here—flowers common not only to the Cascades but native also of the Sierra Nevadas to the south and the Rocky Mountains to the east.

How to reach the area: From I-5, drive east on State Highway 14 from Vancouver, Wash., turning north onto State Highway 141 to Trout Lake. From I-80N in northern Oregon, cross the Columbia River at Hood River, Ore., driving north on Washington State Highway 141 to Trout Lake.

The Bird Creek Meadow complex on the southeast corner of the mountain is within the Yakima Indian Reservation and is managed by the tribe. The southwestern corner of the peak—the Timberline area—is managed by the Gifford Pinchot National Forest.

The campgrounds, roads and trails in the high areas (5000 feet and more) seldom open most years until early or mid-July, closing with the first snows, generally, in October.

And the roads are never "opened". They simply remain closed until the warm temperatures of summer melt them out.

The high-country weather in summer runs to the cool and slightly dry side. Temperatures from mid-June through early September average about 65 to 70 degrees during the day down to 45 and 50 degrees at night.

Rainfall here is generally lighter than in the coastal hills to the west. But the mountain often tends to make its own weather. On days when the peak can be seen clearly in the valley some high places may be socked in with drizzly fog. Generally, however, July and August into early September is the best time to visit the high country.

Hikers here should be prepared for sudden changes in the weather, carrying extra warm clothes and rain gear on even single-day hikes. When the sun's out, the peak can be hot. But once a storm moves in—or even a single cloud—temperatures can drop sharply.

Use here is heaviest on weekends. And it's seldom crowded even then. The distance of the mountain from large urban centers and the condition of most of the high mountain roads appear to hold visitor traffic down.

Which is probably all for the better. Because these fragile meadows cannot stand extremely heavy use and the foot traffic they get in some areas is already destructive.

The flowers here, of course, are the main attraction. They start blooming as the snow leaves in the spring and continue blossoming throughout the summer with the mix of flowers changing as the season progresses. And there is really no best time to visit the meadows. They're lush all season long. The color never seems to end.

WHERE TO DRIVE

This is backroad exploration country, strictly. You can drive in this region to ice caves, through huckleberry meadows, to high lakes, lookouts, vista points, past waterfalls under the almost con-

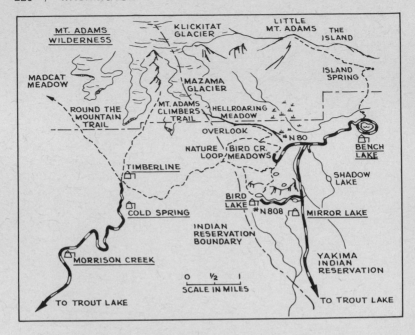

stant surveillance of Mount Rainier, Mt. Adams and Mount St. Helens—sometimes all three at once.

But the roads here are all logging roads. Some are well developed. But many are narrow, steep and rough. All, however, can be driven with the average passenger car or pickup with care. Don't pull a trailer without first checking with local rangers.

To plan trips into this backcountry write for a recreation map and consult with rangers before you start. Logging traffic may be heavy on some roads during the summer.

WHERE TO HIKE

BIRD CREEK MEADOWS

Mt. Adams towers—spectacularly—over the meadows here. But you'll have a hard time taking your eyes off the flower displays, one of the richest in the entire West.

To reach this area, drive north from Trout Lake to the end of the paved road, turning right onto road N700 and then left onto road N80, driving to the Bird Creek Meadows Picnic area in about 21 miles. Extremely rough toward the end.

Meadow Loop Trail—Climb to vistas of Mt. Adams over Hellroaring Canyon before dropping down again into the flowers of Bird Creek. Less than 1 mile.

Find the trail off the very end of the road into the Bird Creek picnic area. The trail switchbacks first to the right and then back to the left as it climbs to vistas back over Trout Lake, Glenwood, and toward Mt. Hood in Oregon.

In about a half-mile, take a spur trail to the right (north) climbing above timber and across a bare ridge to a viewpoint down into Hellroaring canyon and out at Mazama Glacier. Climbers sometimes start up the mountain from here.

Return to the main trail and continue west as it loops down the mountain through still more alpine meadows to the picnic area again.

And stay on the trail. The flowers here can't survive the impact of many human feet. So make certain that you don't contribute to the problem.

Bird Lake Trail—Hike through the best of the meadows past two small waterfalls—from Bird Creek Meadows to Bird Lake. 2.25 miles. Arrange to have someone meet you.

From the Bird Creek Meadow picnic area hike west past a display sign to the Round-the-Mountain Trail. It's the most heavily used trail. In about three-quarter mile, turn downhill (left) on the Bird Lake spur trail.

Take lots of time now, letting the beauty of the meadows soak in as you pass first one waterfall and then another. Color here you'll find few places else.

Bluff Lake Trail—Fewer meadow flowers here but a lot more vistas.

From Bird Creek Meadow picnic area walk west on the Timberline trail about 50 yards to the signed Bluff Lake trail. Turn left, reaching the lake in about .8 mile.

From the south end of the lake look back at Mt. Adams, then look over the bluff at Mt. Hood too.

Return as you came or continue on the trail as it drops over the bluff to Bird Lake campground in another .8 mile.

Bird Creek Meadows

TIMBERLINE

Meadows here too but not so many flowers. This area is grazed by cattle which sometimes get beyond their allotment limits. Lots of vistas, however.

To reach this area, drive north from Trout Lake turning off the paved road in about 1.5 miles onto forest road N80. Follow signs.

Round-the-Mountain trail—Ever-changing views up at Mt. Adams, to the south at Mt. Hood, Mt. Jefferson and the Three Sisters in Oregon and to the west of Mount St. Helens.

Find this trail to the west of the Timberline Campground at the very end of the road.

The trail winds gradually up and down, passing Salt Creek, a briny, mineral water stream, at about 2.8 miles. Pause here to look for small calcium-encrusted plants and rocks along the side of the stream. Not always easy to find.

Hike as far as you have time.

Climber's Trail—It looks steep and it is steep but it's the start of a popular climbing route to the top of Mt. Adams.

Find the trail along the tracings of an old road uphill from the Timberline Campground. Hike until the path becomes faint in about 1.5 miles and then turn back. Don't attempt to climb further unless you've been trained and are equipped.

BACKPACKING OPPORTUNITIES

The Round-the-Mountain trail is probably the most popular overnight-and-long backpacking route in this area.

This trail, despite its name, does not go all the way around Mt. Adams. But it does lead around the south side of the mountain, connecting with the Pacific Crest trail on the western slope.

Start either from Bird Creek Meadows (see hikes) or from the Timberline Campground.

This is truly a spectacular trail—even in the rain—as it climbs through subalpine forest, across lush meadows and around and through weird frozen rivers and ridges of lava spewed out by the peak in some dark century past.

Wilderness permits are required for overnight hikes into this backcountry.

WHERE TO CAMP

These high elevation campgrounds are seldom full except on weekends—and often not even then.

Campgrounds in the Yakima Indian Reservation near Bird Creek Meadows include:

Bench Lake—34 units at 4850 feet in a forest setting around Bench Lake northeast of the meadows. Some with views of Mt. Adams. Entrance road not recommended for trailers. Piped water. Pit toilets. Swimming. 18.2 miles from Trout Lake.

Bird Lake—20 units at 5500 feet in subalpine timber near but not on the lake. Pit toilets. Piped water.

Mirror Lake—7 sites. Pit toilets. Piped water. At 5350 feet. 19 miles from Trout Lake.

To reach these campgrounds, drive north from Trout Lake,

turning right at the end of the paved road onto N700 and then left onto road N80. Not recommended for trailers. Extremely rough toward the end. And steep. But passable if you use great care.

Campgrounds in the Timberline area of Gifford Pinchot National Forest include:

Morrison Creek—9 units in a fenced grassy area. No views. Popular with climbing parties. Pit toilets. 10.3 miles north of Trout Lake.

Cold Springs—A primitive camping area on a short spur road east of the main road about 13 miles from Trout Lake.

Timberline—3 formal sites on subalpine slopes with views of Mt. Adams, Mt. Hood and Mount St. Helens. No water. Pit toilets. 14 miles from Trout Lake.

To reach these campgrounds, drive north from Trout Lake turning off the paved road onto forest road N80 in about 1.5 miles. Follow signs.

Where to Get Information

For information on the national forest areas write:

> District Ranger
> Mt. Adams Ranger District
> Gifford Pinchot National Forest
> Trout Lake, Wash. 98650

For information on facilities and regulations on Indian lands write:

> Forestry Branch
> Yakima Indian Agency
> Bureau of Indian Affairs
> U.S. Department of Interior
> Toppenish, Wash. 98948

OREGON

north oregon beaches

NO BIG GULPS of ocean scenery here. Just lots of tasty samples served up off U.S. 101 in the northwest corner of Oregon.

And in every flavor too: Some sandy beaches here. Others stacked with cliffs and still other tucked around small coves. Explore them all.

To reach the area: Drive west from Portland, Ore., on U.S. 26 to U.S. 101 south of Seaside.

The section of the Oregon coast covered here extends from Astoria south to Neahkahnie Mountain and embraces both rugged rocky sections of coastline and sweeping sand beaches.

The beaches, roads and even a few campgrounds in this section are open to public use all year round. Facilities in most of the campgrounds, however, are closed from November through April.

Weather in this area is not an important factor in its enjoyment. Ocean beaches in the Northwest always tend to be a little soggy and the hiker who waits for a clear day—summer or winter—may never hike at all.

July and August, statistically, are the driest and clearest months with the midwinter months leaning heavily to the drenched side. However, fogs and drizzles can blot the coast almost anytime in the summer and blocks of crisp, clear days are not unknown in the middle of the winter.

Summer temperatures here range in the upper 60s in the daytime down to the low 50s at night with winter temperatures ranging from daytime highs in the upper 40s to nighttime lows in the mid-30s. Snow is uncommon.

Use here is heavy all year, but it is heaviest during the summer vacation period, reaching peaks on weekends and holidays. Highway traffic follows the same pattern, running bumper to bumper on summer holiday weekends. Even bicycle traffic is high then too. The state has provided special lanes along sections of U.S. 101 for bicycle use.

Persons who hike in the coastal area need only be concerned about the dangers of surf and tides. Rocks near surflines can be slippery and dangerous. Cliffs along many of these shores can be treacherous, undercut as many of them are by erosion. And rising tides often trap the unwary on off-shore low-tide rocks.

WHERE TO DRIVE

Highway U.S. 101 down Oregon's Pacific Ocean coast may be one of the most scenic drives in the West. No constant vistas certainly. But the road leads past more views than any other on the coast.

In this region, drive south from Astoria turning off first to Fort Stevens State Park for views of ocean beaches, the wrecked schooner Peter Iredale, and a former Coast gun battery emplacement.

Stop then at Cannon Beach, driving north about 2 miles to Ecola State Park for glimpses of rain forest and high vistas with sea lions and birds on off-shore rocks. Also drive south of Cannon Beach to stop at Tolovana Beach and Hug Point to explore sections of sandy shore.

Stop next at Oswald West State Park to hike about a quarter mile to a small cove where surfers sometimes try their luck and then on south only a few miles to more views over the Pacific from the side of Neahkahnie Mountain.

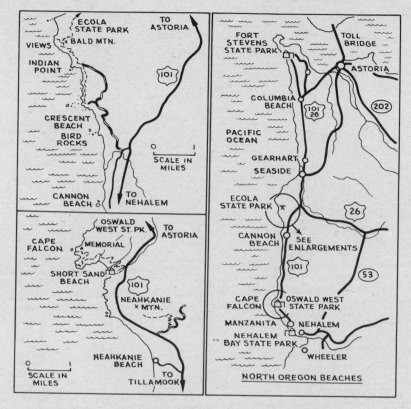

NORTH OREGON BEACHES

WHERE TO HIKE

Enjoy sunsets from sandy beaches, hike high bluffs over basking sea lions, explore rock-bound promontories, and even hike up a coastal mountain.

Fort Stevens State Park beaches—Wait for low tide to explore a wrecked ship and then stroll sandy beaches both north and south.

From the entrance station to Fort Stevens State Park, drive straight ahead to parking areas just off the beach above the wrecked Peter Iredale, a schooner that ran aground here in 1906. Only steel ribs of the hull still show here now.

Hiking either way from the wreck for almost as far as you want to go. Surf fishing.

Ecola State Park—Wander more than 8 miles of trails here over high bluffs for constant views down on rock heaped shores. Picnicking but no camping.

Bring binoculars and watch sea lions.

To hike one of the more interesting trails, drive north from Cannon Beach about 2 miles to a large parking area overlooking the ocean.

Find the trail across the grass in the northeast corner of the parking area. The path drops into a small draw and then climbs back above the ocean and on to Indian Beach in about 2 miles.

High views to the south here of Haystack Rock and Cannon Beach and north to Tillamook Head.

Either return the same way or have someone meet you at the Indian Beach picnic area, north by road in 1.8 miles.

For other views in this area, hike north out of Indian Beach on a national recreation trail about a mile.

Find the trail to the right off the parking lot at the Indian Beach picnic area.

The path switchbacks inland for less than a quarter of a mile before traversing upward along the bluff to viewpoints in a mile. This trail continues north to Seaside in about 6 miles.

Oswald West—Hike through lush rain forest to an open promontory to look out at the Pacific and down on Smuggler's Cove.

Find the trail out of the northwest corner of the picnic area at Oswald West State Park.

The trail switchbacks inland to start with and then turns, toward the ocean traversing the side of a slope first to the north and then to the west to a viewpoint on Cape Falcon in about 1.5 miles. Continue your hike on the main trail north another half-mile to a second vista.

Neahkahnie Peak—Climb to one of the highest points along the entire Oregon coast to look north to the mouth of the Columbia and south to Cape Lookout and out over the small communities nearby.

To reach this trail, turn east off U.S. 101 onto a gravel spur about 2.5 miles south of Oswald West State Park. Watch for a Neahkahnie mountain sign uphill on the left.

Find the trail on the left hand side of the spur road in .4 miles.

The trail (keep left at all junctions) switchbacks up the mountain immediately, first through open meadows and then into timber before starting a long traverse to the west and vista points in about a mile.

There are two small summits on this mountain. An old relay station sets atop the first one you come to. Scramble up the second one to the west for better views.

BACKPACKING OPPORTUNITIES

Except for the quarter-mile walk into the Oswald West campground, no overnight backpacking is permitted in these state park areas.

WHERE TO CAMP

Camping here centers around three Oregon State Parks.

Fort Stevens—379 tent sites and 224 trailer sites in forested and grassy areas. A popular camp near the ocean. Flush toilets. Show-

Wreck of the Peter Iredale

ers. Laundry. Piped water. Reservations available. Open all year. Off Highway 101, 10 miles west of Astoria. Follow signs. State fee.

Oswald West—35 tent sites in rich rain forest on an ocean cove. These sites are all walk-in camps with several wheelbarrows available at the road to pack in your equipment. Piped water. Pit toilets. North of Manzanita on U.S. 101. Open April to October.

Nehalem Bay—292 sites in grassy but exposed area in dunes near the ocean. Wooden fences screen each site. Flush toilets. Showers. Laundry. Water and electricity at each site. Reservations available. State fee. Off U.S. 101, 3 miles south of Manzanita junction. April to October.

Where to Get Information

To get information on state facilities in this region, write:
    State Parks and Recreation Section
    300 State Highway Building
    Salem, Ore. 97310

columbia gorge

ADMIRE THE MIGHTY Columbia River here certainly. It's still the greatest river in the West.

But pause long enough also to enjoy the real jewels of this mighty gorge—the dozens of waterfalls that lace its canyon walls.

Many—including the famous 620-foot Multnomah Falls—can be viewed from the highway. But most of the falls can be seen only by persons willing to hike.

How to reach the area: Drive east from Portland on I-80N, turning south off the freeway at Troutdale to the Columbia River Scenic Highway.

Use of this area, just outside Oregon's largest urban center, is extremely heavy particularly on weekends and holidays.

Over 2 million people visit Multnomah Falls each year and 100,000 of those hike all the way to the top of the falls. And over 40,000 persons start hikes on the popular Eagle Creek trail with as many as 100 to 130 persons hiking there on weekends—in the middle of the winter.

The impact here is heaviest on summer weekends and holidays. However, it continues high on other weekends throughout the year.

Campgrounds—both state and national forest—are always filled each night in the summer. Campers can usually find a place to camp without problems *after* Labor Day and *before* Memorial Day.

Although the season here runs generally from May to early November, camping is confined to the April-October period, starting after the last freeze and closing with the first one.

Summer daytime temperatures here will range in the mid-80s dropping to an average of 50 degrees at night. Rainfall is generally the lightest from June through September and the heaviest between November and March. Rain, however, doesn't have much effect on hiking within the gorge. All of these canyon trails are shady and cool and rain changes them very little.

All a hiker needs here is a good pair of shoes and perhaps a rain jacket. He should be warned, however, to stay on trails and particularly to stay away from the slippery rocks above the waterfalls. These falls are great to look at but treacherous, even fatal, to climb around. Watch out, too, for poison oak which grows in the gorge.

The Forest Service maintains an unmanned information station at Multnomah Falls. Rangers also conduct occasional hikes from the Multnomah area and campground programs at Eagle Creek. Schedules are posted in campgrounds.

WHERE TO DRIVE

Visit anyone in Portland and you'll probably end up taking either a drive to Mt. Hood or up the Columbia River gorge—or both.

Suggested here is a drive from the I-80N freeway east of Portland along the old Columbia River Scenic highway with a spur trip from Crown Point to the top of Larch Mountain at 4056 feet.

The scenic highway which starts at Troutdale winds in and out above the river, sometimes in pleasant forest, other times past waterfalls, to a spectacular view down the gorge from a vista point at Crown Point State park. It ends at the freeway again beyond Ainsworth State Park in about 22 miles.

And don't hurry. Take all of the side trips. Stop at all the view-

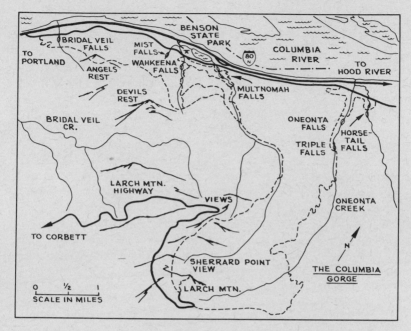

points and waterfall. And walk, for certain, up to the base (at least) of Multnomah Falls.

To drive to Larch Mountain, turn south off the scenic highway about 9.5 miles from the freeway or about a mile west of Crown Point vista house.

The road climbs inland until it reaches a picnic area in 13 miles. For 360-degree views walk a short spur trail uphill to the right to a formal viewpoint with vistas of Mt. Hood, Mt. Jefferson, Mt. Adams, Mount St. Helens and even Mt. Rainier, far north in Washington state.

WHERE TO HIKE

Waterfalls are almost the exclusive reason for hiking here. None is the same. Some plunge into bowls of rock, others fall in long misty plumes and still others drop right over the top of trails.

And watch the ground for trail signs here. They consist of marble or concrete headstone-like slabs.

Multnomah Falls to Wahkeena Falls—Although Multnomah

Falls is the most heavily visited spot in the gorge, trails above it lead to vistas and other falls not often traveled by other hikers. A 2 mile walk. (For other hikes see map.)

Start this climb with everybody else on a paved trail but leave most of the others standing on the bridge directly below the falls as the trail winds around a ridge and gets down to the serious work of climbing to the top of the gorge.

A viewpoint half way interrupts the tedium but the climb resumes again until the trail reaches the top of the bluff in 1 mile.

And stay on the trail here please. Many of these slopes, as you will see, have already eroded heavily—despite efforts of the Forest Service to protect them—as the result of seemingly innocent short-cutting.

At the top of the bluff (catch your breath first) hike inland, turning sharply downhill to the right in .1 mile onto a spur leading to a viewpoint (look straight down the falls here) in a few hundred yards.

To continue on the loop to Wahkeena Falls, return to the main trail, crossing Multnomah Creek and then turning right onto the Perdition Trail.

It soon becomes apparent where this trail got its name. The way here clings to the very edge of the cliff, high over the gorge. It's absolutely safe even though you may find yourself holding your breath.

In about .3 miles take a spur downhill to the right to a viewpoint in a few hundred feet.

From now on the trail winds up—but mostly down—a ridge on a series of steep log stairways, dropping eventually across the foot of Wahkeena Falls and on to the Wahkeena Falls parking area.

To return to Multnomah Falls, find a trail on the south side of the road.

Oneonta and Horsetail Falls—Look up a tiny gorge, then hike above it to first one waterfall and then two others, ending at the base of a fourth! 3.8 miles.

Find the fern-draped gorge on the south side of the scenic highway about 2.2 miles *east* of Multnomah Falls. Start the water-fall loop trail about .1 mile *west* of the gorge.

You'll find no formal trail up the gorge. In the spring, it's often flooded. But in late summer walk up the dry stream bed as

On the Eagle Creek Trail

far as you want. Cool breezes below green draped cliffs.

Find the loop trail across the road from a small parking area just west of the gorge. The trail first switchbacks to the west and then back to the east before climbing into a canyon through pleasant timber to a junction with the Horsetail Falls trail in about 1 mile.

But don't turn left yet. Continue climbing straight ahead another .8 mile, switchbacking to the top of Triple Falls, the second on this trip.

Return now to the junction and continue east as the trail drops over the top of Oneonta Falls and then traverses north to views down onto the Columbia River before cutting back into the canyon again and passing behind Ponytail Falls. From Ponytail Falls the trail switchbacks downhill to the Horsetail Falls.

Punch Bowl—Hike 2 miles above scenic Eagle Creek to vistas down into a bowl full of waterfalls.

Find the trail at the end of the road along the creek in the Eagle

Creek picnic area (see Eagle Creek Campground). The trail climbs quickly but never steeply above the left side of the stream eventually making its way along a path blasted out of the rock cliff, high over the creek.

In about 1.5 miles watch for a concrete, ground-level marker indicating a side trail (right) to a view of Metalko Falls.

Beyond Metalko Falls, the trail crosses a stream and then climbs again reaching the viewpoint above the Punch Bowl in 2 miles.

Turn back here, or continue on if you have time. Tunnel Falls at the end of 6 miles.

BACKPACKING OPPORTUNITIES

A number of loop backpack trips—some as long as 26 miles—are possible on trails within the gorge.

All of them climb stiffly going in away from the river and drop sharply coming back out. But they all lead to remote and interesting waterfalls and camping spots.

The best time to hike here is during the week. Most of the backcountry camping spots will be taken on weekends and holidays.

No permits are yet required here for overnight trips into the area.

WHERE TO CAMP

Camping in Forest Service campgrounds within the gorge is limited to Eagle Creek Campground which fills up every weekend and practically every day during the summer period.

Two state parks and a commercial facility nearby offer additional sites.

Eagle Creek—24 sites on a forest bluff overlooking the Columbia. A pleasant camp. But somewhat difficult fo find. Drive east on I-80N turning right just beyond the Bonneville turnoff. From the west, turn off I-80N at Bonneville Dam, looping back onto the freeway (heading east) turning south off the freeway in about a mile. Flush toilets. Piped water.

Ainsworth—45 sites on an open grassy loop just off the scenic highway about 3.5 miles west of Multnomah Falls. Flush toilets. Piped water. Oregon state fee.

Viento—45 sites in an open grassy slope. 8 miles west of Hood River on I-80N. Flush toilets. Piped water. Oregon state fee.

Where to Get Information

For information on trail and trail conditions in the gorge, write:
District Ranger
Columbia Gorge District
Route 3, Box 44A
Troutdale, Ore. 97060

mount hood

DO MORE THAN look at a mountain here: Meet one.

You can see Mt. Hood from highways and lower meadows in any number of places. It dominates the horizon here.

But to appreciate the violence that shaped—and still shapes—this stately peak pick any one of several short high trails to walk among its glaciers, moraines, jumbled volcanic rocks, pumice slopes and meadows.

To reach the area: From Portland, drive southeast on U.S. 26. From I-80N at Hood River, drive south on Oregon State Highway 35.

The Forest Service maintains trails and campgrounds all the way around this 11,235-foot peak, the highest in Oregon. But only those in the southeast corner of the mountain are covered here.

The camping and hiking season around the mountain varies with the elevation. Lower facilities open earlier and stay open longer than those higher on the mountain. Campgrounds listed here generally open in May and remain open until after Labor Day. Some of the higher camps, however, don't open until the snow melts usually in mid-June.

Trails on the mountains often remain clogged with snow until early in July with the best hiking between mid-July and September.

Temperatures here also vary with elevation. Daytime temperatures in the valleys will range in the 80s with nighttime temperatures dropping into the upper 40s. Higher in the mountains, however, summer temperatures can range from the 60s in the daytime to below freezing some nights.

Hikers here should equip themselves for every weather eventuality. The weather changes here rapidly as it does on all Northwest mountains. So carry extra warm clothing and rain gear even on a day-long trip. Good shoes, of course, are essential.

The Forest Service offers no naturalist programs here. For information about the forest inquire at the district ranger station in Parkdale, south of Hood River.

WHERE TO DRIVE

Even from the roads here: High vistas, spectacular lakes, green meadows and rich valley forests.

From Hood River, drive south on State Highway 35 to Timberline Lodge, high on the south slopes of Mt. Hood, in 51 miles. But add several side trips for a whole series of additional spectacles.

In one mile from Hood River, turn east on a road to *Panorama Point* in 2 miles. Views here down on the Columbia, and the orchards and berry fields of Hood River with views of Mt. Hood and Mt. Adams too.

About 7 miles south of Hood River turn right onto the *Lost Lake* road driving 24 miles on a paved road to Lost Lake with its classic reflected view of Mt. Hood towering over the lake.

In 22.5 miles, turn right (west) onto a paved and gravel road leading to *Cloud Gap* in 13 miles (follow signs). Vistas here of Mt. Hood, of course, and higher views still of the valley and Mt. Adams.

To reach *Timberline Lodge,* turn north off the highway in about 45 miles, driving 6 miles up the mountain to the famous lodge. And allow lots of time here to wander the meadows and stand in awe of the mountain itself.

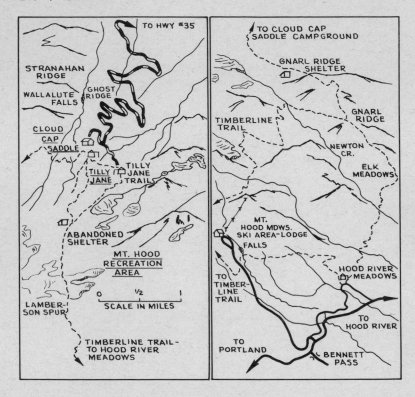

In returning to the main loop highway, drive down the mountain on the little used "west leg" road. Turn off the mountain road about a half-mile from the lodge parking lot, sharply right under a ski-lift. This road wanders—literally—down the slope through trees in a very unhurried sort of way.

WHERE TO HIKE

Hike any of several trails here to discover what the high slopes of a mountain are really like.

Cooper Spur—Climb sharply from timberline along a climber's path to almost instant views from a barren moraine onto Eliot Glacier. About 1 mile.

To reach this trail, drive to Cloud Gap picnic area (see drives) finding the trail uphill to the west.

In about 100 yards, take a spur trail uphill sharply to the right reaching the top of the ridge in half-to-three quarters of a mile.

Views here down on Hood River valley, up at Mt. Hood and out toward Mt. Adams, Mount St. Helens and Mt. Rainier to the north.

Follow the fading path along the ridge top for still higher and higher vistas and views now down on the glacier, from the moraine.

Hike as far as you can see the trail.

Tilly Jane Loop—Hike from subalpine timber to barren scree and meadow slopes—all with vistas up at Mt. Hood and out at the St. Helens-Adams-Rainier volcanoes to the north.

From Cloud Gap picnic area (see above) hike south on the Timberline trail about a mile, turning downhill to the Tilly Jane Campground in another mile, turning north then to return to Cloud Gap in still another half-mile.

Follow the trail uphill out of the picnic area as it climbs out of timber to cross a series of barren scree slopes to high meadows near the junction. If you find snow on this section of trail, follow pole and rock cairns which mark the zig-zag way.

At the junction with the downhill Tilly Jane trail, take time to hike uphill a few hundred yards to an abandoned stone shelter, one of several constructed all around this mountain in the 1930s.

On the Tilly Jane trail, drop smartly into timber and then along the edge of a steep pumice gorge eroded out by Polallie creek, before turning northward to the Tilly Jane recreation complex. Before crossing the creek to the campground explore to the right to find an old log cooking shed and lodge which once served as a starting point for climbing parties.

To reach the trail back to Cloud Gap, drop past an old amphitheater, crossing the creek to the guard station, finding the trail east of the station, on the north side of the campground: Cloud Gap past two creeks in a half-mile.

Elk Meadows—Hike through forest to surprising vistas of Mt. Hood over broad grassy meadows. A 2.7 mile hike.

To reach this trail drive to Hood River Meadows Campground about 37 miles south of Hood River, finding the trailhead to the right just as you enter the campground.

The trail, which starts out on an old road, winds gently up and down crossing two streams before reaching Newton Creek in about 1 mile.

From here the trail switchbacks sharply and stubbornly for another mile, dropping down in the last half-mile to the meadow. Find a shelter on the edge of the large meadow, to the right.

Bask here in view of Mt. Hood, eat lunch, nap and then return.

Mt. Hood Meadow Loop—Sample all of the variety this mountain has to offer on a loop trip from Hood River Meadows, across the side of the mountain to Elk Meadows and back. All day. About 12 miles.

To start from the Hood River Meadows Campground (see above) find the trail off the campground loop road on the west side of the campground. Watch for sign.

The trail wends north first through forest and then up switchbacks to the base of Umbrella Falls in 1.9 miles. Bear to the left here, on grade, to a point where the trail crosses the highway south of the Mt. Hood Meadows Resort.

Here again, the trail enters timber and winds upward, under ski lifts, to a junction with the Timberline Trail in another 1.5 miles.

From Cooper Spur Trail

Turn right now, following the trail as it climbs first up and then down across steep flower meadows deeply scented with lupines under two more ski lifts, past Pencil Falls and Clark Creek to Newton Creek. Another 3.8 miles.

Watch for a spring on the left here as you drop down into timber and around a ridge before reaching Newton Creek.

After climbing out of the barren Newton Creek gorge below the black lava rocks of Gnarl Ridge, turn downhill in 1.2 mile on the Gnarl Ridge trail reaching Elk Meadows in 1.2 more miles. Return to the campground in 2.7 miles (see Elk Meadows Trail).

BACKPACKING OPPORTUNITIES

The 37-mile Timberline trail all the way around Mt. Hood is probably the most popular backpacking trail in this area.

The trail which stays high on the mountain within the Mt. Hood Wilderness, crosses meadows, drops into valleys, and runs along high ridges past lakes and waterfalls in a complete circuit of the peak.

Some hikers make the trip in three days. But others spend much longer, taking side trips or just loitering under the gaze of the mountain.

The hike traditionally starts at Timberline Lodge, however, a number of other spur trails connect with the main trail making other starts—and loops—possible.

No permits are required for overnight camping here.

WHERE TO CAMP

Only campgrounds along the east and southeast side of the mountain are listed here. These camps get heavy use on holidays and weekend. Best time to camp is midweek.

Campgrounds on the east side of the mountain south of Hood River include:

Polallie—8 sites just below the highway along the Hood River. Pit toilets. Well water. 25 miles south of Hood River. Open weekends only.

Sherwood—24 units in a pleasant wooded area. Some sites near the river. Pit toilets. Piped water. 30 miles south of Hood River.

Robinhood—25 units in forested area near the river. Piped water. Well. 35 miles south of Hood River. Open weekends only.

Tilly Jane—12 units on a secluded timbered loop at 5600 feet. Pit toilets. 33 miles from Hood River off the Cloud Gap spur road (see drives).

Campgrounds south of Mt. Hood include:

Trillium Lake—40 units on loops on Trillium Lake. Some sites near the water. Views of Mt. Hood. Pit toilets. Piped water. Turn south off U.S. 26 about 2 miles east of Government Camp. Lake in 1.5 miles.

Still Creek—23 sites on wooded loops. Pit toilets. Piped water. Turn south off U.S. 26 about a mile east of Government Camp.

Alpine Campground—18 sites in subalpine setting at 5400 feet on side of Mt. Hood. Piped water. Pit toilets. 1 mile south of Timberline Lodge.

Phlox Point—4 sites in subalpine setting at 5600 feet. Pit toilets. 1 mile south of Timberline Lodge on west leg road. (See drives.)

Where to Get Information

To get information on this area, write:
District Ranger
Hood River Ranger District
Mt. Hood National Forest
Route 1, Box 573
Parkdale, Ore. 97407

silver falls

A GLISTENING NECKLACE here of waterfalls.

Perhaps one of the largest and certainly the most spectacular groups of falls in such a small area anywhere in the West.

Not a vacation destination, certainly. But if you've come to explore the beauties of western Oregon, you must stop here.

To reach the area: From Salem, Ore., drive south on State Highway 22, turning east in only a few miles onto State Highway 214. Silver Falls State Park in 16 miles.

There are more than 14 waterfalls in this 8300-acre Oregon State park with most of them concentrated in two lush gorges linked by a single trail.

Five of the cascades plunge more than 100 feet with the South Falls, the highest, plunging 177 feet from its eroded basalt cliff.

And most interestingly, hikers can walk behind many of the waterfalls on natural cave-like ledges eroded by the falling water.

The park and its trails are open all year around with most use concentrated from spring to fall.

Winters, however, may be the most spectacular time to visit the park. After several days of freezing weather, the falls change from cascades of water to glistening facades of ice, set in frosted and slippery gorges.

The camping season in the park's one campground generally opens in May and continues through late October with the heaviest use on weekends between Memorial Day and Labor Day.

The weather here is generally mild all summer with mid-July temperatures ranging from about 80 degrees in the daytime to 55 at night. Spring and fall temperatures range slightly cooler.

July and August are the driest months here. Although the weather isn't as important as it is in some areas. There are no big vistas here to be blocked out by clouds. And walking in the dim canyons can be just as pleasant in an Oregon shower as on a sunny day.

Spring hikes have the added advantage of canyon vistas through more open foliage, particularly if you hike before the trees and shrubbery fill out. And fall may be the most colorful as the hardwoods turn to reds and yellows.

And if you hike in the canyons—as you should—don't overlook the plants: Lush growths of salal, ferns, huckleberry, thimbleberry, rhododendrons, plus wildflowers in season.

The park offers no formal naturalist program. Oregon parks— among the most beautiful, well-designed and well-maintained in the nation—are managed by a division of the state's highway department. If you have questions, contact park workers.

WHERE TO DRIVE

Going to and from places in Oregon can often be as interesting as the destinations themselves. And so it is here.

From Salem plan a very unhurried trip to the park through the gently rolling farmland foothills.

The road beyond the town of Shaw eastward climbs gradually and winds gently past one farm and then another over one hill to the next leading to a vista point just west of the park with views back over the entire valley toward Salem.

Rich greens here on a clear day in spring and greener yet in the rain. Golden in mid-summer and rich brown as the fields are plowed.

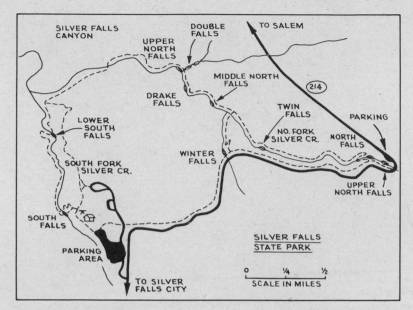

Oregonians, as you'll see here, take pride in the beauty of their state. They hope visitors will too.

WHERE TO HIKE

You can take a short hike to some of the larger waterfalls. But to see them all, walk 6.5 miles around a canyon loop.

South Falls and Lower South Falls—Hike downhill behind the park's highest falls and then down the canyon to still another 93-foot string of white water. About 1 mile.

To find the trail follow signs off a parking loop at the end of a road in the South Falls picnic area.

Take a short spur trail from the parking area turning left and following the trail as it drops down behind South Falls, which plunges 177 feet into the canyon, continuing to a bridge at the bottom with a spectacular view back up at the falls.

Continue past the bridge as the trail drops down a series of steps to pass now behind Lower South Falls. Either return here, the same way you came, or continue downstream as the trail climbs

Lower South Falls

(that's correct) another .3 mile taking a spur trail to the right which winds back atop the canyon rim to the parking lot.

North Falls—Hike less than a quarter mile here to a 136-foot falls plunging into another dark canyon.

Find this trail across a bridge from a parking area on the highway about 4 miles east of the main picnic area road junction.

Bear right as the trail winds around a bluff and switchbacks behind the falls. Full views of the torrent from the trail on either side.

Water Fall Loop—A necklace hike here with waterfall pearls all strung in a row. A 6.5-mile loop.

Start at the parking area (see South Falls) dropping first behind South Falls and then Lower South Falls to continue on the trail leading to lower North Falls in a little more than 1.3 miles.

Just beyond this squat 30-foot cascade, turn uphill (left) for a short side visit with Double Falls, a wispy plume that drops from one ledge to another a total of 178 feet.

Returning to the trail, hike past Drake Falls (27 feet) in .2 mile, and on to Middle North Falls (106 feet) in still another .2 mile. To hike under Middle North Falls watch for a spur trail to the right as you approach the face of it. Best views of this falls from the far wall of the canyon, at the end of the spur.

From Middle North Falls hike .5 mile on to Twin Falls and, in .9 mile more, the base of North Falls.

To return to your car, take a spur trail to the right as you climb uphill from behind North Falls, following that path just below the highway to Winter Falls in about a mile and then back to the picnic ground road in another 1.2 miles.

A peaceful walk with modest ups and downs and accompanied almost constantly with the noisy chatter of first one falls and then another. Flowers in season too. Watch particularly for the Oregon oxalis which folds its clover-like leaves whenever it is warmed by the sun. Monkeyflowers too. And salmon berries as big as your thumb.

BACKPACKING OPPORTUNITIES

Overnight backpacking trips are not permitted in this park. Camping is restricted to established campsites.

WHERE TO CAMP

Camping is limited to a single campground within this park. Nearest commercial camping facilities are in Salem.

Silver Falls Campground—61 sites in grassy forest setting. Some with electrical power hookups. Flush toilets. Piped water. Showers. Laundry facilities.

Where to Get Information

For information on Oregon State parks, write:
Oregon State Highway Department
Parks and Recreation
301 State Highway Building
Salem, Ore. 97310

mount jefferson

A SPECTACULAR PEAK. But one of the most secretive in the Pacific Northwest.

You can see it—from a distance—in any number of places as it rises over ridges and joins far vistas with other Cascade peaks.

But close views of the mountain are reserved almost exclusively for hikers willing to walk in to basins of lakes high around the mountain where the peak washes its reflection in the sun.

To reach the area: From I-5 in Salem, drive east on State Highway 22 to the Forest Service ranger station near Detroit. From U.S. 97, drive northwest from Bend on U.S. 20 turning north to Detroit on State Highway 22.

The 10,947-foot peak is part of the Mt. Jefferson Wilderness which embraces—in addition to its namesake mountain—more than 150 lakes, five glaciers, 160 miles of trails and dozens of other lesser mountains.

The campground season outside the wilderness varies with the elevation of the campgrounds. Low-level camps around Detroit

Lake, for instance, generally open in mid-April. But camps higher up along the Santiam River often remain closed by snow until almost a month later. All of the campgrounds, however, are closed, in part, after Labor Day with some sites kept open through October.

Use here is heaviest during July with the greatest summer impact on holidays and weekends and at campgrounds around Detroit Lake.

For the best camping, therefore, visit here in midweek during the summer season, seeking camping spots along the river.

Trails here open as the snow melts also. Trails to lower lakes are often open in early June. But high elevation trails down the Cascade Crest and to the base of Mt. Jefferson generally do not open until late June or early July.

Temperatures here range from hot in the valley near Detroit to cool at the high lakes around Mt. Jefferson. Valley temperatures range from daytime highs in the 80s to nighttime lows around 60 degrees. Temperatures range from 12 to 20 degrees cooler at the 6000 foot level below Mt. Jefferson.

Hikers face few hazards here. Severe thunderstorms are infrequent and rainy periods are generally of short duration in July and August.

Drivers, however, should approach all side-roads with caution. Logging is heavy here and logging trucks rumble over most of these roads all summer long, particularly during the week. Be aware.

The Forest Service in this area conducts no naturalist programs. However, weekend campfire programs are presented at the Detroit Lake State Park. Inquire at the park.

WHERE TO DRIVE

This is commercial logging country. High roads lead to occasional vistas but the roads are likely to be busy with logging trucks during the week and the vistas, most of them, are over clearcuts.

Oregon is the largest timber producing state in the nation and much of that lumber and plywood comes from forests like these.

The clearcut harvest method used here has been the subject of controversy and hearings before Congress. Forest industry leaders contend that clearcutting is the only economical way of harvesting

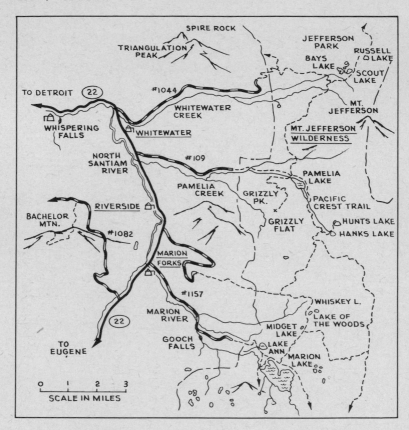

these mature forests and that the method is necessary to the natural forest regeneration process.

Conservationists, on the other hand, argue that the method is unsightly, wasteful and causes serious erosion problems.

So if you do drive these backcountry roads decide the matter for yourself. Observe the amount of material left after the logs are removed, the nature of the regeneration on old cuts, the erosion, if any, and make up your own mind.

WHERE TO HIKE

-All of the best is hiding here. And that's the absolute truth. Few views of Mt. Jefferson from any of these low elevation roads. But from these trails . . . a mountain you'll never forget!

And flowers at every level. Watch particularly in early July for the spectacular pure white Santiam lily that grows along some of these low level trails. Big as an Easter lily and twice as exciting to meet here in the wilderness.

Marion Lake—Hike through flower-filled forest past a small lake to a bigger one with vistas up at Mt. Jefferson and out to Three Fingered Jack. 2.5 miles.

To reach this trail turn east off Highway 22 onto the Marion Creek road No. 1157 about 17.8 miles east of the Detroit Ranger station, reaching the end of the road in 4.5 miles.

Find the trail uphill to the right. The path starts very gently through shady forest to the wilderness boundary and then switchbacks gradually higher into timber passing Lake Ann and then climbing to a rock outcrop with views of Mt. Jefferson.

At Marion Lake, bear to the right following a trail above the shore to a rock promontory in about a quarter-mile. Climb fisherman trails to the top for bigger vistas of Mt. Jefferson and views also in spots of Three Fingered Jack.

Santiam lilies here in early July with pipsisewas, single delights, queen flowers, twin flowers—all evolving in season.

Pamelia Lake—Hike to a pretty lake tucked between cliffs and then on up—if you have time—to the top of Grizzly Peak at 5799 feet. 2.3 miles to the lake and another 2.8 miles to the top of the mountain.

To reach the trail, turn east off Highway 22 about 13.7 miles east of the Detroit Ranger Station onto the Pamelia road No. 109. driving 3.6 miles to a parking lot on the left.

The trail here starts near a large sign heading easterly away from the road. A very gradual path—perhaps one of the most gentle in the book—wends through forests and rhododendrons with occasional glimpse of Mt. Jefferson through the tops of trees.

At the lake, views of the top of Mt. Jefferson across the "outlet" end of the lake to the right. This lake actually drains underground into Pamelia Creek. The lake may be low in the summer.

For a face-to-face look at Mt. Jefferson, hike 2.8 more miles up the Grizzly Peak trail to the top of the mountain. Only up and up here. And persistently.

Jefferson Park—This is where Mt. Jefferson really lives! So spend a whole day prowling what has to be one of the most beautiful alpine meadow and lake systems in the entire Pacific Northwest. A 5-mile hike.

To reach this trail, turn east off Highway 22 and about 12 miles east of the Detroit ranger station onto the Whitewater Road No. 1044 finding the trailhead in 7.3 miles on the right (uphill) side of the road.

The trail starts uphill, from the parking area through a clearcut, switchbacking 1.5 miles through forest to a junction with the Triangulation Peak trail. Keep right here as the trail now climbs over one ridge and then another to an explosive view in about 2 miles of Mt. Jefferson towering over the Whitewater and Russell creek basins. (And notice how the mountain looks from here. It'll look different later on.)

Get water at 4 miles as the path drops from the view ridge into forest and a branch of Whitewater Creek. At a junction with the

Mt. Jefferson from Scout Lake

White Heather

Pacific Crest Trail at 4.2 miles, turn left following the trail to the north, reaching the first lake, Scout Lake, in about another half-mile. (Note the mountain now from here—two crests instead of one!)

No one will need to suggest that you stop here. Mt. Jefferson looms above you wherever you go, sometimes towering over meadows and at others reflected in lakes. Loiter here as long as you can, exploring Bays Lake (with rock bays in it) to the west and Russell, Rock and Park lakes which lie over the ridges to the north.

And don't pass up the flowers. At lower levels, twin flowers, columbines and lupines. At the top, brilliant paintbrush, shooting stars, dwarf huckleberry and both red and white heather.

But treat everything with the greatest of care. This beauty requires tenderness. It cannot survive without it. So disturb nothing. Take only memories and leave no evidence of your visit at all. And camp outside the area if possible.

BACKPACKING OPPORTUNITIES

Backcountry hiking opportunities here center around the Pacific Crest trail that traverses the full length of the Mt. Jefferson Wilderness.

Hikers can either hike the full length of the area, some 40 miles, from Breitenbush Lake at the north to U.S. 120 at the south, or make any number of shorter trips from spur roads and trails along the edge of the wilderness.

Trails here are always busy so hikers will seldom find complete privacy in most lake camping spots. But, by the same token, it's not overrun with people either.

Inquire either at the ranger station in Detroit or at the Willamette National Forest headquarters in Eugene, Ore., about current registration and permit requirements before starting your trip.

Forest officials will also advise hikers on areas which are likely to be crowded and suggest alternatives if asked.

WHERE TO CAMP

Most of the National Forest campgrounds near the trails covered here are located along the Santiam River. These camps are seldom filled except on busy weekends and holidays. Most of the camping pressure in this area falls on the state and federal facilities around Detroit Lake, a reservoir.

Whispering Falls—11 sites on pleasant forest loop near the river. Find the waterfalls off a cliff across the river. Flush toilets. Piped water. 8 miles southeast of Detroit on Highway 22.

Whitewater—5 sites along Whitewater creek. Pit toilets. 11 miles southeast of Detroit off Highway 22.

Riverside—40 units on pleasant forested loops. Some sites above the river. Piped water. Pit toilets. 14 miles southeast of Detroit.

Marion Forks—15 units on a spur road along Marion Creek. Pit toilets. Piped water to some units. Near the state fish hatchery. 16 miles southeast of Detroit on Highway 22.

Detroit Lake State Park—320 sites on loops near Detroit Lake. Flush toilets. Showers. Laundry. Reservations available. An Oregon State Park. Often busy. State fee. West of the Detroit ranger station.

Where to Get Information

For information on this area, write:
District Ranger
Detroit Ranger District
U.S. Forest Service
Star Route, Box 320
Mill City, Ore. 97360

central oregon coast

HIKE HERE INTO two different beach worlds—one of harsh cliffs and smashing waves and the other of rolling dunes and far-off whispers of surf.

And both along the coast of central Oregon on U.S. Highway 101 north and south of the city of Florence, Ore.

To reach the areas: Take any Oregon highway west from I-5, which crosses the state north to south between Portland and Ashland, finding 101 along the state's Pacific coast.

To reach the crashing surf drive north on 101 from Florence about 25 miles or south from Yachats about 2 miles to Cape Perpetua.

To prowl the sand dunes, drive to campgrounds and side roads on 101 between Florence and Coos Bay, 50 miles to the south.

CAPE PERPETUA

Secret coves, cauldrons of roiling surf, forest walks, high vistas and scenic drives—all from a Visitor Center complex and campground operated by the Siuslaw (Sigh-u-slaw) National Forest at the cape.

Trails here are open to hikers the year around. Backcountry roads may be closed occasionally by snow in the winter. The Visitor Center, which operates seven days a week in summer and Wednesdays through Sundays in winter, offers movies and naturalist conducted tours of coastal features, June through September.

WHERE TO DRIVE

Well-maintained gravel forest roads lead inland from the Visitor Center to high views of the rugged ocean coast and the coastal mountain range.

Cape Viewpoint—Turn inland off Highway 101 just north of the visitor center onto Forest Road No. 152. In about .5 mile turn left onto a short spur (No. 153) which leads to a parking area near a vista trail atop the cape in another mile. Find the viewpoint trail off the end of the parking loop. Walk 25 yards to the first view down on the cape. For a longer walk, continue on around a loop past more viewpoints, returning to the parking lot in .3 mile.

Cummins Peak Lookout—Longer vistas at 2475 feet of the ocean coast plus the Oregon coastal mountains. Turn inland off Highway 101 just north of the Visitor Center onto road No. 152 (same as above) continuing west about 8.3 miles to spur road (No. 152W). Turn right, following signs to the lookout area in another 3.5 miles. This trip is part of a formal self-guided tour of forest features. Get printed information at the Visitor Center.

WHERE TO HIKE

Well marked and maintained trails lead into timbered areas, to surf-smashed coves and from high vista points.

Devils Churn—All of that and more. Narrow rock gorges smash waves into plume after plume of spray off a trail that drops from a highway vista point, circling above the surf line for about a half mile.

Find the trail from a viewpoint parking area on the west side of Highway 101 just north of the Visitor Center. The trail drops

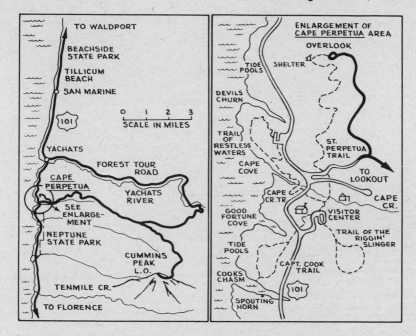

down to a ledge and then loops back to the south overlooking the surf-plumed rocks. Take unmarked spur trails down to the surf line for a closer look at tidepools, spray channels and the Devils Churn itself. But use caution. The surf here is extremely powerful.

Captain Cook Trail—A .6 mile loop past Indian shell mounds to Cook's chasm. Best to park at the Visitor Center and take the trail which starts downhill to the left of the center. Trail crosses the highway, passes an Indian kitchen midden (shell mound) and then loops south above the chasm—watch for spouting-horn, spray holes across the chasm to the south—before returning to the visitor center trail. Spur trails here also drop to lower rock ledges for tide pool walks and even fishing.

St. Perpetua Trail—Walk downhill through spruce groves from the top of the cape to the campground and Visitor Center. Find trail off the viewpoint path beyond the parking area (see Cape Viewpoint above). Trail switchbacks across open slopes and through timber with almost constant views to the south and out over the cape. A 1.25 mile walk one way, to the Visitor Center.

Trail of Riggin' Slinger—A 1.4 mile loop trail through a spruce forest southeast of the Visitor Center tells the forest management story of the coast range. Views, too, of the cape.

WHERE TO CAMP

Cape Perpetua Campground—42 tent sites scheduled for 1975 in open wooded area along creek. Find campground road just north of Visitor Center off Highway 101. Flush toilets. Piped water.

OREGON DUNES

More than 31,000 acres of rolling sand dunes between Highway 101 and the beautiful Pacific. The largest non-desert dune system in the West.

Hike only a short distance here to find yourself swallowed up in a ghostly silence of moving sand. Or hike further to the noisier sand beaches of the ocean itself.

The dune strip, 45 miles long and a half to three miles wide, stretches from Florence to North Bend. Trailheads in campgrounds and from viewpoints give easy access to the dunes. Hike overland through the dunes to find your own private section of beach. Or share the beach with others at road ends. Driftwood here, agates, and if you're extremely lucky in winter or early spring—particularly after a storm—blue glass balls blown from the nets of fishermen near Japan.

WHERE TO DRIVE

For easy access to the ocean beach and parking lot views of the dunes, try spur roads to viewpoints near Florence, Reedsport and Coos Bay (North Bend).

South Jetty—Series of parking areas give easy access to the ocean plus views of some of the highest dunes in the system. A few exceed 300 feet. Watch for swans in the river lowlands behind the dunes during the fall.

Drive south from Florence, crossing the Siuslaw river, turning toward the ocean in about 1.2 miles. End of jetty in another 6 miles.

Reedsport dunes—Another series of parking areas give easy access to beaches and dunes.

Drive south from Reedsport, turning toward Windy Cove and ocean beaches in about 3.4 miles. Follow road downhill and south to the beach spur.

Dunes at the end of the road in about 4 miles. No formal trails. Pick your own beach, your own dune or valley and follow your own footstep in and out.

North Bend Dunes—More beaches and still more dunes.

Turn west off Highway 101 about 2 miles north of North Bend onto the Horsfall road, keeping right in another 1.1 mile to reach beach access at the end of the road beyond campgrounds. Part of a shipwreck is sometimes visible in winter on this beach near the parking lot at the beach in 3.5 miles from the mill junction.

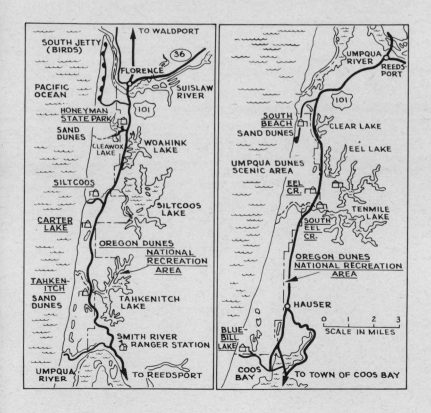

PLACES TO HIKE

Honeyman State Park—Trails here around fresh water lakes and into some of the highest dunes on the coast.

For easiest dune access, walk west from the parking area on Cleawox lake (follow road signs) making your way along the edge of the dune on the lake into the dune area itself. Ocean beach in 1.8 miles as the crow flies. But there's no formal trail.

For a quiet walk around a marsh lake, take the trail from the campground around the west side of Lily Lake, looping back to the east side of the lake and returning to the campground in about a half mile.

Find trail off the campground entry road, to the west, just north of the registration booth.

Umpqua Dune Scenic Area—Trails from Eel Creek Campground climb over dunes into one of the largest complexes of dunes. Motor vehicles are banned here.

Find the main trailhead beyond the first campground loop, uphill from the road. It's signed. A formal trail leads .2 mile to the edge of the dunes. Beach but no trail in 2.1 miles. An entrancing walk into sand valleys and over sand hills. Mark your way. You won't get lost, but your tracks will help when finding your way out.

Other Trail Access—Marked and unmarked trails lead into dune areas from almost every campground along the central coast strip.

Look for marked trails at Carter Lake Campground—near the boat ramp—and at Tahkenitch Lake Campground—off the south end of the south loop. (.8 mile to dunes and 1.6 miles to the beach.)

BACKPACKING OPPORTUNITIES

Ocean Beach Overnight Hikes—Hike as far as you want and pick your own campspot away from crowds almost anywhere along the 45 miles of ocean beach.

No formal trails at all. Simply follow the ocean beach, camping behind the seawall formed by the first low row of dunes. Protection here from the constant wind. No camping permitted on the beaches.

Consult with U.S. Forest Service officials at Gardiner on best places to camp. No water except from scattered creeks and ponds.

Crossing the dunes

The north section of beach stretches from the Umpqua River at Reedsport north to Florence. About 23 miles. The southern section which embraces the Umpqua Dunes stretches 22 miles from the Umpqua to Coos Bay.

WHERE TO CAMP

Honeyman State Park—A fully developed, pleasant campground in a wooded area (rhododendrons bloom in the spring) 3 miles south of Florence. 382 sites, 76 with electricity and 66 of those with sewer outlets too. Swimming in Cleawox and Woahink lakes. Some loops open all year. Busiest on weekends and holidays. Best season, spring and fall. Sites can be reserved during the summer season by writing the park, Box 3514, Florence, Ore. 97439. Be sure to list the number in your party, the nature of your camping equipment and the dates you want. No advance payment required. State fee.

Siltcoos Recreation Area—19 tent and 56 trailer sites on four small pleasant campground loops in a grassy dune area beyond the first dune seawall. 7 miles south of Florence. Job Corps nature trail. Open year round.

Carter Lake—12 tent sites and 20 trailer sites on two wooded loops near dune ridges. Some around the lake. Swimming. 9 miles south of Florence.

Tahkenitch Lake—4 tent and 32 trailer sites on loop near dunes but away from the lake which is across the highway. Boat launch nearby. 9 miles north of Reedsport.

Eel Creek—7 tent and 85 trailer sites on three loops in a relatively open area. Near the edge of Umpqua Dunes Scenic area. 15 miles north of North Bend. Federal fee. Some loops open year around.

Bluebill Lake—19 trailer sites on small loop in a mid-dune area near a small lake. Short trail around south shore of lake. 3 miles north of North Bend. Open year around.

Where to Get More Information

On Cape Perpetua:
> Director
> Cape Perpetua Visitor Center
> P.O. Box 274
> Yachats, Ore. 97498

On Honeyman State Park:
> Honeyman State Park
> Box 3514
> Florence, Ore. 97439

On Oregon Dunes National Recreation Area:
> Area Ranger
> Oregon Dunes NRA
> Gardiner, Ore. 97441

diamond lake

BACKROAD PROWLING COUNTRY, this, with all sorts of hidden gems waiting to be found and enjoyed.

Waterfalls by the cliff-full, a lava cave, a hot spring, vista hikes—all from a big camping lake.

And, oh yes, rhododendrons, wild forests of them every spring.

You'll have to walk here, but not very far.

To reach the area: From I-5 in southwestern Oregon drive east from Roseburg on State Highway 138 reaching Diamond Lake in about 80 miles. From Crater Lake National Park, drive north from the north park entrance to Highway 138, continuing on to the lake.

Diamond Lake, just north of Crater Lake National Park serves as a central point for exploring the Cascade mountain foothill country in this part of the Umpqua National Forest.

Most of the features covered here lie just off paved roads. But a few must be sought down logging roads all of which, however, are well maintained and easy to drive in a passenger car.

The spring and fall may be the most spectacular times to visit this area.

271

Through May and June the wild rhododendrons bloom throughout low elevation forests turning them all into literal parks. In the fall, frost creates another color display as the vine maples and huckleberries turn from green to brilliant yellows and reds.

Campgrounds here open generally early in May and remain open through October. Fishing is one of the major attractions here and facilities are usually most crowded when the fish are biting best, generally in the early spring and late fall. Vacationers take over facilities in midsummer when use is heavy the week around but heaviest on weekends and holidays.

Temperatures here range between 70 and 80 degrees during the day in summer, dropping to the 40s at night with spring and fall temperatures slightly lower. July and August offer the best weather although the autumn here can be cool, crisp and clear as well.

Cloudy weather, however, should have little effect on any visit. There are few big vistas to be blotted out by clouds and hikes to shady forest waterfalls are as interesting on a drizzly day—maybe more so—than when the sun shines.

The Forest Service presents evening campfire programs at the Diamond Lake Campground on weekends. Schedules are posted at the information center across the road from the campground entrance.

WHERE TO DRIVE AND HIKE

Roads here lead to few vistas but to many short trails of less than a mile to waterfalls, hot springs and even a lava tube cave.

The side roads here are all logging roads, identified by number. Watch for logging traffic during the week.

TRAILS OFF STATE HIGHWAY 138

Clearwater Falls—Walk less than 100 yards to a shady, mossy sheltered waterfalls with a picnic area nearby.

Drive north from Diamond Lake on Highway 138 about 11 miles turning south off the highway to the Clearwater Falls picnic area in less than a half-mile.

Find the 30-foot falls just beyond the picnic area.

Whitehorse Falls—A small but pretty falls and a prettier pool. All in a lush green setting.

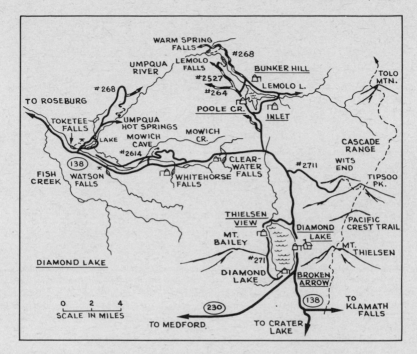

From Clearwater Falls, continue west on Highway 138 for 3.7 miles turning north down a short spur to the falls and campground.

For best views of the falls, walk to the left of a parking area dropping to a large pool.

Mowich Cave—If you've never seen a lava tube cave this is the time to see one.

To find the short trail to the cave, drive about 1.7 miles west from the Whitehorse Falls, turning right (north) passing a powerhouse, to a junction across the river with road No. 2614. Turn right again, watching for the cave trail sign to the left, uphill, in less than a half-mile.

The trail climbs about a quarter-mile relatively sharply through a rhododendron forest to the entrance of the cave in the side of a basalt bluff.

The cave is only about .1 mile long. Take a flashlight. Cool, dank and dark.

Watson Falls—The highest (272 feet) and the most delicate falls in this series—a long misty plume down a moss and fern draped cliff.

Find the trail to this waterfall about 3.1 miles west of the Mowich Cave turnoff (4.6 miles beyond Whitehorse Falls). Turn off Highway 138 to the south, parking off the highway by a stream, to the right, in less than a half-mile.

The trail crosses the road from the parking area then switchbacks first to a viewpoint at the base of the falls and then on up two more switchbacks to a shady and mist-swept view down into the pool below the falls. Rhododendrons here too with twin flowers and columbine in season. About a half-mile walk.

Toketee Falls—Hike through pleasant forest to a vista point looking back at a secretive double falls.

To find this falls turn north of Highway 138 about 2.3 miles west of the Watson Falls turnoff. Watch for sign to Toketee Ranger Station.

After dropping off the highway, bear left at the first junction

Whitehorse Falls

crossing the river and turning left again as you run into a wooden flume. Find the trailhead downhill off a parking area less than .3 miles from the highway.

The trail starts out through a picnic area before climbing sharply over the rim of a gorge and then dropping quickly to a vista point just beyond the only down-staircase on the trail. A very small vista point perched on a rock outcrop. View of the falls through the trees. Way trails drop steeply into the gorge. But don't take them.

SHORT TRAILS IN OTHER AREAS

Lemolo Falls—A little hard to find, perhaps, but if you're a waterfall buff you'll want to add it to your list.

To reach this trail drive north from Diamond Lake on Highway 138 turning north on the Lemolo Lake road in about 8 miles. In 4.3 miles, turn west (left) onto road 264, and then right (north) onto road 2527 in about .4 mile. In 1.7 miles turn right again onto a dirt spur marked for Lemolo Falls.

Find the trail off the end of this dusty spur in about a half-mile. The path drops down an old road to an old campground in about a half-mile and then switchbacks into the gorge to the base of the falls in another half-mile. (Find the trail out of the old campground, downhill from the only picnic table.)

An interesting falls over a columnar basalt cliff which you can probably enjoy all by yourself.

Warm Spring Falls—View this gentle falls over rhododendrons in the spring. A quarter-mile walk.

To find the trail, continue north on the Lemolo Lake road (see above) crossing the outlet of the lake to turn sharply left (west) onto road No. 268. In 4.7 miles watch for a trail sign on the right.

This gentle trail drops off the road to the *left* dipping once past a spring to reach an unmarked viewpoint on a cliff beyond the falls. Best views over flowers in the spring.

Umpqua Hot Springs—Drive down a dusty road to hike to an unlikely hot spring perched atop a rock bluff. A half-mile walk.

To find the trail, turn north off Highway 138 onto road 268 (see Toketee Falls trail) driving first to the far end of Toketee Lake. From the lake, continue on 268 for about 5.3 miles turning right (south) onto a gravel-dirt spur. Watch for a concrete, ground level trail marker and an informal camping area on the left in another 2.2 miles.

The trail switchbacks downhill a couple of times ending at a shed sheltering the hot spring which boils out of a natural eroded rock tub. Soak your feet and return.

WHERE TO HIKE

Tipsoo Peaks from Wits End—The order here is correct. For you will certainly be at your wit's end before you reach the Tipsoo Peaks, atop the Cascade crest. 3 miles.

To find this trail, drive north from the Diamond Lake Campground on Highway 138 for 5.6 miles turning right (east) onto road 2711, later 2788, and driving 5 miles to a trail sign uphill on the right.

The trail starts at the edge of a clearcut, climbing deceptively steeply up a series of switchbacks through forest to lava outcroppings around a circular meadow.

But take care, particularly toward the end, when the trail tread all but disappears as it crosses meadows. Follow blazes on trees and green steel fence posts stuck in meadows, never losing sight of one until you've found the other.

From the circular meadow at the top, hike east picking your way between two small peaks, climbing through rocks to the top of either one—or both.

Vistas from the top of the crest down on Diamond, Lemolo and Miller lakes, across at Mt. Thielsen and north to the Sisters.

And take care in hiking downhill too. In fact, the trail may even be harder to follow in some spots then. So hang on to all blazes and remember the trail never goes straight up or straight down and probably never goes in the direction you expect it to.

Carry water. None on the trail.

BACKPACKING OPPORTUNITIES

The Pacific Crest Trail crosses north and south along the eastern side of this area and can be reached from a number of spur trails.

One of the more popular overnight hikes is to Maidu Lake on

the crest trail from a spur trail up the Umpqua river from Bradley Creek east of Lemolo Lake. A 6.8 mile hike.

No permits are required for overnight hikes in this area.

WHERE TO CAMP

Most of the camping here centers around the large campgrounds on Diamond Lake. But other facilities, some of them not so heavily used, can be found in forested sites off the major roads.

Diamond Lake—304 sites along most of the east shore of the lake. Many on the water. Others on forested shady loop. Sites here are assigned at an entrance station. Flush toilets. Piped water.

Broken Arrow—155 sites on a series of loops in a lightly forested, pumice flat on the south side of Diamond Lake. None near the water. Flush toilets. Piped water.

Thielsen View—68 sites on the west side of Diamond Lake on loops away from the water. Primarily a fisherman's camp. Pit toilets. No water. 3 miles west of Highway 138 on road 271.

Poole Creek—41 sites on the west shore of Lemolo Lake. Some sites along the lake. Piped water. Pit toilets. 15 miles north of Diamond Lake.

Toketee Lake—18 sites on a pleasant forest loop near but not on Toketee Lake. 2 miles east of the Toketee Ranger station. Pit toilets. River water.

Clearwater Falls—10 sites on wooded loop above Clearwater falls. 12 miles northwest of Diamond Lake. Pit toilets.

Whitehorse Falls—5 sites on small loop beyond falls. 6 miles east of Toketee junction. Pit toilets. Well.

Where to Get Information

For information on this area, write:
     District Ranger
     Toketee Ranger District
     Toketee Route, Box 101
     Idleyld Park, Ore. 97447

crater lake national park

BY ANY SCALE, far more here than just a lake. A spectacle, really. And an ever-changing one.

There's the water, for sure. But water like you've never seen before. So pure. So deep, it's almost like a gem. Glistening blue at times, royal purple at others and sometimes, in the shallow part, a blaze of iridescent shades.

If you get this far West, be sure and stop. Spend a day, at least. Or more.

To reach the area: From I-5 in southwestern Oregon, drive to Medford then northeast on Oregon State Highway 62 to the park. From Eugene, drive southeasterly on State Highway 58 to U.S. 97.

Crater Lake, between 4 and 6 miles across, is one of the deepest lakes in the world. Only one other in the western hemisphere—the Great Slave Lake in Canada—is any deeper and then only by 83 feet. Depth soundings have fixed Crater Lake's depth at 1932 feet.

The lake, centerpiece of this 250-square-mile park, lies inside the top of an ancient volcano which erupted and destroyed itself only 6600 years ago.

Volcanic activity, however, did not cease then. Since that time Wizard Island, which projects 760 feet above the lake, was formed by volcanic activity within the caldera itself.

Although the Rim Village area on the south side of the lake is open year around, the main scenic loop road which completely circles the lake is not open before July 4 most years, closing with the first heavy snows in late September.

The park gets its heaviest use during the midsummer with peaks on weekends and holidays. The park's campgrounds are filled almost every night then.

After Labor Day however, through September, crowds drop off and more space becomes available. Naturalist programs will have been discontinued and temperatures will be cooler. But visitors will find an air of peace here not normally found in the summer.

The weather here, due to the elevation, is generally cool. Daytime temperatures range into the 70s with highs of about 85 degrees. Nighttime temperatures range to the low 40s with snow possible in every month of the year. Afternoon summer thundershowers are not uncommon in the park but they usually strike and move on.

Except for the cool weather, campers and hikers face no problems here. However, no visitor should attempt to climb down into the crater at any point except on the trail in Cleetwood Cove which leads to a boat dock. All of the crater slopes around the lake are either dusty pumice or rotten rock and dangerous if not impossible to climb.

Evening naturalist programs are offered at the two park campgrounds. In addition, park rangers conduct daily field trips to points of interest. Rangers also accompany concession boats which make regular trips—for a fee—across the lake.

WHERE TO DRIVE

You can "see" the crater in one stop at the rim. But you can't appreciate its many features unless you complete the 33-mile loop drive around it.

Starting at the Rim Village on the south side of the lake, the road loops first to a viewpoint down on Wizard Island and then to a series of views of bays, points and coves.

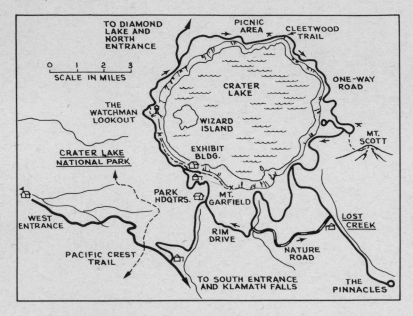

In about 18 miles, take a one-mile spur road to the highest road point in the park—a 7865-foot point about 1700 feet above the lake.

Return to the loop and stop again, for certain, at Kerr Notch to look down on the famed Phantom Ship, a rock-shard island in this section of the lake.

From the notch, the rim road now turns inland around a high ridge through meadows, across subalpine slopes and past wildflower gardens to the rim again. Allow 2 hours at least.

WHERE TO HIKE

As always—and it's most tedious to keep saying so—the best and the most private vistas in the park are reserved for hikers.

Trails here aren't long. Most of them, in fact, are far too short. But fortunately most people don't leave the road so the trails aren't usually overrun.

Mt. Scott—Put the entire park in perspective here. A grand overview with vistas north to Mt. Thielsen and south to Mt. Shasta from the highest point in the park—8926 feet. A 2.5 mile hike.

Find the trail off the east side of the loop road about 18 miles from the Rim Village junction and several hundred yards beyond the White Bark Picnic area.

Park against the road bank on the left. The trail at first drops across a meadow on a two-lane old road track and then circles around the south side of the mountain in timber reaching the first views to the south from open pumice slopes in about three-quarter mile.

The trail now climbs steadily higher to the east with constant and growing vistas toward Mt. Shasta and over the Agency and Klamath lakes and the grazing plains of south central Oregon.

As the trail gets almost south of the peak, it starts a series of switchbacks with views now to the east and occasional views at the end of switchbacks over the lake.

In the last quarter-mile, the trail breaks out on a ridge overlooking the lake and traverses north to the lookout with 360 degrees view everywhere.

No water on the trail. Carry your own.

Garfield Peak—It's a short, sharp walk to a long, sprawling vista.

Find this trail in front of the Crater Lake Lodge. Follow it downhill to the east and then up a series of persistent switchbacks and ridges to the top at 8060 feet.

The first part of the trail offers inland views over the park complex and hills to the south. Wild flowers, too. The top third of the trail, however, climbs along the edge of the rim with constant views to the north. From the top, Mt. Shasta again to the south, Mt. Thielsen to the north. And the entire lake, of course.

The Watchman Tower—It's almost unbelievable how rapidly you can leave the crowds at road level to find cool views here. While thousands may drive the road below on weekends only a few hundred make the hike to the lookout. An .8 mile climb.

Find the trail off a vista point parking area about 4 miles north of the Rim Drive junction. The path heads south along the rim and then climbs around the west side of the mountain, circling back and switchbacking to the tower at 8056 feet. A steady but easy climb.

The lookout is manned during high fire danger periods. Displays

View from The Watchman

are maintained on the lower level pointing out horizon features. And note, too, the prismlike colors in the shallow waters around Wizard Island below you.

BACKPACKING OPPORTUNITIES

There are no overnight backpack trails into or on the crater.

However, the Lightening Springs trail off the west side of the loop road leads to the Pacific Crest Trail in about 4 miles. The Crest trail crosses the park from north to south for about 25 miles.

There are also several long trails near the Pumice Desert on the north side of the park. Little water here.

Fire permits are required on all backcountry treks within the park.

WHERE TO CAMP

During the summer, park campgrounds fill early in the day with the campground near the rim filling often by midmorning.

Overflow camps can be found in national forest areas north of the park near Diamond Lake.

Mazama—200 sites in forest setting. Opens early in July to mid-October. At 6100 feet. Flush toilets. Piped water. Near the south entrance station.

Rim Campground—54 sites on a series of loops in a rolling subalpine setting at 7100 feet. Flush toilets. Piped water. Near but not on the rim. A few sites, however, do have views of the lake.

Lost Creek—14 sites in a remote forest area. 3 miles from the loop on the Pinnacle spur off Kerr Notch. Pit toilets. Piped water. Usually full.

Where to Get Information

For information on the park, write:
        Superintendent
        P.O. Box 7
        Crater Lake National Park
        Crater Lake, Ore. 97604

CALIFORNIA

coastal redwoods

STAND HERE IN awe of living time and wonder how many other men, in how many other generations, have looked upon these great trees.

And the trees aren't the only wonders here: Ocean beaches, vistas, waterfalls, and a delicate fern-draped gorge too.

To reach the area: Drive north from Eureka and south from Crescent City on coastal highway U.S. 101. To find Jedediah Smith Redwoods State Park, drive north from Crescent City on U.S. 101 and U.S. 199.

The one great constant here, as it has been for hundreds of years, is the giant coast redwood, which grows along this coast south to Monterey.

But tragically, the trees in these parks are almost all that remain today of the once-vast forests that cloaked this entire coast. All the rest have been—and are being—logged off to build houses that won't last one-third as long as it took these giants to grow.

Weather conditions can change in a matter of miles inland along this coast. On the ocean beaches, summer days are often cool, damp and foggy, while inland only a few miles, the weather can be sunny and warm.

Ocean daytime temperatures here average near 60 degrees while temperatures inland range to 85 degrees. And while nighttime temperatures along the coast average in the 50s, inland temperatures drop to 45 degrees.

Summers in both areas are much drier than in the winter when more than 100 inches of rain can fall in a single season.

Facilities in all of these state and federal areas are open, at least in part, all year round. But use is heaviest in the summer and particularly on weekends and holidays.

Campgrounds in California state parks—there are no federal camping facilities—are usually full all summer and visitors are urged to get reservations (see Where to Camp) before visiting the area.

But in the fall after Labor Day, and in the spring before July 1, sites are usually available in all of the parks. Naturalist programs will have been discontinued and some of the more remote coastal roads may be closed, but the crowds will have gone.

Visitors here need few warnings. Come prepared for cool and wet weather. And if you hike on beaches, do not attempt to round rock headlands, particularly on incoming tides. Many promontories cannot be rounded at all. And be aware, too, of the dangers of the surf which has a strong undertow here.

WHERE TO DRIVE

The drive down U.S. 101 from Crescent City to Orick leads through some of the richest coast redwood forests in the West.

Each new turn brings a new grove of towering trees and new opportunities to stop and explore the dozens of short trails just off the highway.

But to add the brilliant views of the ocean and more intimate looks at the redwoods take any of several side trips between the two communities.

Howland Hill Road—No rushing traffic here. Instead, a narrow dirt road which winds quietly among redwoods almost touching trees on either side.

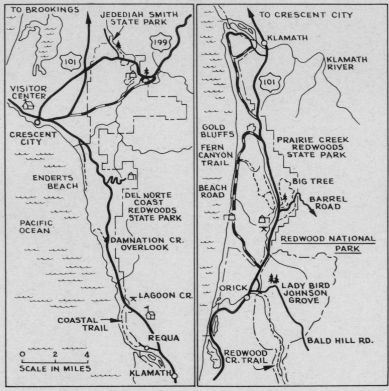

Find this road in Jedediah Smith Redwoods State Park. From the campground entrance, drive east about 1.8 miles turning right at the Stout Grove sign. Cross the river, keeping right again on the other side.

Follow this road past the Stout Grove in about 3 miles (stop and explore the many trails around the famed Stout tree here) and then continue about 6 miles as the road winds and climbs through forest and past open meadows back to the Elk Valley road and Crescent City.

Enderts Beach Road—A short spur with long vistas just south of Crescent City.

Turn west off U.S. 101 about 3 miles southeast of Crescent City driving about 2 miles to the end of the road at a picnic area.

Look back here at the beaches of Crescent City and over still other beaches and rock cliffs to the south.

Coastal Drive—High ocean vistas here from a narrow and twisting road almost directly above the ocean.

To find the road, turn west off Highway 101 onto the Klamath Beach road just across the Klamath River, south of Klamath.

The road, paved to start with, climbs inland and then upward to airplane views down on a rugged, rocky shoreline. Viewpoints and turnouts. Part of an old coastal highway.

Return to U.S. 101 in about 10 miles.

Gold Bluff Beach—Drive along the longest sand beach in northern California past a pretty fern-draped gorge and a waterfall.

To find this road, turn west off U.S. 101 onto the Davidson Road about 3 miles south of the entrance to the Prairie Creek Redwoods State Park. Trailers not allowed.

The gravel road winds inland over a ridge dropping down first to the Bold Bluff Beach Campground and then to Fern Canyon, in 5.7 miles.

Stop here for sure, hiking a quarter-mile or so into a cool, shaded gorge with its cliffs draped with ferns and mosses. Follow the stream bed as far as you want.

From the gorge parking lot, continue another 1.3 miles to Gold Dust Falls, pluming off a cliff in trees to the east of the road.

And stop anywhere else the fancy strikes you to wander several hundred yards over to the Pacific ocean itself. This road may be closed in winter.

Cal-Barrel Road—Just a glimpse here of what these great forests could all look like if they lost the protection they now have.

Turn east off U.S. 101 about .4 miles north of the entrance to Prairie Creek Redwoods State Park.

The road climbs for 3.5 miles through richer and richer forest, leaving the park at the top of the ridge to burst out into a barren logged-over tract. Pretty?

WHERE TO HIKE

The opportunities for short day hikes here are almost limitless. All of the state parks are crossed and recrossed with interesting trails. Only a smattering are listed below.

Jedediah Smith Redwoods State Park—If you camp here, take

any one of several short hikes. From Highway 199, hike around the half-mile Simpson-Reed and Peterson Memorial trail through a prize grove of redwoods. And from the campground, cross the Smith River (summer only) hiking through redwoods, rhododendrons, ferns, mosses, salmon berries and salal to the Stout Grove, another lush stand.

Del Norte Coast Redwoods State Park—Hike 2 miles here to a small ocean beach down a switchback Damnation Creek trail off Highway 101 about 4.3 miles south of the entrance road to Mill Creek Campground.

The trail drops sharply downhill (and climbs back up just as sharply) through groves of redwoods to the beach.

Spend time here prowling tidepools, if you're fortunate enough to arrive on an outgoing tide.

Prairie Creek Redwoods State Park—Dozens of short trails lead off the highway here to stately groves of trees. And several longer trails of more than 4 miles lead from the park headquarters area to

Jedediah Smith State Park

the ocean beach. Obtain a map at park headquarters and plan your own special trip. 55 miles of trail here to explore.

Coastal Trail (Redwood National Park)—Hike 4 miles here from one trailhead to another along a rugged section of ocean coast.

Find the trailhead out of the Lagoon Creek picnic area west of U.S. 101 about 4 miles north of Klamath.

The trail, part of a nature loop to start with, winds around a headland and then climbs south above the ocean, dropping down in about a mile to Hidden Beach and then on to a sea-cave overlook before ending at a Klamath River viewpoint in about 4 miles.

Arrange for transportation. The trail ends on the Requa road off U.S. 101 about 4 miles south of Lagoon Creek. Trail at the end of the road in about 2 miles.

Lady Bird Johnson Grove—Stroll a mile through a grove of prime coastal redwoods named in honor of the wife of President Lyndon B. Johnson.

To reach the trail, turn east off U.S. 101 north of Orick onto the Bald Hill road, driving 2 miles to a trailhead parking area.

Redwoods here plus Douglas fir, rhododendrons, salal, mosses and ferns.

BACKPACKING OPPORTUNITIES

Backpacking opportunities are limited in this heavy use area.

In lands under management of the Redwood National Park, however, overnight trips are possible into the Tall Trees area at the end of an 8.5-mile trail up Redwood Creek. Find the trail about a half-mile off U.S. 101 on the Bald Hill road about a mile north or Orick. Summers only.

Overnight trips are also permitted into the Enderts Beach camp on the ocean at the end of a half-mile trail off the Enderts Beach road (see drives), south of Crescent City. Hardly a backpack trip in the classic sense. But a pleasant place to camp, nonetheless. Only 6 sites.

WHERE TO CAMP

Campgrounds in this area are all within state parks. And visitors planning to camp here during the summer season should obtain reservations before leaving home.

Write for an application from the State Department of Parks and Recreation, 1416 Ninth Street, Sacramento, Calif. 95814. Sites can be reserved up to 90 days in advance.

In addition to the public facilities there are also commercial campgrounds nearby.

Jedediah Smith Redwoods State Park—107 sites on shaded loops in rich redwood forest setting. Piped water. Flush toilets. Showers and laundry. State fee. To reach the campground, turn east off U.S. 101 onto U.S. 199 north of Crescent City. Some sites open all year.

Del Norte Coast Redwoods State Park—145 sites in second growth redwood and alder. Along a creek. Flush toilets. Piped water. Showers. Laundry. State fee. Steep entrance road. Off U.S. 101 south of Crescent City.

Elk Prairie (Prairie Creek Redwoods State Park)—75 sites in redwood forest just off U.S. 101 north of Orick. Watch for elk in meadows near the campground. Nature trail for the blind also nearby. Piped water. Flush toilets. Showers. Laundry. State fee. Some sites open all year.

Gold Bluff (Prairie Creek)—25 sites in an exposed ocean beach setting. Piped water. Flush toilets. Off U.S. 101 on the Davidson-Gold Beach road.

Where to Get Information

For information on this area, write:
    Superintendent
    Redwood National Park
    P.O. Drawer N
    Crescent City, Calif. 95531
For information on state parks, write:
    California Department of
    Parks and Recreation
    P.O. Box 2390
    Sacramento, Calif. 95811

lassen volcanic national park

CLIMB A MOUNTAIN here, for sure, on a trail that leads all the way to the top.

But don't pass up the other features—flower meadows, quiet lakes, vistas and even bubbling, steaming pots of mud and water.

Stay several days.

To reach the area: From I-5 through north central California, turn east at Red Bluff onto State Highway 36, or turn east from Redding on State Highway 44.

Lassen Peak is one of the most active volcanoes in the West. As recently as 1915, for instance, the crater in the peak boiled over spilling hot lava 1000 feet down one side, sparking a huge mudflow that tumbled 20-ton boulders down another, and spewing smoke and dust five miles into the air.

And although the volcano is now quiet, thermal areas around it indicate that it is still alive and that its lassitude may not continue forever.

The park is open all year, however its camping season generally extends from mid-May through October with campgrounds opening as the weather permits and closing with the first snows.

Use is heaviest here during July and August when campgrounds fill almost every day and particularly early on weekends and holidays.

September and October, however, may be the best months for camping here. Although the naturalist programs will have ceased and commercial facilities will have been curtailed, crowds will have disappeared and the weather will generally continue clear.

Temperatures here range in the mild and pleasant range throughout the summer. Daytime temperatures at campground levels average about 70 degrees with nighttime temperatures dropping to about 40 degrees. Temperatures at higher elevations will be cooler, dropping from 3 to 5 degrees in every 1000 feet.

Trails open as the snow melts with low-level trails generally clear by late June. Patches of snow may continue on higher trails, however, until early July.

Hikers here face few problems with the park's hot thermal areas posing the greatest hazard, particularly to children. Water in some of these displays reaches scalding temperatures. Hikers, therefore, should keep off thin crusts near the features and make certain that small children remain under control.

The flower season here can often be spectacular. Beginning in June and reaching a peak in July, it often continues through September with particularly heavy displays on meadows in the Kings Creek area.

The Park Service conducts an extensive naturalist program in the park from mid-June through Labor Day, offering, in addition to the usual campfire programs, all-day and half-day nature walks and hikes. Schedules are posted in campgrounds.

WHERE TO DRIVE

The most scenic drive in this park is the paved north and south road which starts at the Sulphur Works Entrance at the southwest corner and winds more than 29 miles past many of the park's most spectacular features to the Manzanita entrance in the northwest corner.

From the south, starting at the hydrothermal sulphur works, the

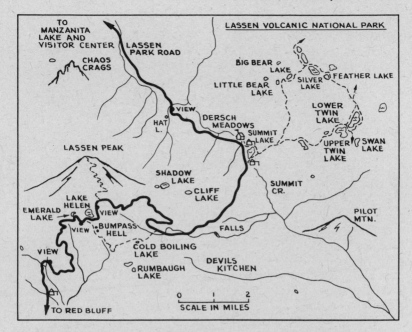

road climbs north past small lakes to the base of Lassen Peak and then on to a series of vista points and mountain flower meadows, reaching Summit Lake in about 17 miles.

From here the road crosses a slope devastated in the 1915 mudflow and past a rock avalanche to the Manzanita Lake complex.

Interest points here are marked with numbered signs keyed to a road guide which can be purchased at visitor information centers.

WHERE TO HIKE

There are more than 150 miles of trails in this park with many of them leading to day-hike destinations. Listed here is a sampling of only a few. Trails are marked with red tags on trees.

Lassen Peak—Climb a mountain! Little more needs to be said. You'll achieve something and you'll know it, that's for certain. A 2.5 mile uphill trudge.

Find the trailhead north off the Lassen Peak parking area, 7.9

miles from the southwest entrance and 21.8 miles from the north-west entrance.

The path here, which starts at 8500 feet and climbs to 10,457 feet, leaves the parking lot climbing upward and never stops until it reaches the top. After a series of long switchbacks past occasional clumps of shading trees (rest under them all) the trail climbs out on completely open slopes and up a series of shorter and shorter switchbacks to the summit.

And start out at a slow pace because you'll certainly end up at one. Carry water, there's none on the trail and don't shortcut any of the switchbacks. Not only is erosion here a problem but falling rock, dislodged on any such attempt, could injure downhill hikers.

At the top, prowl craters to the northwest on informal trails or climb the rock spire which is the official "top" of the peak to the northeast. (However, if you decide not to scramble up these rocks, you'll lose no points—you can still claim you climbed Lassen Peak and don't let anybody tell you differently.)

Vistas here to practically everywhere: North to Mt. Shasta, southerly over the park to Lake Almanor and west toward Redding over the golden hills of California.

And if you get half-way up and decide to turn back, you won't have wasted your time. 360-degree views are reserved for those at the summit, but enroute, increasing vistas from every switchback. And if you're lucky, you may run into a migration of millions of butterflies in the spring.

Bumpass Hell—Hike only 1.5 miles to what could well be the summer home of Macbeth's witches. Certainly the fires burn and the cauldrons bubble.

Find this trail off the Bumpass Hell parking area about 7.1 miles from the southwest entrance or 22.6 miles from the northwest en-trance.

The trail drops off the north side of the parking lot traversing a slope below the highway before climbing upward slightly to a ridge top in about 1 mile.

From here (you can see the steam now and hear the hissing) drop downhill the last half-mile to the middle of the bubbling, steaming, spouting complex of thermal features.

And you'll do more than just see this area. You'll smell it and hear it too. Mud pots burble and burp. Water cauldrons boil and

Craters atop Lassen Peak with Mt. Shasta in distance

bubble. Rock caverns hiss and steam. Wet rock slabs pop, snap and fry. And the whole scene reeks of sulphur. Not all of the features are large. Look too for the small popping and snapping holes, almost raindrop size in some of the rocks.

Stay on the trails. These crusts can break through to scalding water. And do nothing to interrupt the displays.

Return the way you came or continue down the trail to Cold Boiling Lake in about another 1.5 miles.

Cold Boiling Lake—Hike across flower meadows to a bubbling lake. Nothing spectacular, really. But how many lakes do you know that bubble and boil? A .6 mile walk.

To reach this trail, drive to the Kings Creek picnic area south of the main park road about 4 miles southwest of Summit Lake.

Find the trail uphill off the end of the picnic road spur. The trail climbs up this ridge and then wanders along the edge of a meadow system before dropping down to the lake.

Find the "boiling" in the shallow, weedy end of the lake. Cold gasses here bubble out of the earth and up through the water.

This trail can also be reached from Bumpass Hell (see above).

Twin Lakes-Cluster Lake Loop—Spend a day here naming lakes for each of your children and your wife—and maybe even your mother-in-law.

It's an all-day 10-mile walk. But, still, an easy trek.

Find the trail half-way between the north and south campgrounds east of Summit Lake.

The trail starts uphill, climbing steadily to a loop junction in about a mile (look back here at Lassen to the west). Continue straight ahead toward Twin Lakes (you'll come back the other way from Cluster Lakes) dropping first past Echo Lake in 2 miles and then, over a ridge, to the first of two lakes you can name as you please. They have no names on the map.

At 3.5 miles the trail drops over another slight ridge to Upper Twin Lakes and then on to Lower Twin Lake in another half-mile. Don't hurry past either. Prowl the fisherman trails if you have time.

To find the trail to Feather Lake in the Cluster Lake Basin, cross the dike-like outlet of the lower Twin Lake, keeping near the shore, to a junction in a few hundred feet. Turn left (north) here onto an old abandoned road, hiking north about a quarter-mile to a second junction to Feather Lake. Turn left again, hiking past two more tarns you can name arriving at Feather Lake in about another three-quarter mile from the junction.

From Feather Lake the trail winds on to Silver Lake and then to a junction with a trail to Badger Flat. Keep left, continuing first to Big Bear and then to Little Bear lakes.

From Little Bear, the trail now climbs sharply back up the ridge (vistas now north to Mt. Shasta) past another unnamed lake, dropping down in 2.5 miles (views of Lassen again) to the junction with the Twin Lake trail. Turn right, downhill, to the campground.

Start early here. Finish late. And swim enroute in any of the cool, refreshing lakes. You could also extend this trip into an overnight or even a three-day backpack trip. A wilderness permit, however, would be required.

BACKPACKING OPPORTUNITIES

Much of the backcountry in this park has been classified as wilderness and offers excellent opportunities for overnight trips.

Loop trips of several days are also possible from any number of entry points. Study park maps and pick your own on any of the 150 miles of trail.

Permits are required for all wilderness overnight hikes and hikers are urged to defer making any final hiking decisions until they reach the park. Use in some areas may be limited due to heavy human impact.

WHERE TO CAMP

Campgrounds within the park often fill early in the day during the summer season. Entrance stations usually have information on the availability of campsites.

Campers, turned away, can find facilities outside the park in commercial areas west of Manzanita Lake and in National Forest campgrounds both north and south of the park.

Campgrounds within the park which serve the area covered here include:

Manzanita Lake—273 sites on forest loops near but not on the lake. At 5890 feet. Largest campground in the park. Flush toilets. Piped water. Near Manzanita Lake in the northwest corner of the park.

Summlt Lake—94 sites on loops both north and south of the lake. None on the water. At 6695 feet. Flush toilets. Piped water. 12 miles from Manzanita Lake and 17.5 miles from Sulphur Works Entrance.

Sulphur Works—25 walk-in sites for tent campers off a parking area near the Sulphur works entrance. Shady timber sites. At 6700 feet. Flush toilets. Piped water.

There are other campgrounds on other entry roads around the park.

Where to Get Information

For information on the park, write:

Superintendent
Lassen Volcanic National Park
Mineral, Calif. 96063

desolation wilderness

HIGH, BARREN AND harsh country this. But beautiful nonetheless. Dotted with lakes. Patched with flowers and scattered with gnarled, windblown trees.

Camp here. But hike for sure.

To reach the area: To reach Wrights Lake, center of activities covered here, drive east from Sacramento on U.S. 50 turning north onto the gravel Wrights Lake forest service road 5 miles east of the village of Kyburz. Find the lake in about 8 miles.

This area is part of the Crystal Basin recreation complex of the Eldorado National Forest and at the edge of the Desolation Wilderness which embraces most of the high Crystal Range, west of Lake Tahoe. The region is also part of the Sacramento Municipal Utility District watershed.

The camping and hiking season at the higher elevations here usually begins as the snow melts early in July and continues until the snow falls in early October.

Campground use is heaviest here on weekends and holidays

during the summer peak periods. But campers should have little trouble finding space, even at Wrights Lake, during the midweek period beginning Sunday night and ending Friday morning.

Trails are also busiest on weekends with fewer hikers in the middle of the week.

Although the weather is generally good here from mid-July through mid-October, September is rated as one of the best months to visit the backcountry. The crowds are all gone then and the crisp days make every outing enjoyable. Snowstorms don't usually begin until October.

Summer temperatures in the high country range from daytime highs in the 70s to freezing and below at night. Thunderstorms are not uncommon but they do not occur with regularity and seldom pass through at night.

Good hiking shoes are essential here. Also carry a compass and a topographic map. Forest Service maps will not give you the type of information you'll need to follow these sketchy, barren trails.

The Forest Service offers no naturalist programs here. For information stop at the ranger station east of Pollock Pines.

WHERE TO DRIVE

View drives here are confined to logging roads and most of them wend through forest and down canyons with very few views out or up.

But for vistas down on the twisting American River Canyon drive west from the Wrights Lake road or the Granite Springs road to a series of viewpoints from the top of that ridge.

To find the views turn west off the Wrights Lake road about 3 miles south of the lake following the forest road on to the Ice House Reservoir in about 14 miles.

WHERE TO HIKE

The country here is spectacular. Different from any other in this book. But it's not easy to hike in. And not because the terrain is difficult. But because the Forest Service here makes little—and in some cases, no—effort to maintain its wilderness trails. (See backpacking opportunities.)

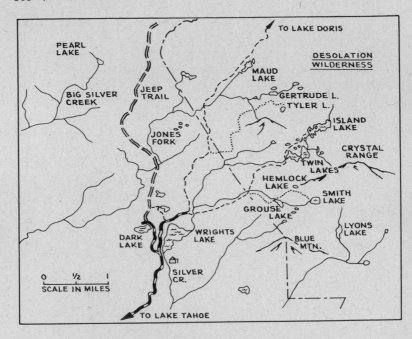

A few of the main arterials in the wilderness, used by commercial horse packers and local horsemen, are generally maintained each year. But others may not be maintained. And without either signs or cairns, to mark even junctions, many of the trails are impossible to follow at all.

Listed here are two into the Desolation Wilderness that are generally maintained but still may pose difficulties to the amateur hiker. Wilderness permits are required, even for day hikers.

Maud Lake—Hike over high barren slabs of rock to a small lake etched in granite. 3.6 miles.

This is one of the few trails on this side of the wilderness which is regularly maintained.

To reach the trail take the middle fork road at the Wrights Lake entrance driving through the campground on the left (west) side of the lake, bearing right at the end of the campground on a rough road that climbs behind a series of leased homesites to end in forest at an undeveloped parking area. Or, park in the meadow before reaching the campground, walking to the trailhead.

Find the trail off the end of the road, to the left. It's signed as the Willow Flat Trail.

The path starts out fairly level through forest but soon begins climbing up rock slabs marked with cairns and occasional blazes to a high rock plateau in about a mile, reaching a junction with trail to Tyler Lake in 1.4 miles.

From this junction, the trail climbs now to a crossing of Silver Creek and then up steadily from one flat spot to another arriving at the lake in another 2.2 miles.

No towering peaks here and no spectacular vistas. But beauty still is what is truly a desolation of rocks, knobs and rugged terrain.

Find a patch of heather, sprawl out in the sun and enjoy the many inlets and islets on this pretty lake. No camping within 100 feet of the lake.

Twin and Island Lakes—Cool lakes here tossed amongst islands of rock below barren granite slopes.

An adventure hike, truly, for the way is not always clear. And if you can't find the trail and don't have a topographic map, turn back.

To reach this trail drive to the end of the parking road (see above) finding the path off the end of the road to the right. It's signed as the Twin Lakes Trail.

The path starts out in forest around the edge of a meadow and past an old homestead before starting up a series of rock ledges, climbing sharply at the end of a mile to the border of the wilderness.

The trail now cuts through timber for a short way, crossing a creek and climbing out again onto barren rocks.

Take particular care now. The mountainside is littered with cairns, left by hikers apparently marking their own way up to other lakes.

The main trail, however, is generally marked with rows of stones and by circular ray-shaped pock marks dynamited in the rock. Plus cairns, too.

And pay close attention to the ground around you. Look up for long and you'll find yourself off the trail.

Generally, however, the trail makes its way to a saddle and then down past waterfalls and wind blown trees to the outlet of Twin Lakes.

Explore here if you have time enough. The second of the twin lakes lies to the right. Otherwise, cross the outlet below the first lake—watch for blazes on the trees—following the trail now along the left side of the lower lake as it climbs sharply up a series of rock terraces to the next level of lakes.

At Boomerang Lake, a small tarn shaped just like its name, follow the trail right, alongside the tarn, crossing its inlet and then turning sharply right, staying in the bottom of the draw and picking up the trail as it switchbacks up a ridge ahead to the Island Lake.

And Island Lake is just what you'd expect. A network of rock tarns, laced with heather islands at the base of a barren mountain cirque.

BACKPACKING OPPORTUNITIES

There are more than 75 miles of trails within the Desolation Wilderness. But the standard of maintenance on them is entirely

Maud Lake

different than that in other wilderness covered in this book.

Where trail signs are maintained in the other areas, they are not maintained here, particularly on the spur trail system. And where primitive sanitary facilities are being installed in heavy-use sites elsewhere, those which already existed here have been removed.

Forest officials in this area—there does not appear to be any national policy—interpret the federal wilderness laws as requiring the elimination of *all* signs of man. And they indicate that in an effort to control use they plan only to maintain major arterial trails for hikers and horse packers.

Foot trails to side-area lakes, popular with backpackers, will not be maintained. As signs fall down they will be removed. Some of the trails will even be eliminated from maps. And hikers, if they wish to visit these areas at all, must navigate their trips with the aid of topographic maps.

Old trails here do not have an established tread as they do elsewhere. Most of the paths here cross solid rock. So once signs or cairns are removed the trail all but disappears.

As indicated, other forests do not follow these policies and many conservation and wilderness groups do not advocate them either. So when you hike here, wonder if Congress, in creating the wilderness, really intended to endorse this type of non-maintenance, non-management, and whether this is the best, or only, way to control use, particularly at a time when there is a growing need for more, not less, backcountry hiking space. And wonder as you hike if you would meet more or fewer people on the main trails if there were more side trails which could be followed and hiked.

Wilderness permits are required here whether for day or overnight hikes. They may be obtained at the Forest Service office east of Pollock Pines either in person or by mail. And carry a stove. Wood is scarce and almost sacred throughout this wilderness.

And, of course, treat the entire area with care.

WHERE TO CAMP

Camping here is confined to Wrights Lake although there is also a lower elevation campground, at Sly Park, five miles south of Pollock Pines.

Wrights Lake—80 sites on two forested loops, one west and one south of the lake. Open from July until the snow falls. None of the sites is on the lake although some on the west side are oriented toward the water. Well-spaced, pleasant camps. Pit toilets. Piped water.

Sly Park—300 sites on a series of loops near but not on Jenkinson Lake, a reservoir. Open March to November. A busy area. Pit toilets. Piped water. This camp is operated by an irrigation district. Daily fee.

Where to Get Information

For information on this area, write:
  District Ranger
  Pacific Ranger District
  Eldorado National Forest
  Pollock Pines, Calif. 95726

point reyes
national seashore

AN UNLIKELY—BUT spectacular—mixture here of high rolling farm lands; sandy ocean beaches, dunes and sheer rock cliffs.

Geologically, the point is an island separated from mainland California by the San Andreas Fault, the notorious earthquake centerline that extends down the northern California coast.

But scenically, it's a rare artist's mixture of brilliant ocean and soft pastorals.

Drive to see much of the splendors here. But hike to more exclusive views.

To reach the area: From U.S. 101, between San Francisco and Santa Rosa, turn west to State Highway 1.

Dairy and beef farmers still pasture the high grasslands within this seashore area. More than 6000 animals graze here every year.

But the Swiss-like mixture of agriculture and recreation detracts not at all from the beauty of the seashore. Drive and hike here, but carefully, remembering that much of the area is still in private management.

305

Seashore facilities are open here all year. But the best time to visit, either to hike for a day or backpack into one of the seashore backcountry camps is probably midweek after Labor Day through late September and early October.

Summer fogs and drizzles chill the landscape and blot out the ocean views from May through June and sometimes into early July.

And once local schools are out use becomes heavy all the time with particularly severe impacts on weekends and holidays. Oddly, however, the point is seldom overrun despite the fact it is so close to San Francisco. The restricted capacity of the Golden Gate Bridge appears to limit the number of persons able to head north here on heavy travel days.

Temperatures here range on the cool side even during the summer with daytime highs averaging in the 60s and nighttime lows around 50 degrees on the coast. And although fogs are common it seldom rains during the midsummer period.

Birds are one of the peninsula's added attractions with more than 300 species identified here. Note particularly the ubiquitous turkey buzzards which soar over all of the high meadows.

The flower season gets underway in February and lasts through July. Watch particularly for the variety of colorful lupines which grow on the higher ridges. The colors range from yellow, through blue to almost green at times.

Hikers should bring warm clothing even in midsummer. Evenings are cool and chilly sea breezes are common. Visitors are also warned not to climb on the high cliffs. They not only can be, but are, extremely treacherous. Be aware too of the dangers of tide and surf when hiking on beaches or over seashore rocks.

Confine your exploration to public lands. And inland, stay on trails particularly in brushy areas to avoid poison oak.

In the summer, the Park Service presents evening campfire programs in the headquarters area. Other activities are also scheduled from headquarters during the summer. Schedules are posted there.

WHERE TO DRIVE AND WALK

Spectacular driving country here. High views out over the ocean from grass, pasture ridges green in the spring and golden in the summer.

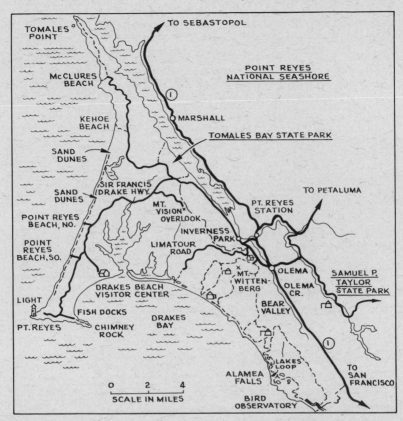

TO SEBASTOPOL

TOMALES POINT

McCLURES BEACH

POINT REYES NATIONAL SEASHORE

MARSHALL

TOMALES BAY STATE PARK

KEHOE BEACH

SAND DUNES

SIR FRANCIS DRAKE HWY.

SAND DUNES

MT. VISION OVERLOOK

TO PETALUMA

PT. REYES STATION

POINT REYES BEACH, NO.

INVERNESS PARK

LIMATOUR ROAD

POINT REYES BEACH, SO.

MT. WITTEN-BERG

OLEMA

SAMUEL P. TAYLOR STATE PARK

OLEMA CR.

DRAKES BEACH VISITOR CENTER

LIGHT

BEAR VALLEY

FISH DOCKS

DRAKES BAY

PT. REYES

CHIMNEY ROCK

LAKES LOOP

ALAMEA FALLS

TO SAN FRANCISCO

0   2   4
SCALE IN MILES

BIRD OBSERVATORY

Drive the full length of the Sir Francis Drake Highway which winds 19 miles from Inverness Park and then take the side trips and short walks too.

Tomales Bay State Park—Drive through groves of Bishop pines to views out over Tomales Bay to the mainland.

Turn north off the Sir Francis Drake Highway about 6 miles from the junction with Highway 1 and then right again in another mile into the state park.

Lots of places to picnic on high slopes and look out over the Bay. Or follow the winding road to water level at Hearts Desire Beach to prowl beaches there.

McClure's Beach—A small sand cove here guarded at either end by headlands and cliffs.

To reach this area, drive to the end of the Pierce Point road about 8.5 miles beyond the entrance to the state park (see above). Park at the end of the road and then hike about a quarter-mile downhill to the beach.

Explore tide pools here in the headland rocks at low tide.

To hike out along ridges to the north, take a path uphill from the parking lot walking along the ridge tops as far as you want. Tomales Point in about 5 miles.

Point Reyes—Cliff views down onto sea lion rocks and out across San Francisco Bay.

To reach the point, drive about 20 miles from Highway 1 looping first to the west and then back to the south to the end of the road just east of the Point Reyes Lighthouse, which is closed to the public and cannot be seen from within the park.

Stop at the end of the spur road (right) and roam the high cliffs, watching sea lions with binoculars. These are steep cliffs. Use care, and stay behind railings.

Chimney Rock Overlook—Climb a ridge to views out at Chimney Rock and back over Drakes Bay.

To reach this trail, turn left (east) off the main highway (see Point Reyes) at the point where the highway turns right to reach the cliff vista points. The road drops through a farm lot—avoid all cows—past a rail fenced parking area in about a mile.

Park there and find the trail to the right beyond a trail sign, hiking about three-quarter mile to an overlook at the end of the ridge.

North Beach and South Beach—Drive down short spur roads to developed picnic areas on sandy ocean beaches.

Turn west to North Beach about 5.5 miles from the Tomales Bay park turnoff and to South Beach in 8.3 miles.

Hike away from the crowds in any direction to find privacy on a sand dune of your own. Don't play in the surf. The undertow is treacherous.

Drake's Beach—Stop at the Visitor Center here with your questions and then roam beaches just off the parking area.

To reach this, turn east off the highway in 7.8 mile from the Tomales Bay Park turnoff.

Mt. Vision Viewpoint—Follow a gravel road to high vistas down on Drakes Estero and out over the ocean from Mt. Vision at 1282 feet.

McClure's Beach

Turn south off the main highway about 1 mile beyond the Tomales Park junction driving about 4 miles to higher and higher and broader and broader vistas of farms, cliffs, lakes and beaches.

Limantour Road—Walk an ocean beach. Or better yet bring a bird book and spend the afternoon identifying water birds.

Drive north from the seashore headquarters on the Bear Valley road, turning west in 1.3 miles onto the Limantour road, driving to the end near the beach in 7.6 miles.

Prowl beaches on Limantour spit or watch the birds in marshes both east and west of the road. A research natural area. So disturb nothing at all.

WHERE TO HIKE

Hike here to ocean beaches, lakes and even low-level mountains on trails that wind through forest, brush and sand.

The Bear Valley area of the seashore is devoted almost exclusively to hiker use. Backpacking is permitted (see backpacking opportunities) but most of the features can be explored on a day-hike basis.

And carry water on all hikes. Surface water may be contaminated.

Mt. Wittenberg—Hike through forest and over meadows to the highest point in the seashore preserve—Mt. Wittenberg at 1407 feet.

Find the trail out of a parking lot beyond the headquarters area. Cross a meadow and then turn right in a few hundred yards onto the Sky Trail, climbing steadily now through pleasant forest to a junction with the Mt. Wittenberg trail in about 1.2 mile.

From the junction, the path switchbacks up open slopes to vistas north toward Tomales Bay and south and west to the ocean. No single viewpoint here. Just wander the meadows looking first one way and then the other.

Either return the way you came or drop over the mountain to the west, bearing left to a junction with the Meadow Trail, returning to the parking lot.

Bear Valley Trail—Hike a gradually graded trail to the ocean. 4.4 miles.

Take the Bear Valley trail from the headquarters parking area following the heavily traveled path first through forest and then through brush and grass to the ocean.

For a loop trip, hike north on the trail above the beach about a half mile returning to the headquarters area on the Sky trail in a little more than 4 miles.

Others—Obtain a park map and plan any of several day loop trips throughout this area. There are nearly 70 miles of easy trails to choose from.

BACKPACKING OPPORTUNITIES

Camping in this seashore area is confined to backpacking camps. But you'll need to get a reservation.

The Park Service maintains four backcountry camp spots on trails within the Bear Valley complex. Hikers who want to camp there must obtain reservations either at the seashore headquarters or by mail and telephone. Reservations are accepted up to 90 days in advance and must be picked up in person.

Use here is heaviest on weekends and holidays with most sites reserved several weeks in advance.

No fee is presently levied for reservations.

And carry your own fuel. No wood fires are permitted.

Camps within the seashore area include:

Sky Camp—2.8 miles by trail on the western slope of Mt. Wittenberg with views of Drake Bay and Point Reyes.

Glen Camp—4.5 miles by trail. In a wooded valley. 2.5 miles from the ocean.

Coast Camp—8 miles by trail. In a grassy hollow above the ocean.

Wildcat Camp—7 miles by trail in a grassy meadow near Wildcat beach. A group camp.

Each camp has piped water and toilet facilities.

WHERE TO CAMP

There are no vehicle camping facilities within the national seashore. However, there are commercial and state park facilities nearby.

The state park is generally busy during the summer season. Sites, however, can be reserved. Applications for reservations can be obtained from the State Department of Parks and Recreation, 1417 Ninth Street, Sacramento, Calif. 94814, or within the state through a special computerized (Ticketron) system.

Samuel P. Taylor State Park—72 sites on pleasant redwood forest loops. Some near creek. There are a number of hiking trails on the river and to viewpoints in the park. Flush toilets. Piped water. Showers. State fee. 6 miles southeast of seashore headquarters on the Sir Frances Drake Highway. Drive south from the seashore a half-mile to Olema, turning uphill to the east.

Where to Get Information

For information on the national seashore, write:
            Superintendent
            Point Reyes National Seashore
            Point Reyes, Calif. 94956

tuolumne meadows (yosemite national park)

WHEN CALIFORNIANS RAVE about the High Sierras, here's one of the better reasons why.

A mountain paradise of towering, gray rock domes, craggy peaks, brilliant crystal lakes, twisted weathered trees, and colorful flower-crammed meadows.

If you stop no other place in the High Sierras, spend a few days in this area.

And it's nothing at all like the camping scene in Yosemite Valley to the south. Most of the people here come to enjoy the mountains, not each other.

How to reach the area: From I-5 or U.S. 99, turn east on State Highway 120 north of Modesto, continuing into Yosemite National Park. From U.S. 395 through eastern California, turn west from Lee Vining at Mono Lake.

The Tioga road, open only in the summer, climbs into the very heart of the high country in this great park. The valley with its waterfalls and domes gets the heaviest use and the greatest publicity. But the visitor to this area will experience the truth of the Sierras and appreciate the vastness of this high world of granite and ice.

The camping and hiking season here is relatively short, opening and closing with the high-elevation snows. The campgrounds generally don't open before the end of May, closing in September and October, with the high trails remaining clogged by snow a little longer and closing down a little sooner.

Area use is heaviest, as you'd expect, during the midsummer months with the greatest impact on weekends and holidays. So, therefore, camp, drive or hike midweek and avoid the crowds. Campgrounds here cannot be reserved.

As in many areas, the post-Labor Day period may be one of the best times to visit. The weather will be cooler, particularly at night, but the crowds will have gone and finding a campsite will no longer be a problem.

The park weather is at its best during late summer when it seldom rains at all. However, good weather often continues until October. Summer daytime temperatures range into the low 70s and higher dropping occasionally to freezing at night, even in midsummer.

Thunderstorms are not uncommon during the summer, raging over the mountains periodically every week. Hikers are warned to stay off exposed ridges whenever a storm develops.

Campers face no particular problems here. Warm clothing, of course, is essential and suntan lotion is probably necessary when hiking at this high altitude on bright, sunny days.

The elevation of these trails, all over 8500 feet, may cause some low-elevation residents a problem for a day ot two. If you find yourself short of breath—which will be likely—simply slow down and take your time.

The Park Service offers interpretive programs here throughout the summer. Campfire programs are conducted nightly at the Tuolumne Meadows Campground. Auto caravans and hikes are also scheduled periodically throughout the summer. Inquire at the Visitor Center for a schedule.

WHERE TO DRIVE

Once you arrive at these meadows, you will have already driven through some of the most spectacular scenery in the park, no matter which way you made the trip.

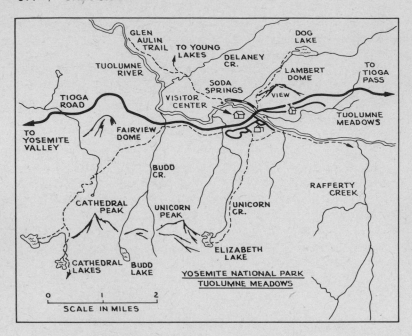

GLEN
AULIN
TRAIL   TO YOUNG
LAKES

DOG
LAKE

TUOLUMNE
RIVER

DELANEY
CR.

LAMBERT
DOME

TO
TIOGA
PASS

TIOGA
ROAD

SODA
SPRINGS

VISITOR
CENTER

VIEW

FAIRVIEW
DOME

TUOLUMNE
MEADOWS

TO
YOSEMITE
VALLEY

BUDD
CR.

RAFFERTY
CREEK

CATHEDRAL
PEAK

UNICORN
PEAK

UNICORN
CR.

CATHEDRAL
LAKES

BUDD
LAKE

ELIZABETH
LAKE

YOSEMITE NATIONAL PARK
TUOLUMNE MEADOWS

0   1   2
SCALE IN MILES

But don't stop now. If you came from the west, over the high pla-teaus past Tenaya Lake, continue now on to the east climbing to Tioga Pass at 9941 feet, the highest auto pass in the state. The road leaves the park then and drops down sharply through a rugged canyon to Lee Vining and Mono Lake.

If you entered the park from the east, continue westward across the high glaciated rock country around Tenaya Lake, past a series of formal viewpoints with vistas far off to the south.

Continue on this road down into the valley if you'd like to join the crowded, carnival atmosphere there. Scenery too. But it's some-times difficult to see—or at least appreciate—through all the peo-ple. From Tuolumne Meadows, about 55 miles.

WHERE TO HIKE

The trails listed here barely sample this spectacular country and if you can afford the time, stay and hike the many others in this area.

The trails are all easy to follow. "T" blazes on trees along these trails were first used by the army early in the century. And the "T" doesn't mean anything as nice as Tioga or Tuolumne. It simply means trail. Ugh.

Elizabeth Lake—Hike to a pretty horseshoe shaped lake with peaks towering from 10,000 feet above it. 2.3 miles.

Find the trail off the end of the campground spur road along the west side of the Tuolumne River on the east side of the campground.

The trail continues off the end of the road, forking uphill to the right in about 25 yards and then traversing through forest about a half-mile to another trail from the campground.

From this junction, the trail continues south (left) climbing sharply at times and not so sharply at others, crossing several streams and then leveling out in open forest and through increasingly open meadows to the lake.

Camping along the north and east shores of the lake. By permit, however. Wander the shores for constantly changing vistas.

Cathedral Lakes—A pair of high slab-and-boulder bound lakes at 9350 feet below the spires of Cathedral Peak. 3.5 miles.

Find this trail out of a parking area on the south side of the Tioga road 1.7 miles west of the Tuolumne Meadows Visitor center. You can also hike to this junction on a spur trail that follows the highway from the campground.

The trail starts out climbing relatively sharply over a knoll, dropping down to cross several creeks in about 1.5 miles. Now, the path climbs less steeply over another knoll and then more gradually through a blackened, ghost forest, killed by an insect infestation, to a junction with the trail to the first lake at 3 miles.

To visit the first lake, turn right dropping through a maize of boulders along a creek to the most beautiful meadows in this area. Pause here to follow the meandering streams, watch for darting trout, look back at Cathedral Peaks and wonder at the flowers.

Find the lake—just as spectacular—on the other side of the meadows: Rock slabs along an entire shore and note, too, the huge boulders dumped atop them by some ancient glacier.

To reach the second lake, return to the junction and hike uphill again through soggy meadows about a half-mile watching for the lake on the right. Prowl the small inlets here too before returning.

Dog Lake—Take a shaded afternoon walk to a pretty forested lake with mountains peaking over the end. 1.3 miles.

To reach this trail, drive or walk to the Lembert Dome Picnic area north of the highway just east of the Tuolumne River bridge. Find the trail off the left (west) side of the parking area, near the road.

The trail parallels this spur road a short distance, passing a meadow to the right. Just beyond the meadow, watch for a trail to the right uphill—it's sometimes marked with an arrow. The way now climbs relatively sharply but irregularly to the lake.

Picnic here. More meadows to explore. But no fires or camping.

Lembert Dome—A sharp 1.2 mile climb to the top of a glaciated dome which towers 800 feet above the surrounding meadows.

Find the trail from the Lembert Dome Picnic area (see above) along the west base of the dome, following it along the north side as it climbs to something of a saddle on the east. Here make your way across the rock itself to vistas at the top.

Cathedral Peak above Cathedral Lake

Take care here. For both yourself and others. First, don't roll any rocks downhill. There may be other hikers and climbers below. And second, don't try to hike down the side of the dome. Return the way you came. These slopes are much steeper than they look and fall off sharply at the bottom.

BACKPACKING OPPORTUNITIES

This is the heart of Yosemite backpacking country. From these meadows, trails fan in every direction into the park's backcountry. And with one great advantage over the valley: Many tend to go down instead of up.

All overnight backpackers must obtain wilderness permits. The park, however, has not yet adopted a reservation program limiting the number of hikers.

And carry a stove. Wood here is generally scarce and the existing wood should be left for others to see. Bears can often be a problem too, particularly in heavy use areas. Carry your food in plastic bags and hang it high above the ground between trees.

A park concessionaire operates a circle of backcountry camps for hikers from July 4 to Labor Day. However, reservations must be made before the hiker starts his trip. Fees include bed, dinner and breakfast.

WHERE TO CAMP

Campgrounds here are generally less crowded than those in the valley. However, most camps will fill each day during the summer season with the heaviest use on weekends and holidays. None of the camps in this section of the park can presently be reserved through the nationwide reservation system.

Tuolumne Meadows—600 sites on forest loops on hillside near but not on the meadows. Pleasant camping. Flush toilets. Piped water.

Tenaya Lake—50 sites, some of them on the lake shore. All are walk-in tent camps. Park in a parking area and pack your gear 50 to 200 yards. A beautiful camp. Fantastic views. But lots of mosquitos in early summer. Flush toilets. Piped water. About 9 miles west of Tuolumne Meadows.

Porcupine Flat—50 sites in a primitive camp off the Tioga road 6.5 miles west of Tenaya Lake. Pit toilets. Stream water.

Porcupine Creek—10 sites in a primitive camp. 6 miles west of Tenaya Lake. Pit toilets. Stream water.

Where to Get Information

For information on this area, write:
>   Superintendent
>   Yosemite National Park
>   Box 577
>   Yosemite National Park, Calif. 95389

yosemite valley

ALL OF THE grand rock domes and towering waterfalls are still here—just as they have been pictured in the great studies by photographer, Ansel Adams.

But in addition now—unfortunately—mobs!

And unless you hike away from it all, it's much more of a social than a scenic scene.

But stop here for a short time anyway. John Muir thought it was beautiful. And it still is. You simply have to ignore your fellow men.

To reach the area: From Fresno, drive north on State Highway 41; from Merced, drive east on State Highway 140; from Modesto, enter via State Highway 120, and from the east, over the Tioga Road.

The great tragedy of this beautiful place is people. On the busiest days 20,000 crowd into the valley alone and many of them come, not to enjoy the great spectacles of nature, but simply to look at each other.

So let's be candid: Elbow to elbow people. Mobs of bicycles.

319

Rivers full of rafts and innertubes. Guitars on every corner and under every tree. And campgrounds at night choked, literally, with campfire smoke, and radios.

One of the park's few saving graces, aside from the spectacle of the mountains, is the free shuttle bus system designed to move all of these people around. Park your car and ride. Busses run every few minutes to most points and trailheads in the valley.

Some camping facilities remain open in the valley all year but most of the camps don't open until spring, closing in the fall.

The park is busiest from Memorial Day through Labor Day— the park gets half of all its visitors then—and campgrounds are full most of the time. Reservations therefore are essential if you plan to visit then.

The fall of the year, after Labor Day, is probably the best time to visit the valley. The weather is generally still pleasant. The trails remain open. And best of all, most of the people have gone. However, some years the waterfalls may dry up between July and October.

The weather in the park is at its best during the summer. Rains taper off in April and May reaching April levels again in November. August is the driest month.

Temperatures in the valley range from pleasant in the spring and fall to warm in midsummer. Spring temperatures range from 75 to 37 degrees, while summer temperatures range into the 90s and down to the 50s. September and October temperatures average about 55 to 65 degrees.

Lightning storms rage over the park during the summer on an average of twice a week. But they last only a short period. Hikers on bare ridges above the valley are warned to retreat to lower levels at the first sign of such storms.

Bears are probably the park's biggest nuisance to campers. Keep all food locked up in the trunk of your car and make certain none is ever put in your tent.

No particular clothing is required here although warm jackets are needed at night.

The Park Service here offers one of the most extensive programs in the West—everything from demonstrations of blacksmithing to star-gazing programs.

Evening programs are also presented throughout the park. A

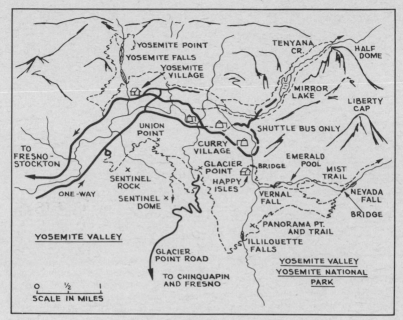

YOSEMITE POINT
YOSEMITE FALLS
YOSEMITE VILLAGE

TENYANA CR.
HALF DOME

MIRROR LAKE

LIBERTY CAP

UNION POINT

SHUTTLE BUS ONLY

TO FRESNO-STOCKTON

CURRY VILLAGE

GLACIER POINT

BRIDGE

EMERALD POOL

MIST TRAIL

SENTINEL ROCK

HAPPY ISLES

ONE-WAY

SENTINEL DOME

VERNAL FALL

NEVADA FALL

BRIDGE

YOSEMITE VALLEY

PANORAMA PT. AND TRAIL

GLACIER POINT ROAD

ILLILOUETTE FALLS

TO CHINQUAPIN AND FRESNO

YOSEMITE VALLEY
YOSEMITE NATIONAL PARK

0   ½   1
SCALE IN MILES

schedule of events can be obtained at entrance stations or visitor centers.

WHERE TO DRIVE

One can see most of the classic valley scenes from the loop road in the Valley. Printed guides will even tell you where to stop and take your pictures.

Every visitor should make at least one trip around the valley loop just to get an idea of what it's all about. But for better vistas with less people, try other roads.

Glacier Point—Drive to airplane views down on Yosemite Village and out at Half-Dome and other peaks in the High Sierras.

From the Valley drive toward State Highway 41 on the Wawona Road, turning east at Chinquapin, driving 16 miles to the end of the road at 7,214 feet, nearly 3000 feet above the valley floor.

And don't hurry. The road passes a series of flower meadows before reaching the high vistas. And at the end of the road take time to walk to the formal vista points for the biggest views.

Tioga Road—Set aside a full day here and drive about 100 miles to Tuolumne Meadows and back through some of the most spectacular high country in the West.

Drive west out of the Valley on Highway 120 toward Stockton, turning north onto the Tioga Road in 10 miles.

The road now climbs up through forest to a barren, glaciated slab-rock country typical of this section of the Sierras.

Viewpoints along the way identify the peaks and lakes which string out along the road. Take lunch and, if available, a full tank of gasoline. No service stations between Crane Flat and Tuolumne during the summer. The Tuolumne station closes in early fall.

And drive midweek if you can. Weekend traffic can get heavy. The road generally doesn't open until late May or June usually closing in early November.

WHERE TO HIKE

Hiking is the only way to escape crowds. And there's one basic rule. The higher you hike the fewer people you'll meet, even if you start from a road at the top and walk down.

Most of the Valley trails here are paved. And signs are punched out of steel plate.

Glacier Point-Happy Isles—Drop downhill—which is the only way to go—from the grand vista atop Glacier Point past three waterfalls to the valley. An 8.7 mile one-way hike.

Find the trail from Glacier Point off the road into the parking area just before it loops downhill. Watch for a sign on the uphill side of the road.

The trail climbs over the rim and then starts steadily downhill in timber with occasional views out toward Giant Stairway, Half-Dome and Liberty Cap.

At 1.4 miles turn left at a junction with the Buena Vista trail and continue downhill to a view of Illilouette Falls through trees before crossing the creek above the falls in .6 miles.

From the creek the trail now climbs into the open past Panorama Point with its view straight down into the valley and on to a junction (still in the open) with the Mono Point trail. Keep to the left again as the trail drops into timber and switchbacks sharply downhill to a view of Nevada Falls and Liberty Cap through the trees.

Bus below Yosemite Falls

At a junction in a mile with the Merced Lake Trail, turn right for a short walk to the top of Nevada Falls—and the crowds again.

From here, either continue across the river above the falls about .2 mile to a junction with the Mist Trail, or return to the Merced Lake trail, to find your way down to Vernal Falls.

The Mist trail switchbacks sharply down alongside Nevada Falls and past Vernal Falls to the Vernal Falls bridge in 1.9 miles. The Merced Lake trail makes the trip more gradually in 2.7 miles with fewer glimpses of Nevada Falls and views of Vernal Falls from a short spur trail.

From the Vernal Falls bridge, the paved trail drops above the river to the Happy Isles Trail Center and the valley loop road. Catch a shuttle back to camp. No autos are permitted in this area.

Four Mile Trail—Hike uphill here if you must, but downhill if you can, between Glacier Point and the valley. 4.6 miles either way but it will seem like 10 if you try going up.

Find this trail at Glacier Point (see drives) behind the tourist facilities there. The trail starts downhill instantly and seldom stops. It's not a steep trail. But going down don't expect to spend much time walking up and if you hike up, don't expect to walk down.

But the vistas seldom cease. Views across the valley at El Capitan, both the upper and lower Yosemite Falls and all of the valley village and road complex. And at the start, vistas down the entire Tenaya Canyon with Half Dome too.

Arrange to be picked up at the bottom. Or better yet, catch a bus.

Yosemite Falls—Climb to the top of Yosemite Falls and then back down again. 3.5 miles one way.

Find this trail off a parking area near the Sunnyside Campground just west of Yosemite Lodge. Trailhead is marked with a sign.

The trail starts out climbing in timber to a vista point at 5000 feet in 1.4 miles and then on to the base of the falls in another .7 miles.

From here, the trail switchbacks up a brushy side-canyon to a junction with the Yosemite Point trail at the end of 3.2 miles. Turn right dropping down a series of stairs for an overview in .3 mile.

BACKPACKING OPPORTUNITIES

A number of extended backcountry trips are possible from trails starting either in the valley or from Glacier Point, above the valley.

None will be suggested here. Campers interested should purchase trail guides from the Yosemite Natural History Association.

Backpackers must obtain wilderness permits for all overnight hikes, prior to leaving on trips. Backpackers with stoves can camp anywhere. Those wishing to build campfires, however, must camp in designated sites.

High trails here are generally open from early July through September or October, depending on the weather.

WHERE TO CAMP

Any persons planning to camp in the valley during the rush season should make advance registrations through National Park Service nationwide reservation system.

Not all sites in the valley are reserved. But the chances of getting one in competition with others is remote. The park maintains other camps, generally less crowded, outside the valley. And campers can find commercial facilities in nearby communities.

All of the campsites in the valley are on crowded loops in open forest. All are served with flush toilets and piped water. Showers and laundry facilities are available from concessionaires.

Sunnyside—55 sites. A quarter mile east of Yosemite Lodge.

Lower River—152 sites. A trailer-pickup camper campground only. No tents. On Merced River north of Curry Village.

Upper River—212 sites. Tent only. Along the Merced River north of Curry Village.

Upper Pines—239 sites in forest near Happy Isles.

North Pines—150 sites, near the stables. On the Merced River.

Lower Pines—250 sites, some on the river. Northeast of Curry Village.

Where to Get Information

For information on the park, write:
> Superintendent
> Yosemite National Park
> P.O. Box 577
> Yosemite National Park, Calif. 95389

mammoth lakes

WALK HERE ON the roof of the world.

Roads end at 9000 feet and trails seldom drop below 10,000 feet as they climb over high ridges and barren plateaus to vistas and lakes.

Cool country. Crisp country. Brilliant country, too.

To reach the area: Drive north from Bishop, Calif., or south from Carson City, Nevada, on U.S. 395, turning west on California State Highway 203 north of Crowley Lake.

The Mammoth Lakes Recreation Area is part of the Inyo National Forest, one of the prime recreation forests on the east side of the Sierra Nevada mountains.

A popular ski resort in winter. Most of the small community, in fact, is built around skiing. But in the summer, attention turns to camping at the lakes and hiking in the John Muir—Minarets Wilderness.

This area is generally its busiest during the peak of the vacation season in August when campgrounds in the lake basin are full most of the time. Pressures may be slightly heavier on weekends with the biggest camping turnaround on Sunday afternoon as old vacationers return home and new ones arrive.

The full camping season here, however, generally extends from early June through late October, opening as the snow melts and closing with the first heavy snow in the fall.

Area trails follow about the same schedule, opening a little later, in mid and late June, and remaining open until heavy snow falls in the high country in October or later.

Fall is one of the better times to visit this area. After Labor Day most of the crowds have disappeared. The weather generally remains pleasant and in the late part of September, the aspens deck the countryside in a blaze of autumn color.

Summer daytime temperatures here range on the cool side of the 70s dropping at night into the upper 40s. Thunderstorms are not unusual but they seldom disrupt activities, striking and then passing. Nighttime storms are uncommon.

The elevation here may pose the greatest problem to visitors. A hiker who starts up a trail fresh from a sea-level home may find himself puffing and snorting even on the most level spots. And some persons may have difficulty getting to sleep the first night or so. Give yourself a day or two to acclimate your body to the change and take it easy when you first start out.

WHERE TO DRIVE

Although all of this country lies at an elevation of nearly 9000 feet, road vistas are generally subdued except from a few spectacular vista points.

Minarets Vista—Look west here at the splintered tops of the Sierra Nevada crest. A magnificent sunset vista point.

To reach this vista turn north off the main street of Mammoth Lakes onto highway 203 following the road as it curves past the Earthquake Fault picnic area and then on to the vista point. 5 miles.

Stop at the fault to take a short nature trail along a gaping 55-foot deep crack in the earth's surface.

At the vista point look west at the sharp peaks of the Ritter range and the Minarets Wilderness along the Sierras. And take

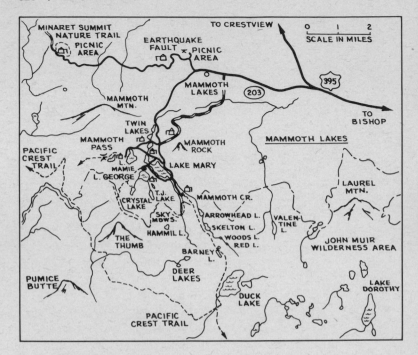

time to walk the nature trail nearby which interprets plant life and geological features.

The road continues on to the Devils Postpile National Monument in 8 miles. A short trail there leads to a cliff display of towering columns of basalt which fracture off into multi-sided post-length shards of rock.

June Lake Loop—Drive past a series of high lakes below a towering ridge of granite mountains. With waterfalls in season.

To reach this area drive north on U.S. 395 east of Mammoth Lakes, turning west on State Highway 158 about 5 miles north of Crestview. The road loops around past the lakes with constant mountain vistas, returning to the highway in about 14 miles. Views at the end of the drive out at the rows of Mono Craters, filled now with pumice, on the ridges to the east.

WHERE TO HIKE

Barely a sampling here of the many hikes in this area. And

omitted entirely are some of the very short walks to waterfalls and small lakes you'll find from campground trails.

All of the trails listed lead to the edge of the John Muir Wilderness. And even day hikers must obtain permits from the ranger station-visitor center in Mammoth Lakes.

Barney Lake—Climb from forest into a high rock-girded basin and a jade-colored lake. 2.5 miles.

Find the trail off to the right at the end of the main spur road through the Coldwater Campground. Find the sign.

The trail starts in forest on long, gradual switchbacks which climb immediately to views of an old mining prospect on ridges to the left.

In 1.2 mile the trail reaches a junction with a short spur, left, to Arrowhead Lake in less than a quarter mile. The small lake, shaped, as you'd expect, like an arrowhead, is tucked into the bottom of a steep forested valley.

From the lake junction, the trail then climbs sharply into lightly forested rock country with increasing views now of surrounding peaks, reaching Skelton Lake in another half-mile at 9900 feet.

From the end of Skelton Lake (and there's no need to hurry past it) the trail climbs to a small, soggy-but-pretty meadow with waterfalls and then switchbacks sharply to a ledge and around a ridge past little Red Lake to Barney Lake, surrounded by steep peaks and girded by scree and slab rock.

Stop here or hike on another 2.5 miles to Duck Lake over Duck Pass on the Sierra Nevada Crest at 10,790 feet.

Emerald Lake and Sky Meadow—Hike past a jewel of a lake to a high meadow tucked below towering mountains and crossed by meandering streams. A long 2 miles.

Find this trail off the right side of the main road into the Coldwater Campground from a parking area several hundred yards back from the end of the road. (See Barney Lake trail.) The trail is signed.

The path here starts uphill on an old service road, bearing right around a water tower to the banks of Cold Water Creek. The trail now follows the creek uphill sharply but very pleasantly leveling off as the stream does in about a half-mile.

The trail then climbs inland to the left, bearing right as it continues to climb through a boulder area toward Emerald Lake, tucked in forest and watched over by mountain peaks.

To continue to the meadow, pass the lake, climbing sharply on the trail along a creek, first on the left side and then on the right, topping out at Gentian Meadows, a small spot thick with flowers in season.

From this meadow, the trail switchbacks uphill to the head of the canyon and then traverses right to go over one ridge and then another climbing, finally, from a creek up a steep open slope to the end of the meadow.

Take care in hiking the last section of this trail. Early in the season parts of it may be covered with snow. Watch for occasional cairns and blazes.

Hike up the narrow meadows and along the stream to find a place to eat lunch and gaze up at the peaks above you.

Mammoth Crest and Crystal Lake—High views here over the entire Mammoth Lakes basin with a side trip to a pretty rock-girded

Sky Meadow

lake. 3 miles.

Find the trailhead near the entrance to the Lake George Campground. The trail starts uphill, to the north, from a small parking area across from the entrance road. It's signed.

The path at first climbs sharply through open forest below a road and then switchbacks up a ridge to a series of higher and higher views directly down on Lake George. Junction near the top of the ridge with the Crystal Lake trail in about 1 mile.

Turn left here to reach the lake, tucked below Crystal Crag and Mammoth Crest. The lake trail climbs briefly from the junction and then drops sharply to the outlet of the lake in about a half mile.

To continue on to the crest, follow the main trail uphill as it continues to switchback, climbing finally out of timber onto an open red and chocolate pumice ridge with sudden and constant views out over the valley.

At the top of the crest in 3 miles, soak up the vistas and then drop over the other side following trails either south to explore still other crest-side views or north to the top of a cinder peak for 360-degree vistas toward the Minarets, over the valley and south along the Sierra crest.

No water on this trail at all.

BACKPACKING OPPORTUNITIES

Longer trails here lead into some of the most spectacular high country in the Sierra Nevadas.

The famed John Muir Trail passes along the western side of this area and can be reached from several spurs from the lakes basin. Other trails here loop far into the wilderness with destinations of their own.

Wilderness permits are required here for day or overnight hikes. However, no restrictions have yet been placed on where backpackers may camp or hike. Use in this area is heavy, imposing particular burdens on individual hikers to protect it from over-use. Carry your own stove. Wood is scarce-to-nonexistent and the old gnarled trees that still cling to some of these high slopes shouldn't be destroyed.

Several detailed trail guides cover all of this backcountry and are available at the Forest Service Visitor Center or in most western book stores.

WHERE TO CAMP

Camping in this high area centers around a cluster of lakes in the Mammoth Lakes basin southwest of the town of Mammoth Lakes.

All campsites in this complex are assigned through a central campground registration office.

Twin Lakes—88 sites on forested loops in a shady valley between two lakes. None on the lakes. Pit toilets. Piped water.

Lake Mary—51 units on forested loops on both sides of the main campground road. No sites on the lake. Pit toilets. Piped water.

Lake George—42 sites on hillside above Lake George. Views up at the mountains. Pit toilets. No piped water.

Coldwater—79 sites on a series of loops between two creeks on a spur road off the main campground loop system. Piped water. Pit toilets.

Swimming is allowed only in Horseshoe Lake. The other lakes are domestic water sources.

Where to Get Information

For information on this area, write:
District Ranger
Mammoth Ranger District
Mammoth Lakes, Calif. 93546

north lake-south lake

MOUNTAINS HERE CERTAINLY—the very summit of the Sierra Nevada range.

But much more than that too—rare lakes, glacial rock, valley vistas and alpine flowers.

Just a glimpse of why so many hike into the John Muir Wilderness every year. And all from two lakes east of Bishop, Calif., in the Inyo National Forest on the edge of the John Muir Wilderness strip.

To reach the area: From Bishop, Calif., drive west on State Highway 168, taking forks to North Lake, Sabrina Lake and South Lake.

September may be the best time to visit this high country.

Campgrounds here generally open in mid-May with high trails opening in late June or early July, depending on winter and spring snow conditions. But they no sooner open than summer crowds arrive, filling campgrounds and parading over the trails, as many as 400 a day some weekends.

The pressure generally continues through Labor Day with the

heaviest strain on weekends. But after Labor Day, use drops substantially. Camping is still good, albeit cooler. Lots of campsites are available. Trails remain open. The high country is still spectacular. And by late in September, the changing aspens have added color to the local scene.

Summer temperatures here range into the 80s, depending on the elevation of the trail or campground, dropping occasionally to freezing levels at night in the high camps.

Thundershowers roar through the area with some regularity in the afternoons during July and August. But they rarely strike at night. Rains pass quickly and hikers on trails will dry out almost as rapidly as they get wet. Stay off high exposed ridges, however, whenever, any storm threatens. No bears here, either in the high country or around campgrounds. There is not enough for them to eat.

The Forest Service offers no formal naturalist programs here. Persons with questions should stop at the ranger station in Bishop.

WHERE TO DRIVE

There are no scenic drives, as such, in this area. But roads out of Bishop lead to spectacular although unmarked views.

Drive north from Bishop on U.S. 395 as that highway climbs from the valley at 4100 feet up to Sherwin Summit at 7000 feet, with vistas all the way.

Find other high views over Bishop and the Owens River valley as you drive westward from Bishop on State Highway 168, climbing to almost 10,000 feet in the drive to the lakes.

The greatest views, however, are saved for the lakes themselves with snow-capped peaks of the Sierra Nevada crest towering over both Sabrina and South lakes. Drive to North Lake for more restrained vistas from the road up at nearby peaks.

WHERE TO HIKE

Take short hikes into the edge of the John Muir Wilderness and then wish you had more time to spend on longer treks. The trails covered here only sample the wild barren beauty of these high plateaus and lakes.

Permits must be obtained for even day-hikes into the wilderness. And all the hikes listed here cross the wilderness boundary. Obtain permits at the Bishop ranger station (see also Backpacking Opportunities).

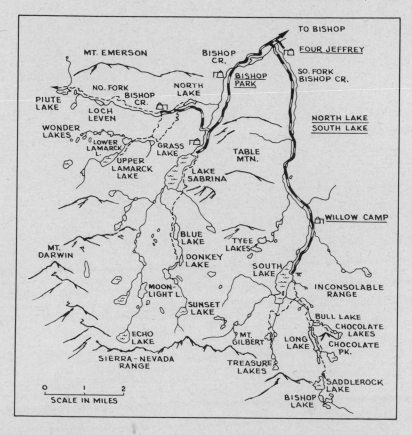

MT. EMERSON
BISHOP CR.
TO BISHOP
FOUR JEFFREY
SO. FORK BISHOP CR.
NO. FORK BISHOP CR.
NORTH LAKE
BISHOP PARK
PIUTE LAKE
LOCH LEVEN
WONDER LAKES
LOWER LAMARCK L.
GRASS LAKE
NORTH LAKE
SOUTH LAKE
UPPER LAMARCK LAKE
LAKE SABRINA
TABLE MTN.
WILLOW CAMP
MT. DARWIN
BLUE LAKE
TYEE LAKES
DONKEY LAKE
SOUTH LAKE
INCONSOLABLE RANGE
MOON-LIGHT L.
SUNSET LAKE
BULL LAKE
CHOCOLATE LAKES
CHOCOLATE PK.
ECHO LAKE
MT. GILBERT
LONG LAKE
SIERRA-NEVADA RANGE
TREASURE LAKES
SADDLEROCK LAKE
BISHOP LAKE
0   1   2
SCALE IN MILES

Long Lake—Climb to a typical High Sierra Lake set below a snow-capped ridge and a chocolate mountain. 2 miles.

Find the trail at the end of the road at South Lake about 24 miles from Bishop. The path starts off to the left of the parking area, dropping abruptly above the lake and then climbing very steadily, further and further back into timber to a junction with Treasure Lakes trail in about three-quarters mile.

Keep left here as the trail levels off, dropping across a creek and then climbing quite sharply again up a series of switchbacks to a bench on which the lake is situated. Good views at the top of the switchbacks back over South Lake and the valley.

At a junction with the Bull Lake-Chocolate Lake trail keep right again, passing a small tarn to reach the outlet of Long Lake. Stop here or cross the outlet and follow the trail along the left (east) side of the lake to other rest and picnic spots.

Mt. Gilbert, Mt. Johnson and Mt. Goode dominate the Sierra Crest skyline to the west. Chocolate Peak—a truly brown mountain—towers over the lake to the east.

For a side trip, take the trail left from the junction uphill to Bull Lake, set in a small forest basin. And if you have time, continue on that trail around the left side of the lake as it climbs steeply and erratically along a creek to the first of three Chocolate Lakes, at the end of a mile.

Treasure Lakes—Climb again to a high, rocky alpine lake basin at about 10,000 feet in a cirque below Gilbert, Johnson and Hurd peaks. 2.5 miles.

Find this trail out of the end of the parking lot at South Lake (see above) turning right at a junction in about three-quarters mile.

The trail drops downhill then across a stream, leveling out for a short distance and then dropping very sharply down, along and across a series of little streams above the head of South Lake.

After crossing the third stream, the trail turns sharply uphill to grind its way rigorously along a stream for about a half-mile to a relatively flat, open meadow. Fantastic views now high over South Lake and down the Bishop Creek valley.

Follow the trail across the open area, crossing a stream and then climbing up another rock ledge to arrive at the lakes.

Rocky, granite country here with patches of heather, rushing water and towering mountains all around.

Loch Leven—An icy, string of a lake strung out between two rock-bound peaks. About 3 miles.

To reach this trail turn north off State Highway 168 onto the North Lake spur road about 19 miles from Bishop. Find the trail out of the end of the North Lake Campground at the end of the road. (But don't park in the campground. Use a special lot about a quarter mile back down the road to the right.)

The trail here starts in aspen and climbs about half way to the lake with few views except through the trees. At the half-way mark, however, the trail climbs out to an open scree and boulder slope at the head of the valley to start a series of switchbacks to the lake on top of the rock cirque.

The trail here is both exciting and depressing. Great views back

Long Lake

down the valley. But the view ahead brings nothing but more cliffs to climb.

But once on top—a whole new world! The lake first and then another barren valley.

Stop at the lake or continue on for another half-mile or so to Piute Lake about 200 feet higher.

BACKPACKING OPPORTUNITIES

Heavy use has brought with it limitations on backpacking particularly from this area into Sequoia and Kings Canyon National Parks.

Hikers who confine their travels to the John Muir Wilderness on the west side of the crest need only obtain a daily wilderness permit. But hikers who want to cross either Piute Pass or Bishop Pass into the parks must also obtain a special reservation.

Only 25 persons a day are permitted over Piute Pass from North Lake and only 50 permits are issued over Bishop Pass from South

Lake. The limitation has been imposed by the park in an effort to protect the heavily impacted high area from further human damage. Hikers into the popular Dusy Basin of the park are also prohibited from building open fires. Hikers must carry stoves.

Permits and reservations can be obtained at the Bishop ranger station. Regulations change from year to year so hikers should check each year before planning any trip.

WHERE TO CAMP

Construction of a $2 million sewer project may interrupt camping in the North and South Lake campgrounds through 1975. Some camps may be closed as a system is constructed to protect the quality of Los Angeles water.

Camps along State Highway 168 to Sabrina Lake include:

Big Tree—7 sites near Bishop Creek on a spur road off the highway about 12 miles from Bishop. Flush toilets. Piped water.

Intake—10 sites near a small dam. Some near the water. Flush toilets. Piped water. 16 miles from Bishop.

Bishop Park—34 sites on stream. Flush toilets. Piped water. 16 miles from Bishop.

Sabrina—32 sites near a stream in an open area. Not on the lake. Flush toilets. Piped water. 19 miles from Bishop.

North Lake—14 sites on forest loop near creek. Near the trailhead. But no trailhead parking. Stream water. Toilets.

Campgrounds along the spur road to South Lake include:

Four Jeffrey—106 sites, some in trees and the others on open slopes. Flush toilets. Piped water. 16 miles from Bishop on county road to South Lake.

South Fork 2, 3 and 5—20 sites in three camps along the county road to South Lake between 4 and 5 miles from the state highway junction. Toilets. Stream water. Walk-in sites.

Where to Get Information

For information on this area, write:

District Ranger
White Mountain Ranger District
151 Grandview
Bishop, Calif. 93514

sequoia national park

THE TOWERING VELVET-RED Sequoias—some of them 3000 years old—may be the first reason for visiting this area.

But the next half-dozen include lakes, waterfalls, mountains, cliffs, meadows and even a cave.

See the General Sherman tree for sure, the largest and one of the oldest living plants in the world. But allot enough time to see the other features too—some from roads but many from trails.

To reach the area: From California State Highway 99 through south-central California, turn east near Visalia onto Highway 198, or east from Fresno onto Highway 180. Both lead into the park.

This 640-square-mile park embraces not only some of the world's older and grandest trees, but some of the Southwest's most spectacular mountain peaks and alpine basins along the Sierra crest.

Lower level campgrounds here are open all year. But the camps near the Giant Forest area, covered in this book, often do not open before the last of June or early in July, depending on when the snow melts.

Use is heaviest during the school vacation period, reaching a peak in August. The impact, however, is most severe on weekends and holidays with campgrounds filling up two days in advance on most holiday weekends.

Fall camping, after Labor Day, is becoming increasingly popular particularly with retired persons and families with pre-school children.

The weather generally continues in the pleasant range through October. The days are shorter and naturalist programs have generally been discontinued, but visitors face no problem finding campsites and hiking on trails can almost be a private affair.

Temperatures here range from downright hot at lower elevations to chilly higher in the park. Temperatures near the park headquarters at Ash Mountain in the southwestern corner of the park will average in the upper 90s from June through August during the day, dropping into the mid-and upper-60s at night.

In the Giant Forest, however, daytime temperatures will range in the mid 70s and low 80s while nighttime temperatures will drop to the low 40s and even below freezing on occasion. Temperatures on some of the higher trails will range even lower.

Thundershowers here occur only occasionally in midsummer, generally in the afternoon, lasting usually less than an hour and passing on. Hikers are warned to get off any exposed ridges whenever they see a storm developing.

Campers face few special problems here. But all visitors are warned to be extremely careful around the park's swift streams. These rivers and creeks can be violent particularly early in the spring and after storms. Children should not be encouraged to play in them.

Owners of trailers and large motor homes are urged to enter the park via Highway 180 from Fresno. The Generals Highway from Visalia is steep, twisty and narrow with a number of sharp hairpin turns difficult to negotiate in long, or wide, vehicles.

The Park Service offers an extensive interpretive program during the summer including campfire programs, walks, hikes and even photographic demonstrations. Schedules are posted in campgrounds and can be obtained at entrance stations and visitor centers.

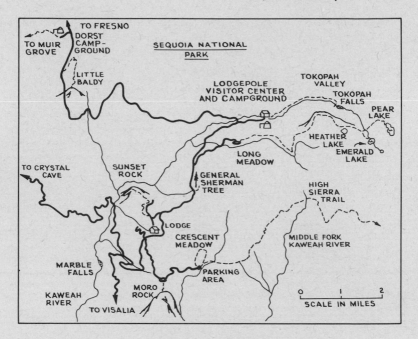

WHERE TO DRIVE

The main roads into and through this park offer access to some of its best vistas.

The highway 180 from Fresno, which enters the northwest corner of the park, climbs through open country with constant views back over the valley. And the park road from the low-level Ash Mountain headquarters twists and climbs from desert into a high cool forest with equally constant views down over that valley.

At the top, the Generals Highway winds through a string of lush Sequoia redwood groves and past a series of vistas overlooking Kings Canyon and Redwood Mountain.

And be sure also to take spur roads to Moro Rock and Crystal Cave.

Moro Rock—One of the best views in the park from the top of this rock.

Turn east off the main park road just south of the Giant Forest concession complex driving about 2 miles to the Moro Rock parking area.

Stairways climb to the top of the rock in two phases—about 300 feet to the first level and another 400-foot climb to the top. A very busy place, particularly on weekends.

Crystal Cave—Take a guided tour of about an hour through a marble cavern draped with curtains of rock and columns of stalactites and stalagmites. Closed in winter.

Drive south from the Giant Forest about 2 miles turning right (west) and driving another 7 winding miles to a cave parking lot.

From the lot, walk downhill for a half-mile past a series of waterfalls to the cave entrance. Tours start about every half hour. Wear good shoes and a jacket. A fee is charged.

WHERE TO HIKE

Trails here, as always, lead to the best of everything—secretive groves of Sequoias, waterfalls, tremendous high vistas and even quiet meadows.

Muir Grove—Leave the noise of the highway—and people—to enjoy the pristine silence of this remote grove of giant sequoias. 2 miles.

Find this trail off the end of the group campground loop in the Dorst Campground (see Where to Camp). Find sign.

The trail slopes downhill to start with through a pretty but small meadow and then switchbacks gradually uphill to a rock-slab vista point. Stop here to look across at the grove and then follow the trail downhill, to the left, across a creek and back up into the grove itself.

No cars here to disturb the beauty. Only the sound of the hurrying stream, the wind and an occasional woodpecker high on a tree.

From the heart of the grove, the trail continues on another 1.5 miles, ending at an overlook.

Little Bald Mountain—Climb an easy 1.5 miles to put all of this high country in instant perspective.

Find this trail off the east side (uphill) of the park road about 1.5 miles south of the entrance to the Dorst Campground. Park on the east side of the road.

The trail starts very gently uphill in forest away from the road and then switchbacks to an outcropping with the first views in less than a mile. The trail drops, then climbs to a second outcrop with new views and finally, climbs sharply to the 360-degree vistas at the top.

Take a topographic map and identify all of the major areas in the park. Lots of flowers, changing with season. And listen for the sound of grouse strumming in the early summer.

Tokopah Falls—Whistle at marmots sunning themselves on rocks along this 1.7-mile trail to Tokopah Falls.

Find this trail out of the Lodgepole Campground just across the Kaweah River bridge, turning sharply right. Park on the store side of the river, walking across the bridge.

The trail follows the north shore of the river as it winds through forest and past a pleasant meadow, climbing into the open in about a mile through patches of huge boulders (whistle at your marmot here) to the base of the cirque and waterfall.

The trail ends at the falls. Don't try to climb further unless you are trained or properly equipped. A permit is also required.

Heather Lake

And don't pass up the small but pretty rapids in the river below the falls as you hike the trail.

Crescent Meadows—If you're tired of the hub-bub of traffic and people, stroll here through groves of red-barked sequoias around a peaceful meadow.

To reach this trail drive to the end of the Crescent Meadow-Moro Rock road (see Where to Drive), finding the trail to the right of the restroom off the parking lot. The loop path starts on the High Sierra Trail, turning left at the first junction to circle completely around the soggy meadow and back to the road-end parking lot again, never letting the meadow out of sight.

To reach the center of the meadow, walk out a fallen tree that almost crosses the meadow at its upper end.

Heather Lake—Climb out of forest to a spectacular cliff-top view of the Tokopah Valley and then on to a pretty high alpine lake. 4.5 miles.

And check on snow conditions before you start early in the year. This trail can be dangerous if covered with snow or ice.

To reach the trailhead, turn west off the park road onto the Wolverton road about 2.6 miles south of the Lodgepole Campground entrance. Find the trail at the end of the road uphill (to the north) off the middle of the parking lot. Watch for sign.

The trail starts in forest and then climbs persistently and tediously but interestingly through timber (watch for deer) about two-thirds of the way before finally lurching out to a rock cliff on The Watchman and fantastic views straight down on Tokopah Falls and up the valley. (Keep left at all junctions to this point.)

From here the trail clings to the edge of a cliff on a path blasted out of rock (views all the way) as it climbs, southerly now, to the head of a cirque and Heather Lake, just over the ridge, nestled in rock and scattered trees.

Stop here, or continue, if you want, another 1.5 miles first past Emerald and Aster lakes to Pear Lake.

BACKPACKING OPPORTUNITIES

Backcountry trails criss-cross this park with almost endless opportunities for overnight trips.

Backpacking use, however, is extremely heavy here during the peak season requiring officials to impose restrictions on use of some trails.

Wilderness permits are required for all overnight hikes into park backcountry and camping is limited to designated places only. The Park Service is also controlling the number of persons in some backcountry sections by limiting the number of permits issued each day on certain trails. Before planning any backpack trip, therefore, check with park officials on current restrictions.

Open fires are also banned in some sections. So carry your own stove.

WHERE TO CAMP

The only campgrounds listed here are those near the main road through the park.

Check at entrance stations on camping conditions as you enter the park. They have information on campgrounds that are open or filled.

High elevation campgrounds which open early in May, closing in mid-October, include:

Lodgepole—317 sites on loops, some near the river, in a rocky but pleasant forest area. 4 miles northwest of the Giant Forest Village. Flush toilets. Piped water.

Dorst—257 sites in a pleasant forest setting off the main road. 12 miles northwest of the Giant Forest Village.

Lower elevations camps open the year round include:

Potwisha—44 sites in a forested area. Flush toilets. Piped water. 3 miles from park headquarters.

Buckey Flat—29 sites. 1 mile from Hospital Rock. Flush toilets. Piped water. Not recommended for trailers.

Where to Get Information

For information on this park, write:
Superintendent
Sequoia and Kings Canyon National Parks
Three Rivers, Calif. 93271

death valley
national monument

PICTURES AND BOOKS can prepare you for the desert of Death Valley but the truth of its barrenness and intense heat must be physically felt to be appreciated.

An exciting area if you accept it for what it is but don't expect something like your summer backyard.

And one note about its wildlife: Despite the illusion created by some nature films, you won't see creature life here wherever you look. In fact, you'll be lucky if you see any at all. For this is a barren place. Life survives with difficulty with fewer and fewer creatures at each higher level of the sparse food chain.

To reach the area: From U.S. 395 in southeastern California, drive east on State Highways 136 or 190. From U.S. 95 in Nevada, drive west on State Highway 58.

This monument, two and a half times the size of Rhode Island and one of the richest geological areas in the United States, embraces five separate mountain ranges and covers 3000 square miles of desert, 500 square miles of it below sea level.

If you have a choice, the best time to visit this desert is probably between February and April in the spring and between September and November in the fall.

In the winter, the scenic high country is closed by snow and the valleys are taken over almost exclusively by the winter-touring sun seekers who cram them 10,000 strong on major winter holidays.

In the summer, the heat is so oppressive both in the highlands and in the valley that only the hardiest record seekers spend much time here. Valley daytime temperatures in August and July *average* between 113 and 116 degrees, seldom dropping below 85 degrees at night.

During the spring and fall, however, temperatures are much more moderate. In March, for instance, daytime temperatures average about 80 degrees in the valley with nighttime temperatures dropping to a comfortable 53 degrees. In October it's a little warmer with daytime temperatures about 92 degrees and nighttime temperatures in the 60s.

Campgrounds in this monument open and close with the weather. High camps—generally to be preferred to the low ones—open in April, closing in late October. Some of the valley desert camps, however, don't open until October, closing in April.

The desert wildflower season is almost impossible to predict. It depends entirely on the weather each year. But it's usually at its peak in January and February, extending sometimes into March.

The intense heat, of course, causes the greatest problems for drivers, campers and hikers. Motorists are urged to make certain that their car tires and cooling systems are in good shape. The one great disability of the modern car here is the boiling radiator. Water—for radiators only—is generally stored in tanks along steep roads. But it's seldom where your car breaks down.

Drivers should also keep an eye on their gasoline supplies. Service stations here are few and far between.

Hikers, even in the fall-spring season, are urged to protect their bodies from the sun and carry lots of water. Good shoes are essential. And before starting any hike, first acclimate yourself to the heat. And hike early in the day. The desert hits its peak heat about 4 o'clock in the afternoon.

The Park Service here offers an extensive interpretive program, generally geared to winter-time campers, including guided walks and auto tours in addition to naturalist evening programs.

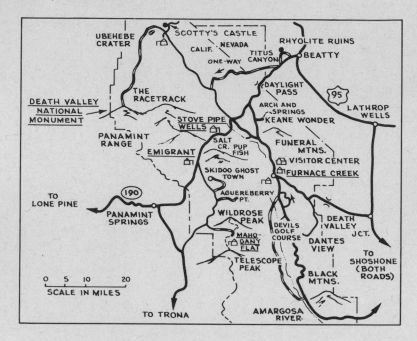

WHERE TO DRIVE

Roads—thankfully in this area—lead to most of the monument's scenic splendors. And listed here is only a sampling of some of the more out-of-way places.

From the Emigrant Canyon road through the high country on the west side of the monument:

Charcoal Kilns—There's something almost artlike in the shapes of these near-perfect kilns, still standing in a row.

To reach the kilns, turn east off the Emigrant Canyon road about 21 miles from Emigrant Junction, arriving at the kilns in about 7 more miles.

Aguereberry Point—The only high road vista point over the Furnace Creek area from the west: From 6433 feet to below sea level in one big drop.

Drive south from Emigrant Junction on the Emigrant Canyon road about 12 miles turning east on a dirt road, following signs, to the point in about 6 more miles.

Park and walk a short way downhill to a formal vista to the east. From roads on the valley floor visit:

Titus Canyon—Drive across desert to wind through a tight gorge with walls only yards apart in places. Check with rangers before you start. The road is sometimes closed.

Find this one-way road off State Highway 58 about 7 miles east of Daylight Pass. Turn north and follow the narrow track about 25 miles, first across the desert and then through the canyon to the road to Scotty's Castle.

Dantes View—Watch a cool sunset here over a very hot valley from 5475 feet.

To reach the view, drive east from Furnace Creek on Highway 190 turning south in 10.8 miles to the viewpoint in 13.3 miles more.

Watch the sunset from your car. But for better vistas hike tourist trails along the ridge, stopping whenever you find a scene that suits you.

WHERE TO HIKE

You don't have to walk very far here to discover what a desert is really like. But walk you must.

Wildrose Peak—Hike through piñon and limber pine in an area once cut over to feed the nearby charcoal kilns to the top of a 9064-foot mountain. 4 miles one way.

Find this trail to the west of the Charcoal Kilns (see Where to Drive). The trail climbs steadily around a ridge and then east to a saddle before turning northward to the top. Views here out to the Charleston Mountains to the east and the Sierra Nevadas to the west.

Keane Wonder—Hike uphill to an abandoned mining site or along a ridge to see a small natural arch and hot spring. And wonder, as you hike, what sort of riches made men suffer the barrenness of this place for long.

To reach these trails from the junction of highway 190 and the Hells Gate road drive northeast about 5.5 miles turning easterly onto the Keane Wonder road. End of the road, in the middle of an old mine-mill complex, in about 3 miles.

Charcoal kilns below Wildrose Peak

To reach the old mines (but don't attempt to explore the dangerous tunnels) hike uphill about 1.5 miles below the remnants of an old tramway.

To reach the warm spring and a view of the arch, follow a faint-but-easy-to-follow path, on grade, a mile to the north. Stay above an old pipeline to start with, dropping below it to a jeep road in the last quarter mile. Watch uphill now for the pipeline to end and then make your way uphill to the smelly warm spring and the arch.

Salt Creek—Having viewed the harshness of this land, look now at its fragile life, in a stream yet.

To find this creek, drive north from Furnace Creek about 12 miles turning west onto a short spur road which ends at a creek.

Look first for the tiny, inch-long pup fish—the only fish like it in the world—that lives in this briny shallow and warm stream. Don't drink this water, but dip a finger in it and take a small taste—saltier even than the ocean.

Continue upstream about 2 miles to the stream source—a spring—noting as you go the occasional tracks of small animals and birds.

WHERE TO CAMP

High campgrounds include:

Wildrose—12 sites at 4000 feet on an exposed bench just off the Emigrant Canyon road on the road to Mahogany Flats. Pit toilets. Piped water. Open all year.

Thorndike—8 sites at 7500 feet in a grove of trees. Pit toilets. Boil water. Road not passable for motor home or trailer. 8 miles from Emigrant Canyon road. Open April to October.

Mahogany—10 sites at 8200 feet. Pit toilets. No water. May be difficult to reach with low-slung autos. 9 miles from Emigrant Canyon road. Open April to October.

Valley campgrounds include:

Furnace Creek—64 sites in partially shaded desert flat at minus-196 feet. Flush toilets. Piped water. Near Furnace Creek Visitor Center. Open all year.

Sunset—500 sites. Open October to April. Piped water. Flush toilets. At Furnace Creek.

Texas Spring—85 sites. Open October to April. Flush toilets. Piped water. At Furnace Creek.

Stove Pipe Wells—200 sites. Open October to April. Flush toilets. Piped water. At Stove Pipe Wells.

Emigrant—19 sites. Open April to October. Flush toilets. Piped water. At Emigrant Junction.

Mesquite Springs—60 sites. Open all year. Flush toilets. Piped water. Near Scotty's Castle.

Where to Get Information

For information on this monument, write:

Superintendent
Death Valley National Monument
Death Valley, Calif. 92328